Environment and Development Challenges

Environment and Development Challenges

The Imperative to Act

The Blue Planet Prize Laureates

UNIVERSITY OF TOKYO PRESS

Published by University of Tokyo Press
4-5-29 Komaba, Meguro-ku
Tokyo 153-0041
Website: http://www.utp.or.jp
ISBN 978-4-13-067120-0

Production assisted by is works CO., LTD.
Jacket design: Fumihiko Nishioka
Typeset by Tauhaus

First Edition: October, 2014

Printed in Japan

Table of Contents

PART 2: INDIVIDUAL CONTRIBUTIONS

Preface

Part 1 of this paper presents a synthesis of the key messages from individual papers written by the Blue Planet Laureates (Part 2) and discusses the current and projected state of the global and regional environment, with implications for environmental, social, and economic sustainability. It addresses the drivers for change, the implications for inaction, and what is needed to achieve economic development and growth among the poor, coupled with environmental and social sustainability, and the imperative of acting now. The paper does not claim to comprehensively address all environment and development issues, but a subset deemed to be of particular importance.

In 1992, the year of the Rio Earth Summit, the Asahi Glass Foundation established the Blue Planet Prize, an award presented to individuals or organizations worldwide in recognition of outstanding achievements in scientific research and its application, which have helped provide solutions to global environmental problems. The Prize is offered in hopes of encouraging efforts to bring about the healing of the Earth's fragile environment.

The award's name was inspired by the remark "The Earth was blue," uttered by the first human in space, Russian cosmonaut Yuri Gagarin, upon viewing our planet from space. The Blue Planet Prize was so named in hopes that our blue planet will be a shared asset capable of sustaining human life far into the future. The Blue Planet Prize celebrated its 20th anniversary in 2012. The Asahi Glass Foundation wishes to mark this anniversary with a fresh start in its efforts to help build an environment-friendly society.

On the occasion of publication

To commemorate the 20th anniversary of the Blue Planet Prize, the Asahi Glass Foundation asked past laureates to write a joint paper that would touch upon the issue of conserving the environment. Fortunately, many agreed to participate in this endeavor. The laureates subsequently gathered at the headquarters of the International Institute for Environment and Development in London, where they completed the paper after sessions of passionate discussion.

By publishing the paper, the Asahi Glass Foundation hopes to share with a wider audience the Blue Planet Prize laureates' earnest recommendations to humankind, help build a truly sustainable world, and pass down "an invaluable natural environment" that future generations can continue to enjoy.

The Foundation would like to express its deep gratitude to the laureates of the Blue Planet Prize who agreed to write the paper, as well as to the editor, Professor Sir Bob Watson. In addition, we would like to thank Professor Fumihiko Nishioka of Tama Art University for handling the publication concept and design, is works CO., LTD. for communicating with and managing the authors, and the University of Tokyo Press for agreeing to serve as the publisher.

* * *

The Asahi Glass Foundation was founded in 1933 to foster researches.

The Foundation believes that the very important mission for us humankind is to ensure the sustainability of irreplaceability planet and pass it on to the future generations. For this reason, it established the Blue Planet Prize in 1992, an international environmental award, to recognize individuals or organizations who have contributed to the preservation of the earth's environment.

October, 2014

The Asahi Glass Foundation

Part 1
Synthesis Report

The Blue Planet Prize Laureates

Key Messages

- We have a dream—a world without poverty; a world that is equitable; a world that respects human rights; a world with increased and improved ethical behavior toward poverty and natural resources; a world that is environmentally, socially, and economically sustainable, where challenges such as climate change, loss of biodiversity, and social inequity have been successfully addressed. This is an achievable dream; however, the current system is deeply flawed, and our current path cannot help us achieve it.
- Population size and growth and related consumption patterns are critical elements in the many environmental degradation and social problems we currently face. The population issue should be urgently addressed through the education and empowerment of women, including work-force equity; property rights, ownership, and inheritance; health care of children and the elderly; and making modern contraception accessible to all.
- There is an urgent need to break the link between production and consumption on the one hand and environmental destruction on the other. Doing so can raise material living standards for a period that would allow us to overcome world poverty. However, indefinite material growth on a planet with finite and often fragile natural resources will eventually become unsustainable. Unsustainable growth results from environmentally-damaging subsidies in areas such as energy, transportation, and agriculture and should be eliminated; external environmental and social costs should be internalized; and decision making should take into account

the market and non-market values of ecosystem goods and services.

- The immense environmental, social, and economic risks arising from our current path will be more difficult to manage if we are unable to measure key aspects of the problem. For example, governments should recognize the serious limitations of GDP as a measure of economic activity and complement it with measurements of the five forms of capital: built, financial, natural, human, and social, i.e., a measure of wealth that integrates economic, environmental, and social dimensions. Green taxes and elimination of subsidies should ensure that the natural resources needed to protect the poor are universally available rather than merely via subsidies that often benefit only those who are better off.

- The present energy system, which is heavily dependent on fossil fuels, underlies many problems we face today: exhaustion of easily accessible physical resources, security of access to fuels, and degradation of health and environmental conditions. Universal access to clean energy services is vital for the poor, and a transition to a low-carbon economy will require rapid technological evolution in efficient energy use, environmentally sound low-carbon renewable energy sources, and carbon capture and storage. The longer we wait to transition to a low-carbon economy, the more we are locked into a high-carbon energy system with consequent environmental damage to ecological and socioeconomic systems, including infrastructure.

- Emissions of greenhouse gases (GHGs) are one of the greatest threats to our future prosperity. World emissions (flows) are currently around 50 billion tons of carbon dioxide equivalent (CO_2e) per year and are growing rapidly. As the terrestrial and oceanic ecosystems cannot absorb all of the world's annual emissions, concentrations (stocks) of GHG emissions in the atmosphere have increased to over 400 ppm of CO_2e today (even after taking into account the offsetting radiative effects of aerosols) and increasing at a rate of approximately 2.5 ppm per year. Thus, we have a flow-stock problem.

Without strong action to reduce emissions over the course of this century, we are likely to increase the atmospheric concentration by at least 300 ppm, taking concentrations to 750 ppm CO_2e or higher by the end of this century or beginning of the next. The world's current commitments to reduce emissions are consistent with at least a 3°C rise (50-50 chance) in temperature, a temperature not seen on the planet for about 3 million years, with serious risks of a 5°C rise, a temperature not seen on the planet for about 30 million years. Given the uncertainties present in all steps of the scientific chain (flows to stocks to temperatures to climate change and impacts), this is a large-scale problem of risk management and public action.

- Biodiversity has essential social, economic, cultural, spiritual, and scientific values, and its protection is crucial for human survival. The rapid loss of biodiversity, unprecedented in the past 65 million years, is jeopardizing the provision of ecosystem services that underpin human well-being. The Millennium Ecosystem Assessment concluded that 15 of the 24 ecosystem services evaluated were in decline, four were improving worldwide, and five were improving in some regions of the world but declining in others. Measures to conserve biodiversity and ensure a sustainable society must be greatly enhanced and integrated with social, political, and economic concerns. There is a need to value biodiversity and ecosystem services and create markets that can appropriate the value for these services as a basis for a "green" economy.

- The decision-making systems at local, national, and global levels on which we rely in government, business, and society exhibit serious shortcomings. The rules and institutions for decision making are influenced by vested interests, with each interest having very different levels of influence on how decisions are made. Effective change in governance demands action at many levels to establish transparent means for holding those in power accountable. At the local level, public hearings and social audits can bring the voices of marginalized groups to the forefront. At a national level, parliamentary and press oversight are key. Globally, we must find better means to agree and implement measures to achieve collective goals. Governance failures also occur because decisions are being made in sectoral compartments, with environmental, social, and economic dimensions addressed by separate, competing structures.

- Decision makers should learn from ongoing grassroots actions and knowledge in areas such as energy, food, water, natural resources, finance, and governance. This is necessary, not least in rural communities with a view to their management, control, and ownership of these resources. Decision makers need to scale-up the grass roots actions by bringing together a complementary top-down and bottom-up approach to address these issues. Global cooperation can be improved by building upon the on-going regional cooperation to deal with common sustainable development issues.

- Effective training programs should be implemented to multiply the number of competent decision makers in business and government. They must learn to integrate programs and policies within sustainability constraints, understand the business cases thereof, and acquire the skills to strategically move toward such sustainability goals.

- All the problems mentioned above demand that we increase investments in education, research, and knowledge assessments. The goal of education for all must be achieved. The Future Earth Program recently launched by ICSU and ISSC will provide the multi-disciplinary knowledge base (social science, humanities, economics, natural sciences, engineering, and technologies) needed for sustainable development. Future Earth must be complemented by a web-based, multi-disciplinary knowledge assessment system that critically reviews, integrates, and synthesizes new knowledge with previous information in as close to real time as possible to strengthen the science-policy interface.

- If we are to achieve our vision, the time to act is now, given the inertia in the socioeconomic system and that the adverse effects of climate change and loss of biodiversity cannot be reversed for centuries or are already irreversible (for example, species loss). We know enough to act; however, the current scientific uncertainties confront us with an immense risk management problem. Failure to act will impoverish current and future generations.

1. The Problem

1.1 Introduction

We have a dream– a world without poverty; a world that is equitable; a world that respects human rights; a world with increased and improved ethical behavior toward poverty and natural resources; a world that is environmentally, socially, and economically sustainable and where economic growth occurs within the constraints of achieving social objectives of poverty eradication and social equity and nature's life supporting capacity; and a world where the challenges such as climate change, loss of biodiversity, and social inequity have been successfully addressed. This is an achievable dream; however, the system is broken, and our current path cannot help us achieve it.

Unfortunately, humanity's behavior remains utterly inappropriate toward dealing with the potentially lethal fallout from a combination of increasingly rapid technological evolution and extremely slow ethical–social evolution. The human ability to act has vastly outstripped the ability to understand. As a result, civilization faces a perfect storm of problems driven by overpopulation, overconsumption by the rich, use of environmentally malign technologies, and gross inequalities, including loss of the biodiversity that runs human life-support systems, climate disruption, global toxification, alteration of critical biogeochemical cycles, increasing probability of vast epidemics, and the specter of a civilization-destroying nuclear war or accident. These biophysical problems are interacting closely with human governance systems, institutions, and civil societies that are currently inadequate to deal with them.

The rapidly deteriorating biophysical situation is bad enough, but, this is barely recognized by a global society infected by the irrational belief that physical economies can grow forever and disregarding the fact that while the rich in developed and developing countries get richer, the poor are left behind. In addition, politicians and economists enthusiastically embrace the perpetual growth myth as an excuse to avoid tough decisions facing humanity. This myth promotes the impossible idea that indiscriminate economic growth is the cure for all the world's problems, although it is actually (as currently practiced) the root cause of our unsustainable global practices.

In the face of an absolutely unprecedented emergency, society has no choice but to take drastic action to avert a collapse of civilization. Either we will change our ways and build an entirely new kind of global society, or they will be changed for us.

To achieve our dream of a more sustainable world, decision makers must understand the triple interdependence of economic, social, and environmental factors and integrate them into governmental and private sector policies and programs. One challenge that many countries face is the management of natural resources to eradicate poverty while maintaining the ecological life support system. Economics deals primarily with what, where, and how much of the natural resources are required to eradicate poverty, whereas social issues deal with for whom and how much of the resources are developed; environmental issues address how natural resources can be managed with minimum negative impact on ecosystems. The interaction between economic, social, and environmental issues is enhanced and its coordination made more effective if their respective goals are translated into quantitative terms within a defined time scale. Decision makers must achieve economic growth within the constraints of social and environmental sustainability.

1.2 Underlying Drivers of Change

The major indirect drivers of change are demographic, economic, socio-political, technological, cultural, and religious (Figure 1). These affect climate change and biodiversity loss somewhat differently, although the number of people and their ability to purchase and consume energy and natural resources are common to both issues. Human-induced climate change is primarily driven by the aggregate consumption and choice of technologies to produce and use energy, which is influenced by energy subsidies and unaccounted costs, causing the current over-reliance on burning fossil fuels. The loss of biodiversity and the degradation of ecosystems and their services result primarily from the conversion of natural habitats; over-exploitation of resources; air, land and water pollution; introduction of exotic species; and human-induced climate change.

Figure 1

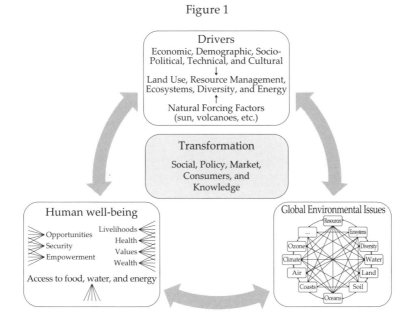

1.2.1 Demographic

The global population, currently exceeding seven billion, and the average per capita energy consumption have both increased sevenfold over the past 150 years, for an overall fiftyfold increase in the emissions of carbon dioxide into the atmosphere, and both continue to increase. As a global average, total fertility rates (TFR) are decreasing as a result of more females completing primary and secondary education, along with availability of fertility control. However, this global average conceals many local difficulties. In some parts of the world, fertility remains high, and its decline in these countries is quite uncertain. More than 200 million women in developing countries still have unmet family planning needs, and therefore, it is crucial for decision makers to increase investment in reproductive health care and family planning programs along with education programs. Although the desire and need for such programs are increasing, it is estimated that funding for these programs globally decreased by 30% between 1995 and 2008, largely because of legislative pressure from the religious right in the USA and elsewhere.

The aging population in many countries around the world is also a relevant sustainable development issue. The economic, social, and environmental implications are currently unclear. However, this trend will undoubtedly have an impact; whether it is positive or negative depends largely on how countries prepare, for example, evaluating what an aging population will mean for economic productivity; consumption of goods and services; urban planning; and financial, health, and social welfare systems.

Both culturally and genetically, human beings have always been small-group animals, evolved to deal with at most a few hundred other individuals. Humanity has been suddenly, in ecological time, confronted with an emergency requiring that it quickly design and implement a governance and economic system that is both more equitable and suitable for a global population of billions of people and sustainable on a finite planet.

1.2.2 Economics

Uncontrolled economic growth is unsustainable on a finite planet. Governments should recognize the serious limitations of GDP as a measure of economic growth and complement it with measures of the five forms of capital: built (produced), financial, natural, human, and social—a measurement of wealth that integrates economic, social, and environmental dimensions and offers a better method for determining a country's productive potential.

The failure of the economic system to internalize externalities sustains environmentally damaging activities. If externalities are uncorrected, markets fail: they generate prices that do not reflect our economic activities' true cost to society. Emissions of greenhouse gases represent a market failure because prices do not reflect the damages caused by emissions from burning fossil fuels. The price of fossil fuels should reflect the true cost to society, resulting in a more level playing field for environmentally sound, renewable energy technologies and a stimulus to conserve energy. Diverse economic instruments facilitate the correction of the emissions market failure, from taxes and emissions trading schemes to standards and other regulations. All are likely necessary.

Furthermore, decision makers must correct many other relevant market failures if we are to manage the risks of climate change: correcting the emissions externality alone will be insufficient. For example, there are market failures around research and development (innovation); imperfections in capital markets that prevent the financing for low-carbon infrastructure; network externalities, for example, around electricity grids and public transport; failures in the provision of information; failures in valuing ecosystems and biodiversity. In addition, environmentally damaging subsidies in areas such as energy, transportation, and agriculture, totaling approximately

$1 trillion per year, cause further market distortion and over-all environmental degradation, and should be eliminated. We must act strongly across all these dimensions.

Correcting the biodiversity and ecosystem market failure is particularly urgent and important. The benefits we derive from the natural world (biodiversity and ecosystem services) and its constituent ecosystems are critically important to human well-being and economic prosperity but are consistently underval-ued in economic analysis and decision making. Contemporary economic and participatory techniques allow us to take into ac-count the monetary and non-monetary values of a wide range of ecosystem services. Decision makers must adopt these tech-niques in everyday policy-making. Failure to include the valu-ation of non-market values in decision making results in a less efficient resource allocation, with negative consequences for social well-being. Recognizing the value of ecosystem services would allow the world to move toward a more sustainable fu-ture, in which the benefits of ecosystem services are better real-ized and more equitably distributed.

Correcting these market failures is also important if devel-oping countries are to continue to advance and improve their living standards. The economic emergence of the BRICS (Brazil, Russia, India, China, and South Africa) over recent decades has been a major success story. Their combined share of world GDP has increased from 23% to 32% over the last six decades. In contrast, over the same period, the OECD share of world GDP has declined from 57% to 41%. This rapid economic growth has seen great improvements in health, literacy, and income. However, this rapid growth and development was achieved mostly through the increased use of fossil fuels (which in 2008 represented 90% of their energy consumption) and the unsus-tainable exploitation of natural resources including oceans and forests. As a consequence of this energy intensive develop-ment, the emergence of the BRICS is associated with a signifi-cant increase in their GHG emissions (particularly CO_2), which have increased from 15% to 35% of global emissions over the last 60 years. This energy intensive development path is clearly unsustainable and impacts are already being felt, e.g., rapid increases in desertification in China and collapsing oceanic biodiversity. Failure to shift to a low-carbon development path, which will, among other actions, require correcting market failures and removing harmful energy subsidies, may result in damaging climate change and environmental damage. This would jeopardize future growth and put at risk these great advances in development over the past several decades. However, there are encouraging signs from BRIC countries. For example, in Brazil, deforestation in the Amazon has been reduced by around 80% in the last seven years, and in China, the 12th 5-year plan (2011–2015) indicates a change in strategy to a more sustainable low-carbon economy. However, much greater action is urgently needed.

1.2.3 Technology

The over-reliance on fossil fuel energy (coal, oil, and gas) and inefficient end-use technologies have significantly increased the atmospheric concentrations of carbon dioxide and other greenhouse gases. Currently, we are releasing one million

Figure 2

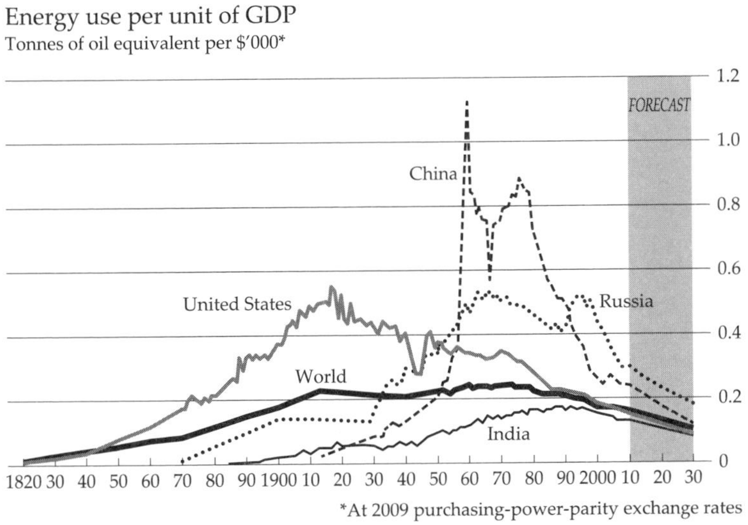

Energy use per unit of GDP
Tonnes of oil equivalent per $'000*

*At 2009 purchasing-power-parity exchange rates

Source: BP Energy Outlook 2030 London 2011

15

years worth of sequestered carbon into the atmosphere each year. Recent efforts to reduce the carbon intensity (CO_2/GDP) were made in a large number of countries, particularly in China and Russia, where the carbon content has declined significantly in the last 30 years, albeit from very high levels (Figure 2). However, the carbon intensities of India, South Africa, and Brazil (including deforestation) have not declined significantly in that period. Therefore, it is clear that all countries must take serious measures to reduce their CO_2 emissions in the next few decades, recognizing the principle of differentiated responsibilities. Despite their efforts to reduce their carbon intensity (and carbon emissions), OECD countries alone will not be able to avoid the growth of the world's carbon emissions.

1.2.4 Socio-Political

There are serious shortcomings in the decision-making systems on which we rely in government, business, and society. This is true at local, national, and global levels. The rules and institutions for decision making are influenced by vested interests; yet, each interest has a very different level of influence on how decisions are made. Effective change in governance demands action at many levels to establish transparent means for holding those in power accountable. Furthermore, governance failures occur because decisions are being made in sectoral compartments, with environmental, social, and economic dimensions addressed by separate, competing structures.

The shift of many countries, in particular the United States, toward corporate plutocracies, with large quantities of wealth (and thus, power) transferred from the poor and middle-classes to the very rich, is clearly doing enormous environmental damage. The successful campaign of many fossil fuel companies to downplay the threat of climate disruption to maintain their industry profits serves as a prominent example.

1.2.5 Cultural

The importance of reducing inequity to increase the likelihood of solving the human predicament is obvious in the differences in access to food and other basic resources caused by the tremendous power gap between the rich and poor. The lack of funding for issues such as provision of family planning services and badly needed agricultural research contrasts sharply with the expenditures of the United States and other rich nations for ensuring uninterrupted oil supplies for themselves and the rest of the industrialized world. The central geopolitical role of oil continues unabated despite the dangerous conflicts that oil-seeking has already generated and the probable catastrophic consequences its continued burning portends for the climate.

1.3 Current and Projected State of Global and Regional Environment: Implications of climate change and loss of biodiversity and ecosystem services for environmental, economic, and social sustainability

The Earth's environment is changing on all scales, from local to global, largely because of human activities. The stratospheric ozone layer has been damaged, the climate is warming at a rate faster than at any time during the last 10,000 years, biodiversity is decreasing at an unprecedented rate, fisheries are declining in most of the oceans, air pollution is an increasing problem in and around many major cities, large numbers of people live in water-stressed or water-scarce areas, and large areas of land are being degraded. Much of this environmental degradation is because of the unsustainable production and use of energy, water, food, and other biological resources and is already undermining efforts to alleviate poverty and stimulate sustainable development, and, even worse, the projected environmental changes will probably have even more severe consequences.

1.3.1 Climate Change

There is no doubt that the composition of the atmosphere and the Earth's climate have changed since the industrial revolution, predominantly because of human activities, and if those activities do not shift markedly, these changes will inevitably continue regionally and globally. The atmospheric concentration of carbon dioxide has increased by over 30% since the pre-industrial era primarily from the combustion of fossil fuels and deforestation. Global mean surface temperature, which had been relatively stable for over 1000 years, has already increased by about 0.85°C, primarily because of human activities since the pre-industrial era, and an additional 0.5–1.0°C is inevitable because of past emissions. It is projected to increase by an additional 1.2–6.4°C between 2000 and 2100, with land areas warming significantly more than the oceans and the arctic warming more than the tropics.

Precipitation is likely to increase at high and middle latitudes and in the tropics, but likely to decrease in the subtropical continents. At the same time, evaporation will increase at all latitudes. Over continents, water will probably be more plentiful in already water-rich regions, increasing the rate of river discharge and the frequency of floods. In contrast, water stress will increase in the subtropics and other water-poor regions with seasons that are already relatively dry, increasing the frequency of drought. Therefore, global warming will most probably magnify the existing contrast between the water-rich and water-poor regions of the world. Observations suggest that the frequencies of both floods and droughts have been increasing as predicted by the climate models.

The Earth's climate is projected to change at a faster rate than during the previous century. This change is likely to adversely affect freshwater, food and fiber, natural ecosystems, coastal systems and low-lying areas, and human health and social systems. The impacts of climate change are likely to be extensive and primarily negative, and to cut across many sectors. For example, throughout the world, biodiversity at the genetic, species, and landscape level is being lost, and ecosystems and their services are being degraded. Although climate change has been a relatively minor cause of the observed biodiversity decrease and ecosystem degradation, it is projected to be a major threat in the coming decades.

There is a limit to the amount of fossil fuel carbon that we can release into the atmosphere as carbon dioxide without guaranteeing tragic and unethical climatic consequences for future generations and nature. Given the decadal time scale required to phase out existing fossil fuel energy infrastructure in favor of carbon-neutral and carbon-negative energies, it is clear that we will soon cross the limit on carbon emissions. The inertia of the climate system, which delays full climate response to man-made changes of atmospheric composition, is simultaneously our friend and foe. The delay not only allows moderate over-shoot of the sustainable carbon load but also brings the danger of passing a point of no return that triggers a series of catastrophic events. These could include melting of the Greenland and West Antarctic ice sheets, leading to a considerable rise in sea level by many meters; melting of permafrost, leading to significant emissions of methane, a potent greenhouse gas; and disruption of the ocean conveyor belt (thermohaline circulation), leading to significant regional climate changes. These impacts would be largely beyond human control if we pass that point of no return.

In addition to loss of biodiversity, the risks from unmanaged climate change are immense and demand urgent action. Global warming caused by human-induced carbon dioxide increases is essentially irreversible on timescales of at least a thousand years, mainly because of the ocean's storage of heat. Therefore, today's decisions about anthropogenic carbon dioxide emissions will determine the climate of the coming millennium. Even if policies and technologies could stop emissions entirely in the 21st century, the sea level would continue to rise. The level of carbon dioxide reached in this century will determine whether low-lying areas become inundated by ice mass losses from Greenland and Antarctica, even if it occurs slowly over many centuries because the warming will persist.

The world's current commitments to reduce emissions are consistent with at least a 3-degree C rise (50-50 chance) in temperature. Such a rise has not been seen on the planet for around three million years, much longer than *Homo sapiens* has existed. Human-induced carbon dioxide emissions pose a serious risk of a 5°C increase to an average temperature not seen on the planet for 30 million years. This problem requires large-scale risk management and public action. The fundamental market failure is the unpriced "externality" of the impact of emissions. Other crucial market failures exist, including those associated with R&D and learning, networks/grids, information, and further market failures around co-benefits such as valuation of ecosystem services and biodiversity issues. Policy that considers only the emissions market failure will not generate the scale and urgency of the necessary response.

The global community's attempts to address climate change have been hopelessly inadequate. The costs of climate change, already projected at 5% or more of global GDP, could one day exceed global economic output if leaders do not act soon. The world requires bold global leadership in governments, politics, business, and civil society to implement the solutions that have been scientifically demonstrated and supported by public awareness to save humanity from a climate change catastrophe.

1.3.2 Biodiversity, Ecosystems, and Their Services

Biodiversity – the variety of genes, populations, species, communities, ecosystems, and ecological processes that make up life on Earth – underpins ecosystem services, sustains humanity, is foundational to the resilience of life on Earth, and is integral to the fabric of all world cultures. Biodiversity provides various ecosystem services on which humankind relies, including provisioning (e.g., freshwater, food and fiber, and fuel); regulating (e.g., of climate, flood, and diseases); cultural (e.g., esthetic, spiritual, educational, and recreational), and supporting (e.g., nutrient cycling, soil formation, and primary production). These ecosystem services contribute to human well-being, including our security, health, social relations, and freedom of choice and action; yet, they are fragile and diminishing across the globe.

We risk losing much of the biodiversity and the benefits it provides to humanity. As mankind's footprint has expanded, unsustainable use of land, ocean, and freshwater resources has caused extraordinary global changes, from increased habitat loss and invasive species to anthropogenic pollution and climate change. Threats to terrestrial and aquatic biodiversity are diverse, persistent, and, in some cases, increasing. The Millennium Ecosystem Assessment concluded that 15 of the 24 ecosystem services evaluated were in decline, four were improving worldwide, and five were improving in some regions of the world but declining in others. Action is critical. Without it, current high rates of species loss are projected to continue to what is becoming the 6th mass extinction event in Earth's history. It has been estimated that every 1°C increase in global mean surface temperature, up to 5°C, threatens 10% of species with extinction. All species count, some more than others at any given time and place. Losing one key species, within an ecosystem, can have cascading effects on the delivery of its ecosystem services.

Ecosystem services are ubiquitous, benefiting people in diverse socioeconomic conditions, across virtually every economic sector and over a range of spatial scales, currently and in the future. Throughout history, human well-being has enjoyed ecosystem benefits free of charge and continues to exert an increasing demand for them. Although the global economic value of ecosystem services may be difficult to measure, it almost certainly rivals or exceeds aggregate global gross domestic product, and ecosystem benefits frequently outweigh costs of their conservation. Yet, leaders seldom consider environmental benefits in conventional economic decision-making, and costs and benefits often do not accrue to the same community or at the same time or place.

A very large sector of society–extending from local stakeholders, the business community, agriculture, conservation, and government policymakers, including development agencies – has increasingly appreciated the value of these ecosystem services. Their economic value is enormous and a fundamental element of green economic development. However, we are degrading these services and squandering our natural capital for short-term gains. Currently, two-thirds of the ecosystem services are being degraded globally, which will soon amount to an estimated annual loss of $500 billion in benefits. Green economic development will require technology development and transfer to increase value added from biological resources, particularly in developing countries. This action would help shift from the resource exploitative method of conventional development to the resource enrichment method of sustainable development.

1.3.3 Food Security

Total food production has nearly tripled since 1960, per capita production has increased by 30%, and food prices and the percentage of undernourished people have fallen. However, the benefits have been uneven, and about one billion people still go to bed hungry each night. Furthermore, intensive and extensive food production has caused significant environmental degradation. In addition to the loss of much biodiversity through outright habitat destruction from land clearing, tillage and irrigation methods can cause soil salinization and erosion; fertilizers, rice production, and livestock contribute to greenhouse gas emissions; unwise use of pesticides adds to global toxification; and fertilizer runoff plays havoc with freshwater and nearshore saltwater habitats.

One of the key challenges that the world faces is increasing agricultural productivity while reducing its environmental footprint through sustainable intensification, given that the demand for food is likely to double in the next 25–50 years, primarily in developing countries. Unfortunately, climate change is projected to significantly decrease agricultural productivity throughout much of the tropics and subtropics where hunger and poverty are endemic today.

The right to food should become a basic human right; a combination of political will, farmers' skill, and scientists' commitment will be needed to achieve this goal.

1.3.4 Water Security

Projections show that by 2025, over half of the world's population will live in severely water-stressed places, and by 2040, demand is projected to exceed supply. This situation is irrespective of climate change, which is likely to worsen it. Water quality is declining in many parts of the world, and 50–60% of wetlands have been lost. Human-induced climate change is projected to decrease water quality and availability in many arid- and semi-arid regions and increase the threats posed by floods and droughts in most parts of the world. This will have far-reaching implications, including for agriculture: 70% of all freshwater withdrawn from rivers and aquifers is currently used for irrigation. Of all irrigation water use, 15 – 35% of irrigation water use already exceeds supply, and is thus unsustainable.

Freshwater availability is spatially variable and scarce, particularly in many regions of Africa and Asia. Numerous dry regions, including many of the world's major "food bowls," are likely to become drier even under moderate levels of climate change. Glacier melt, which provides water for many developing countries, is likely to decrease over time and exacerbate problems of water shortage over the long term. Runoff will decrease in many places because of increased evapotranspiration. In contrast, more precipitation is likely to fall in many of the world's wetter regions. Developed regions and countries will also be affected. For example, summer in southern Europe is likely to be hotter and drier.

1.3.5 Human Security

Climate change and loss of ecosystem services coupled with other stresses threaten human security in many parts of the world, potentially increasing the risk of conflict and in-country and out-of-country migration (Figure 3).

Climate change risks the spread of conflict by undermining

Figure 3

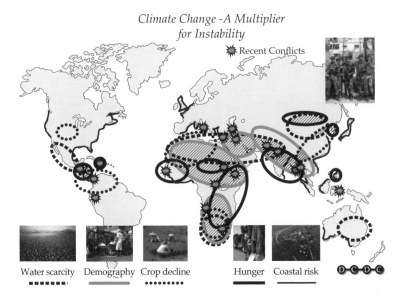

Climate Change -A Multiplier for Instability

Recent Conflicts

Water scarcity   Demography   Crop decline   Hunger   Coastal risk

the essentials of life for many poor people: (i) food shortages could increase in regions where hunger and famine currently exist; (ii) water shortages could become severe in areas where there are already water shortages; (iii) natural resources could be depleted with loss of ecological goods and services; (iv) tens of millions of people could be displaced in low-lying deltaic areas and small island states; (v) disease could increase; and (vi) severe weather events could be become more frequent and/or intense.

Many sub-Saharan African countries have millions of people in abject poverty (per capita incomes of less than $1 per day), who lack access to adequate food, clean water, and modern energy sources and are particularly dependent on natural resources for their very existence. In some cases, governments lack good governance and have to deal with political instability, with some in conflict and others emerging from conflict. Therefore, climate change, coupled with other stresses, risks local and regional conflict and migration, depending on the social, economic, and political circumstances.

2. The Way Forward

2.1 Our Vision

The current global development model is unsustainable. We can no longer assume that our collective actions will not trigger tipping points as we breach environmental thresholds, risking irreversible damage to both ecosystems and human communities. Therefore, our vision must be to eradicate poverty and reduce inequality; make growth more sustainable and inclusive; make production and consumption more sustainable; combat climate change; and respect other planetary boundaries, such as environmental limits. This goal demands that we recognize, understand, and act on interconnections between the economy, society, and the natural environment.

Sustainable development is fundamentally a question of people's opportunities to influence their future, claim their rights, and voice their concerns. Effective governance and respect for human rights are key prerequisites for empowering people to make sustainable choices. A serious shift toward sustainable development requires gender equality and an end to persistent discrimination against women. The next major increment of global well-being could well come from the full empowerment of women.

Because most goods and services sold today fail to bear the full environmental and social costs of production and consumption, we must reach consensus on methods to price them properly. Costing environmental externalities could generate new opportunities for green growth and green jobs. Another option is a manner of doing business as if nature and people were properly valued, without needing to know or signal that value. These options are not mutually exclusive, and because the first may take longer than we have, the second provides a useful safety net.

2.2 The Need to Act

We must act now to limit climate change and loss of biodiversity, and adapt to the already inescapable changes. To transition to a more sustainable future will require governmental and corporate policies that simultaneously redesign the economic system, support a technological revolution, and, above all, stimulate change behavior.

To lower the risks of climate change to acceptable levels, the world must reduce absolute emissions levels by at least a factor of 2.5 by 2050, which requires a reduction in emission per unit of output by around a factor of 8 if the world economy will be 3 times larger in 2050 than today. We clearly need a new industrial revolution. In addition to mitigating climate change, we must be prepared to adapt because we cannot avoid substantial changes in climate. Development, mitigation, and adaptation are intertwined, e.g., irrigation and urban design.

Now is the time to accelerate action. The world economy risks a prolonged slowdown as a consequence of the financial and economic crises of the past few years. Low-carbon growth is the only sound basis for a sustainable recovery. High-carbon growth would gravely imperil humanity's future, and therefore has no future.

Delay is dangerous and would be a profound mistake. The ratchet effect and technological lock-in increase the risks of dangerous climate change: delay could make stabilization of CO_2 concentrations at acceptable levels even more difficult than it already is. If we act strongly and the science is wrong, then we will still have new technologies, greater efficiency, and more forests. If we fail to act and the science is right, then humanity will be in such deep trouble that it will be very difficult to extricate ourselves. Both basic decision theory and common sense point to strong action, particularly because the science is very likely to be right. The Stern Review (2006) sets out the analytical case for early and strong action. The costs of action increase with delay.

The challenge is to generate substantial benefits simultaneously across multiple economic, environmental, and social objectives. This important synergy is advantageous, given that societies are more likely to adopt measures that create local and national benefits, such as improved local and immediate health and environment conditions, and support the local economy than measures serving primarily global and long-term goals, such as climate protection. An approach that emphasizes the local benefits of improved end-use efficiency and increased use of renewable energy creates a tapestry of solutions addressing global concerns.

In addition to addressing climate change, it is of equal importance to reduce the loss of biodiversity and rate of deforestation and forest degradation. Leaders must meet the 2020 Aichi targets to protect and conserve biodiversity.

2.3 Technology Options for Transition to a Low-Carbon Economy

The world's ~78% reliance on fossil fuels (~90% excluding traditionally scavenged biomass) is at the root of many of the world's toughest problems. Economic, security, health, and environmental reasons compel a vigorous transition beyond fossil fuels.

Many combinations of energy resources, end-use, and supply technologies can simultaneously address the multiple sustainability challenges. The various combinations share two common features: (i) radical improvements in energy end-use efficiency and (ii) significant shifts toward energy supply systems that emphasize renewable energies and advanced fossil fuel systems with carbon capture and storage.

The effectiveness of such solutions depends greatly on countries' geography and the level of affluence. Generally, developing countries located in tropical areas can benefit most from solar energy technologies, although cost-effectiveness is also becoming more common at higher latitudes. In industrialized countries with very high energy consumption per capita, energy efficiency measures can be very effective. Yet, developing countries with low energy consumption per capita can achieve economic progress by adopting early in their growth trajectory energy efficient technologies rather than obsolete technologies that will generate problems requiring later remediation. That is, though rich countries use a great deal of energy and waste much of it, poor people, despite using less energy, waste an even larger fraction of what they do use and can ill-afford that waste.

Efficiency improvement is usually the most cost-effective option and can generate benefits across multiple objectives, including alleviating poverty, reducing adverse environmental and health impacts, enhancing energy security, creating net employment and economic opportunities, and increasing flexibility in the selection of energy supply options.

Most countries have not achieved the 3–4% per year rate of decreased global energy and carbon intensity needed to stabilize the climate, and that goal is several times the global average. However, some private sector companies have decreased their energy intensity by far more than 3–4% per year. Most global economic growth is in places like China and India, which are currently building their infrastructure and can more easily build it right initially rather than fix it later. Poor people and countries most urgently need energy efficiency, have the greatest potential for it (they are poor partly because their use is so inefficient), and can thereby attain the most dramatic development gains. We can achieve universal access to electricity and cleaner cooking/heating stoves by 2030; however, this effort requires innovative institutions and national enabling mechanisms such as appropriate subsidies and financing. Clean stoves would substantially reduce indoor air pollution, which causes millions of premature deaths per year, and should also produce climate benefits by avoiding the byproducts of incomplete combustion.

The share of renewable energy in global primary energy could increase to 30–75%, and in some regions (particularly, but not limited to, tropical regions) could exceed 90% by 2050. The main task is to scale-up, reduce costs, and integrate renewables in future energy systems. Carefully developed, renewable energies can provide multiple benefits, including employment, energy security, human health, environment, and climate change mitigation.

Empirical evidence proves that switching from oil and coal to efficient use and diverse, climate-safe, renewable supplies will be profitable, not costly. Saving fuel is almost always cheaper than buying it, and integrative design can often even make large savings cheaper than small ones (expanding returns). Scores of market failures block efficiency but can be transformed into business opportunities. A number of renewable sources, as their costs plummet, now outcompete fossil fuels; most of the rest will do so very soon. Competitive clean energy has comprised half the world's new electric capacity since 2008, reaching a record $260 billion of private investment in 2011 and $1 trillion since 2004, and provides one-fifth of the world's electricity from one-fourth of its capacity. Fast-growing distributed resources add valuable resilience and can bring electricity to the 1.6 billion people who presently lack it.

Most components of Carbon Capture and Storage (CCS) systems are technically available; however, the primary task is to reduce costs and achieve rapid technology improvement. We hope that a number of pilot projects around the world will soon demonstrate their viability although issues of cost and siting remain to be resolved. End-use energy efficiency and renewable energy technologies will be potent competitors to CCS.

These new energy realities should shift the climate conversation from cost, burden, and sacrifice to profits, jobs, and competitive advantage. Even if one rejects climate science, transitioning to a low-carbon economy is sensible and profitable for many other compelling reasons. China, for example, is leading the global efficiency and clean-energy revolutions not because of international treaties and conventions but to speed its own development and improve public health and national security. Thus, climate leadership is shifting from international negotiations to firms, national and sub-national governments, and civil society and from North to South.

2.4 Adapting to Climate Change

Climate change impacts are already occurring, and further effects are inevitable. Although some impacts in certain parts of the world may have short-term benefits, most of them, particularly in poorer developing countries in Asia, Africa, and Latin America, will damage poor countries and communities.

All countries, developed and developing, will need to adapt to the impacts of climate change over the next few decades. However, there are limits to how effectively countries and communities can adapt. Adaptation becomes more difficult if temperatures exceed 2°C, which is of significant concern because the world is on a pathway to becoming 3–5°C warmer than it was during pre-industrial times.

The good news is that many countries, starting with the least developed, have already begun to plan adaptation to climate change and mainstream adaptations into development planning, such as Bangladesh's long-term Climate Change Strategy and Action Plan, the implementation of which has begun.

All countries, rich and poor, must develop national adaptation plans. Although many adaptation actions will be country- and location-specific, there are opportunities for learning lessons across countries, in south–south as well as south–north partnerships.

The most effective adaptation strategy is mitigation to limit the magnitude of climate change, particularly given the significant physical, financial, technological, and behavioral limits to adaptation.

2.5 Approaches to Conserve and Sustainably Use Biodiversity

The loss of biodiversity and degradation of ecosystem services can be stopped and reversed by concerted planning based on adequate data, a well-managed protected areas network, enhancement of the conservation value of agricultural areas supported by the new science of countryside biogeography, use of InVEST and other new tools for mapping and evaluating the services, and transformational shifts in the public and private sector that value the role of natural capital in economic development. The Convention on Biological Diversity (CBD) is the international umbrella for biodiversity, and its 2020 regional and global targets for protecting biodiversity, particularly targets on protected areas and preventing extinctions, are critically important.

To stop biodiversity loss and maintain the services humanity depends on, leaders must incorporate the value of ecosystem services and natural capital into national accounting and decision-making processes across all sectors of society, ensure equitably shared access to ecosystem benefits and costs of ecosystem conservation, and treat biodiversity and ecosystem services as the most fundamental components of green economic development. Therefore, we must further develop and use tools such as InVEST to motivate nations to establish a national inclusive wealth accounting system, including accounting for ecosystem services imported and exported, which could stimulate further approaches to ecosystem service marketplace development. These tools can assist decision makers in determining how to balance the trade-offs among ecosystem services in land use decisions at multiple spatial scales and include both economic and non-economic valuation. In addition, we must also initiate a campaign to build societal awareness, including building the concept into elementary and secondary school education.

Biodiversity and natural ecosystems are foundational to solving the climate crisis, as conservation can slow climate change, increase the adaptive capacity of both people and ecosystems, save lives, and sustain livelihoods in myriad ways as Earth's climate changes. Tropical forests, coastal marine habitats, and other ecosystems play major roles in global biogeochemical cycles, and are thus essential to mitigation. They are also widely available, and via protection and restoration, we can deploy them immediately to reduce atmospheric greenhouse gas concentrations without waiting for new technology. Nations must finance and implement an effective mechanism for Reducing Emissions from Deforestation and forest Degradation (REDD+) to support either reducing deforestation or, for some countries, maintaining already low deforestation rates.

A great advantage of ecosystems as a climate solution is that they play many roles simultaneously. Beyond mitigation, climate adaptation services provided by healthy, diverse ecosystems will become increasingly important in the face of climate change because they can somewhat counteract impacts such as changing freshwater flows, rising sea levels, and shifts in disease-carrying organisms and other pests. For example, mangroves store carbon, support fisheries, harbor diverse species, and can reduce storm impacts. In addition, ecosystems support human livelihoods by providing income and food alternatives that will be important where climate change disrupts current sources. Such diversification helps everyone, but particularly the most vulnerable communities and countries with the least capacity to cope with climate change.

National leaders can no longer think of climate mitigation and adaptation, for both nature and people, as separate problems, for they will not be solved in isolation. If human adaptation to climate change compromises forests or other ecosystems, this loss will speed climate change. If nations attempt climate change mitigation by, for example, reforestation using single-species stands rather than ensembles of native species, that tactic will reduce biodiversity. These losses will increase the need for adaptation even as our capacity to accommodate it diminishes. An integrated approach makes this cycle virtuous: by conserving biodiversity, we decelerate climate change while increasing the adaptive capacity of people and ecosystems alike.

A comprehensive, integrated ecosystem approach is a powerful strategy for identifying, analyzing, and resolving complicated environmental problems, rather than the piecemeal approaches to multifaceted environmental problems that do not work. The inclusiveness of the ecosystem approach provides a powerful framework for identifying new environmental problems or reshaping existing ones and then tackling their complexity, particularly when leaders combine ecosystem processes with social and economic considerations.

2.6 Food Security

Theoretically, we could feed the world today with affordable food while providing a viable income for the farmer with appropriate distribution of harvested foodstuffs. However, business-as-usual precludes this strategy in the foreseeable future. Leaders can address most of today's hunger problems with the appropriate use of current technologies, particularly appropriate agro-ecological practices (e.g., no/low till, integrated pest management, and integrated natural resource management); however, these must be coupled with decreased post-harvest losses and broad-scale rural development. This strategy will require recognizing the critical role of women and empowering them through education, property rights, access to financing, and access to markets via improved roads. In addition, nations must negotiate and implement global-scale trade policy reforms to stimulate local production in developing countries.

Emerging issues such as climate change and new plant and animal pests may increase our future need for higher productivity and may require advanced biotechnologies, in which case we must carefully evaluate the risks and benefits.

To impart the dimension of economic and ecological sustainability in farming requires promoting integrated attention to conservation, cultivation, consumption, and commerce. A country can become a knowledge and innovation superpower only if its leaders pay attention to nutrition and education for all children, women, and men from cradle to grave.

2.7 Water Security

Addressing the challenges associated with water scarcity will require (i) river basin management (often transnational), multi-sectoral management (e.g., agriculture, industry, and households), and coupled land-and-water management; (ii) comprehensive stakeholder involvement (e.g., state, private sector, and civil society–particularly women) with management action at the lowest level; and (iii) improved allocation and quality enhancement via incentives and economic principles. The mere 20% global average cost recovery for water poses a major problem for water management; therefore, it is crucial, yet controversial, to price water correctly as well as reform IMF and World Bank policies to ensure access for poor people.

2.8 Competence in Leadership

Sustainable development implies a major paradigm shift with unprecedented global implications. It is a trivial statement to say that we cannot expect substantial and effective international geopolitical decisions to be made without a precedent. When we need major change, new institutional and governmental models, with the competence needed for appropriately scaled change, will rely on pioneering role models. In paradigm shifts, such models demonstrate that the obsolete paradigm is less beneficial, and that the new paradigm is not only more beneficial but also feasible. Pioneering role models pave the way for the required large-scale policies. Such role models are already providing leadership, and the paper by Karl-Henrik Robert describes several of these. What we must now do is empower and coach the existing pioneering role models to help them scale up sufficiently to empower the required policies. In that context, science can do more than merely demonstrate the need for change and/or explain the complexity of the problems we encounter. In addition, science can demonstrate modes of thinking and planning to exploit the opportunities that follow from the required paradigm shift, not the least from the pioneer's "enlightened" self-interest perspective, and suggest more robust methods of managing the complexity.

Recently, leaders have often attempted policies and plans for sustainable development through piecemeal, narrowly driven agendas. To avoid this ineffective approach it is helpful but insufficient to take a "holistic" systems perspective, recognizing that as we add more and more essential aspects from the system into models and then relate them to all the others, complexity grows and eventually becomes unmanageable. What is needed is truly holistic thinking and action and not just holistic modeling. Each leader wanting to solve a problem typically confronts the fact that he or she has generated another problem elsewhere in the system, such as phasing out the irritating gas ammonia and replacing it with CFCs, only to run into an even larger problem risking the entire ozone layer. How can we learn to design the sustainability problems out of the system? Would it be possible to find such principles for redesign, rather than reacting to emerging realities and "fixing" more and worse problems as they surface?

We need a robust definition of sustainability that we can operationalize for any topic/sector/region/organization. Leaders frequently employ such principles for all kinds of innovation including those outside the domain of sustainable development. This approach is particularly important when current trends are part of the problem, and we may be sorely tempted to spend money on superficially "fixing" problems instead of solving their root causes. Such principles can then work as constraints or, to employ a more technical term, "boundary conditions for redesign." For adequate planning in complex systems, such a set of boundary conditions or constraints serve as a "lens" between the system and the strategic policies and plans and build on an understanding of the basic mechanisms of destruction that underlie the myriad problems. Fixing problems individually will not work. To employ such boundary conditions for sustainability is mandatory for rationally (i) dealing with system boundaries, (ii) dealing with multi-dimensional trade-offs, (iii) making sustainable potentials for various technical systems calculable, and (iv) facilitating cooperation between sectors and disciplines. People from different sectors and disciplines could then raise problems and solutions in relation to the same set of boundary conditions, compare notes, and then find opportunities for synergies and cooperation.

35

A Framework for Strategic Sustainable Development (FSSD) has been developed during a 20-year peer-reviewed consensus process amongst scientists to empower and train leaders and policymakers to plan this way and to provide them with the FSSD aligned tools and concepts that they may need, such as tools for sustainability analysis, goal setting, product/service development, modeling, simulation, monitoring, and other processes. A growing network of universities across the globe is currently designing a joint research program to further this approach. In this effort, they use the FSSD to structure diverse research projects by putting them in the context of global sustainability and to enable more efficient interdisciplinary cooperation.

A growing number of executives in business and leaders of regions/cities across the globe are currently learning how to employ the FSSD and its related tools in everyday operations. They approach the sustainability principles systematically and stepwise while improving on bottom-line finances, exercising "enlightened self-interest." They use not only forecasting, "improving" what they did before, but also bridge the gap to sustainability (backcasting from the boundary conditions). In addition, they empower, rather than discourage, proactive policymakers in legislation procedures and at international summits. This initiative feeds into the next section. We need governance models that can empower the pioneering role models. Shared mental models of boundary conditions for sustainability will not suffice unless we establish infrastructures for bringing people together to co-create solutions.

2.9 The Importance of Good Governance

The decision-making systems on which we rely in government, business, and society exhibit serious shortcomings. Building more effective governance and institutions is central to achieving more sustainable patterns of development–globally, nationally, and locally. Yet, we often neglect the central importance of governance issues, partly because of the different definitions used for "governance" and the abstractness of these norms and structures. An analysis of governance needs to ask, "How, where, and by whom are decisions made?"; "Who gets to write the rules by which decisions are made?"; "What gets decided, and who gains what?"; and "How can people monitor the decision-making process?" Governance is more than just a question of the institutional architecture and how elements relate to each other. Each element presents issues of credibility and legitimacy concerning the processes by which rules are made and remade, interpreted and re-interpreted.

The rules and institutions for decision making are influenced by vested interests, each with very different levels of influence on the process. For example, lobbyists spend a large amount of time and money trying to influence the way elected representatives vote in many legislatures. Furthermore, we must see governance as a dynamic phenomenon, an ongoing process of negotiation between interests, played out in a series of arenas and institutions, nationally and globally. The legitimacy of technical evidence marshaled within such negotiations is critical and often contested, as has been evident in the climate change talks.

Governance involves much more than the ensemble of government framework and includes multiple and overlapping governance systems, with the private sector, civil society, subnational, and local levels all engaged in making decisions in relation to their interests. A widespread assumption exists that governments are the central actors in governance; however, a deeper investigation reveals that government is often an instrument of both its own and others' interests, rather than playing the role of an objective arbiter. The existence of plural and overlapping systems of governance can lead to competition between rival structures and institutional "shopping."

Transformation of governance systems must accommodate a far broader range of interests (poor and rich, young and old, future and present) and ensure access to information regarding the possible impacts of different decision. Subsidiarity, control at the lowest possible level, should be a central principle for sustainable development governance to assure that decisions about resource allocation and use are made at the appropriate level by the appropriate authority for the resource in question. Shifting power to lower levels is vital to bring in local knowledge, increase accessibility to decision making, and ensure a broader range of voices in the debate. Innovations must ensure that the marginalized have a voice that counts through, for example, coalition building, organization, and mobilization to make those voices' heard more effectively. Public hearings, social audits, and participatory budgeting can bring the voices of marginalized groups to the fore.

At the national level, effective changes in governance require a transparent means for people to hold those in power to account. Parliamentary and press oversight are key alongside freedom of information; however, in many countries, these mechanisms remain weak. The accountability challenge is compounded by alliances cemented between government officials and powerful individuals and corporations. The international nature of much of the corporate sector involved in natural resource use means that even the governments of the countries in which they are headquartered have limited influence on their actions and decisions.

Globally, we urgently need better means to agree upon and implement measures to achieve our collective goals. Given the large numbers of states and their separate jurisdictions, we need more effective and far-reaching international institutions and rules. Yet, nation-states are unwilling to submit to collective agreements that constrain their freedom of action. Similarly, we need greater control over international financial and corporate actors to reduce their ability to escape fiscal and other responsibilities through freedom of movement between jurisdictions. Global efforts to address climate change have resulted in a complex international governance architecture, which has largely replicated geopolitical and global economic power relations among nations. These evolving governance arrangements allow little room for the priorities of weaker countries and marginalized people to be heard and addressed. Growing reliance on the G20 as a forum for sorting out global problems risks disempowering the large number of smaller, less economically prominent nations.

Development policymakers and practitioners are increasingly turning to markets as a tool for addressing sustainability and alleviating poverty. Yet, market governance also presents major challenges. Markets and business have the potential to generate new and decent jobs, and use natural assets more sustainably. However, market signals and incentives must be established in ways that mobilize businesses and others to support sustainable growth, create the "missing markets" for environmental goods and services, and ensure more equitable participation. In addition, they need government to ensure the institutional and regulatory infrastructure that allows markets to operate effectively, such as support of property rights. A second worry concerns the lack of accountability of market chains and transnational operations that can evade national laws and regulatory frameworks. A third relates to finding the incentives for environmentally sustainable practices pertaining to the mainstream, as opposed to "niche" sustainable businesses.

Governance failures also occur because decisions are being made in sectoral compartments, with environmental, social, and economic dimensions being addressed by separate competing structures. At government level, this means moving sustainable development concerns from beyond Ministries of Environment to focus on Ministries of Agriculture, Energy, Finance, Planning, Health, and Education as entry points. Cross-ministerial buy-in demands that sustainability be led by the head of government, and that environmental and social valuations are brought into decision making. In business, environment and social issues need to move from corporate social responsibility (CSR) departments into core business operations, with companies required to report in terms of the triple bottom line. In society, more generally, groups such as NGOs need to work together to bridge divides and recognize both common interests and trade-offs between different objectives.

In policies for economic development, anti-corruption

measures have received increased attention. We can speak of an international "good governance" regime supported by many national and international aid organizations and their research institutes. The policy advice from this "regime" has previously been largely geared toward incremental change by finding institutional solutions that will create a "virtuous circle." It is very unlikely that small institutional devices can initiate a process toward establishing good governance in countries with systemic corruption. On the basis of an understanding of corruption as a "social trap," theorists propose that to establish a new equilibrium of social and economic exchange we need a "big-bang," that is, sufficient financial resources to establish public institutions–schools, hospitals, police, courts, and the like–characterized by three qualities: impartiality, competence, and ethical behavior.

2.10 Regional Cooperation

Global cooperation along the conventional path of economic development has been unsustainable because of prevailing nations' self-centered economic interests in a world without politically viable global institutions for sustainable development. Therefore, regional cooperation can play a key role in the transformation to a more sustainable world. Regional cooperation in ASEAN has through the years developed trust within its member-states, which has grown into a common vision and interests in jointly addressing regional developmental issues and created common interests in pursuing sustainable development together.

It is of the utmost importance that we forge an effective link between economic policies–with their impacts on poverty eradication and enhancement of life supporting natural ecosystems at the sub-regional level–and measurable indicators as the basis for geospatial natural resource management planning, superimposed on layers of social poverty location mapping and economic potentials of resource distribution. Indonesia's search for an implementable sustainable development model has demonstrated that macro-economic policies intended to raise GDP may well reach their economic objectives, though not necessarily achieving the social development objective of reducing poverty or the environmental goal of sustaining natural resources.

We can draw important lessons from regional cooperation efforts to pursue sustainable development on issues of common interest in the ASEAN region, such as the Coral Reefs Triangle Cooperation, Forests Cooperation, and Joint Efforts in Reducing Emissions of Deforestation and Degradation of Land (REDD). These efforts can become global building blocks, despite the fact that global cooperation is not advancing. Similar regional cooperative efforts in East Asia, Africa, Latin America, and others may develop support, providing a base that ultimately generates global cooperation on sustainable development.

2.11 Innovation and Grassroots Action

"The Earth has enough for every man's need but not for one man's greed"- Gandhi.

At the outset, we must acknowledge that since Rio 1992, community-based groups in the poorer, most inaccessible rural areas around the world have demonstrated the power of grassroots action to change policy at regional and national levels. In consultation with communities, governments have implemented innovative methods and approaches and scaled them up to cover thousands of individuals living in communities on less than $1/day.

Unfortunately, though, they have not been collectively visible enough to catch the attention of policymakers and the power brokers who formulate crucial global policies without engaging with them at the cutting-edge levels.

Without devaluing the tremendous contribution of such grassroots action and while showing them the respect and recognition they deserve, we must urgently bring them to the attention of powerful policymakers and policy influencers and convey the belief that all is not lost and that we can still save the planet and humanity.

New ideas have been implemented as a result of collective grass roots action from which we can learn lessons only if policymakers and power brokers have the humility and ability to listen. The main lessons could be summarized as follows:

- There is no urban solution to the problem of rural poverty. The simple solutions which the rural poor have used to tackle the issues of climate change and water security (Box 1) already exist; however, we have yet to put a mechanism in place for learning from them. Best practices with the potential to scale up exist and must be highlighted.

Box 1

We must revive the traditional practice of collecting rainwater for drinking and irrigation. It has been used, tested, and proved over hundreds of years. However, ever since the academic engineers arrived on the scene, this practice has been devalued, and the technology solution of exploiting (and thus abusing) ground water through powerful and polluting drilling rigs that install deep well pumps has seriously depleted groundwater. Thousands of open wells for irrigation and hand pumps for drinking water have gone dry. We must collect water from the roofs of public buildings (e.g., schools and dispensaries) into underground tanks to be used for drinking and sanitation. We must construct small dams to allow for groundwater recharge, thus revitalizing the dry open wells and hand pumps, reclaiming collective assets worth millions of dollars. We need simple, practical solutions multiplied on a large scale across the world. This approach will provide a tremendous long-term return on a relatively small investment.

- We must address the critical issues of poverty and climate change through primarily social, not technical, means. The problems of corruption, wasted funds, poor technology choices, and deficient transparency or accountability are social problems for which innovative grassroots solutions have emerged. For example, the model and practice of public hearings and social audits came from the people who were fed up with government inaction in India. Now it has been institutionalized and benefits nearly 600,000 villages in India.

- Grassroots groups have found the value and relevance of a South–South Partnership where the use and application of traditional knowledge, village skills, and practical wisdom between communities across continents have resulted in low-cost community-based solutions that have had an incredible impact in improving the quality of life. Migration from rural to urban areas has decreased, as has dependency on urban and technology skills.
- The empowerment of women represents the ultimate sustainable rural solution. By improving their capacity and competence to provide basic services in rural areas (such as training them as solar engineers–Box 2), they could become the pioneering role models for the world.

Box 2

Without using the written or spoken word and through sign language alone, 300 illiterate rural grandmothers aged 35–50 have been trained as solar engineers. In six months, they have solar-electrified over 15,000 houses, reaching more than 100 villages, and covering the entire continent of Africa (28 countries in five years) at a total cost of $ 2.5 million. This is what is spent on one Millennium Village in Africa. If a grandmother is selected from any part of the developing world, the Indian government pays the airfare and six months training costs in India. The funds for the hardware have been provided by the GEF Small Grants Program, UNWOMEN, UNESCO, the Skoll Foundation, and individual philanthropists.

- The long-term answer is not a centralized system but a demystified and decentralized system where the management, control, and ownership of the technology lie in the hands of the communities themselves and do not depend on professionals, with little relevant experience, from outside the villages.

- Listen and learn how poor communities across the world view the problems of energy, water, food, and livelihoods as interdependent and integrated parts of a living ecosystem and not separately.

2.12 Knowledge Generation and Assessment

Given the importance of credible peer-reviewed knowledge to inform national and international policy formulation and implementation, we need to support research and development and national and international assessments.

National and international, coordinated, and interdisciplinary research is a critical underpinning for informed policy formulation and implementation. We urgently need to strengthen the scientific and technological infrastructure in most developing countries. The International Council (ICSU) and International Social Science Council (ISSC) have led the effort to integrate the World Climate Research Program (WCRP), the International Geosphere Biosphere Program (IGPB), the International Human Dimensions Program (IHDP), Diversitas, and the integrated Earth System Science Programs (ESSP) into the Future Earth program. Future Earth will provide the multi-disciplinary knowledge base (social science, humanities, economics, natural sciences, engineering, and technologies) necessary for sustainable development.

Despite the uncertainties, knowledge gaps, and controversies in our evidence base with respect to biodiversity and ecosystem services, we have sufficient information to more sustainably manage our ecosystems and the flows of services from them. To refine our understanding of the fundamental ecosystem processes underpinning the delivery of ecosystem services, we must both extend our observations and experimental manipulations and improve our models of the key mechanisms. Better holistic ecosystem thinking and models offer a potential way forward for understanding some of the uncertainties and highlighting the sensitivities of multiple interacting drivers of ecosystems, the processes within them, and the flow of services and goods.

We must quantify and understand the inputs and outputs of individual ecosystems that are the functional connection among all ecosystems, constituting the "pulse" of the planet, which, when measured quantitatively, have major management relevance for understanding and resolving environmental problems. Long-term research and monitoring frequently provides new insights into complicated environmental problems. Therefore, we must develop a global and comprehensive experimental and monitoring network that probes the nature of diversity and ecosystem processes and services in present and anticipated future environments and accelerates the capacity for future scenario work.

We need improved high spatial resolution regional climate projections to improve the quantification of extreme weather events and assess the impact of climate change on socioeconomic sectors (e.g., food and water), ecological systems, and human health.

Governments should support research and testing of new technologies, such as low-loss smart electric grids, electrical vehicles interacting with the power grid, energy storage, improved nuclear power plant designs (in the view of some), and carbon capture and storage, as well as education and planning to foster and achieve a sustainable human population and lifestyles.

Independent, global expert assessments that encompass risk assessment and management have proven to be a critical component of the science–policy interface. Such assessments must be policy-relevant rather than policy-prescriptive. International assessments such as the Stratospheric Ozone Depletion Assessments, Millennium Ecosystem Assessment (MA), the Intergovernmental Panel on Climate Change (IPCC), and the International Assessment of Agricultural Science and Technology for Development (IAASTD) have all provided national governments and the international negotiating processes with credible, multi-disciplinary, peer-reviewed knowledge, acknowledging what is known, unknown, and controversial. The newly developed Intergovernmental Platform on

Biodiversity and Ecosystem Services (IPBES) will provide vital information through periodic assessments of the knowledge needed for ecosystem service delivery and the status of the delivery system.

However, we need a web-based multi-disciplinary knowledge assessment system that critically reviews, integrates, and synthesizes new knowledge with previous information in as close to real time as possible to produce the information needed to strengthen the science–policy interface and implement sustainable development nationally, regionally, and globally.

The concept of an electronic, web-based system for the critical, peer-reviewed, integrated assessment and synthesis of multi-disciplinary knowledge for creating a world that enhances and sustains human security (economic, social, and environmental) in the context of local, regional, and global environmental change is gaining general acceptance through a series of formal and informal discussions. Peer-reviewed and gray literature on all aspects of poverty alleviation, human well-being, food, water, energy, materials and human security, climate change, biodiversity loss and ecosystem degradation, land and water degradation, and air quality would be uploaded into a web-based system, critically reviewed, and synthesized with previous information.

3. Conclusion

Climate change and loss of biodiversity undermine sustainable development. However, there is no dichotomy between economic progress and protecting our environment by limiting climate change and loss of biodiversity. Indeed, the cost of mitigating climate change is less than the cost of inaction if one takes the ethical position of not discounting future generations, and delaying action can significantly increase costs. Efficient resource use (e.g., energy or water) saves money for businesses and households. Valuing and creating markets for ecosystem services can provide new economic opportunities. A green economy will be a source of future employment and innovation. Governments, the private sector, and voluntary organizations and civil society at large all have key roles in the transition to a low-carbon economy, adaptation to climate change, and a more sustainable use of ecosystems.

If we are to achieve our dream, the time to act is now, given the inertia in the socioeconomic system, and that the adverse effects of climate change and loss of biodiversity cannot be reversed for centuries or are irreversible (e.g., species loss). Failure to act will impoverish current and future generations.

Part 2
Individual Contributions

Resilient People, Resilient Planet
A Future Worth Choosing

Gro Harlem Brundtland

This is the title chosen by the High Level Panel on Global Sustainability, appointed by the UN Secretary General in 2010. It was presented to His Excellency Ban Ki Moon in Addis Ababa on January 30, 2012, by one of its two co-chairs, President Jacob Zuma of South Africa.

In his remarks, the Secretary General made the following key observations: "Increasing strains and crises in recent years point to the deterioration of the natural environment. The changing climate is one key manifestation. We are reaching, and increasingly overstepping, planetary boundaries. Efforts to reach the Millennium Development Goals and other social and economic targets are hampered by the inability to agree on decisive and coordinated action in national and multilateral fora. This reveals the weaknesses of our governance structures and our outdated development models. It shows the limits of our current approach, which continues to deal with individual symptoms rather than the causes and their interrelationships." He called for us to "reflect on and formulate a new vision for sustainable growth and prosperity, along with mechanisms for achieving it."

Also co-chaired by President Tarjei Halonen of Finland, the Panel comprised 22 members from all continents of the world, including former and present prime ministers, foreign ministers, ministers of development cooperation, and environment ministers, as well as people with experience from the private sector.

The Panel concluded that although the need to integrate the

economic, social, and environmental dimensions of development to achieve sustainability was clearly defined a quarter of a century ago, it is now time to make it happen!

The report "Our Common Future" introduced the concept of sustainable development to the international community as a new paradigm for economic growth, social equality, and environmental sustainability. It argued that an integrated policy framework embracing all of those three pillars could achieve that vision.

Since then, the world has gained a deeper understanding of the interconnected challenges we face, and the fact that sustainable development provides the best opportunity for people to choose their future.

The High Level Panel on Global Sustainability proposes that by making transparent the costs of action and inaction, the political process can summon both the arguments and the political will necessary to act for a sustainable future.

Therefore, long-term vision of the Panel is "to eradicate poverty and reduce inequality, make growth inclusive, and production and consumption more sustainable while combating climate change and respecting a range of other planetary boundaries."

In light of this goal, the report makes a range of concrete recommendations to implement its vision for a sustainable planet, a just society, and a growing economy. Sustainable development is not a destination, but a dynamic process of adaptation, learning, and action. It is about recognizing, understanding, and acting on interconnections – above all, those between the economy, society, and the natural environment. The world is not yet on this path. Progress has been made, but it has been neither fast nor deep enough, and the need for farther-reaching action is growing ever more urgent.

At the same time, the status quo is increasingly facing challenges from powerful drivers of change: the impacts of current production and consumption patterns and resource scarcity, innovation, demographic change, changes in the global economy, green growth, growing inequality, changing political dynamics, and urbanization.

What, then, can we do to make a real difference for the world's people and the planet? We must understand the dimensions of the challenge.

We must recognize that the drivers of that challenge include unsustainable lifestyles, production and consumption patterns, and the impact of population growth.

As the global population grows from almost seven billion to nine billion by 2040, and with the emergence of three billion new middle-class consumers over the next 20 years, the demand for resources is rising exponentially.

By 2030, the world will need at least 50% more food, 45% more energy and 30% more water – all at a time when environmental boundaries are creating new limits to supply. This is markedly true for climate change, which affects all aspects of human and planetary health.

The current global development model is unsustainable. We can no longer assume that our collective actions will not trigger tipping points as environmental thresholds are breached, risking irreversible damage to both ecosystems and human communities.

At the same time, such thresholds should not be used to impose arbitrary growth ceilings on developing countries seeking to lift their people out of poverty. Indeed, if we fail to resolve the sustainable development dilemma, we risk condemning up to three billion members of our human family to a life of endemic poverty. Neither of these outcomes is acceptable, and we must find a new way forward.

Importantly, sustainable development is not a synonym for "environmental protection." Instead, it is fundamentally about recognizing, understanding, and acting on interconnections– above all, those between the economy, society, and the natural environment. Sustainable development is about seeing the whole picture, such as the critical links between food, water, land, and energy, ensuring that our actions today are consistent with where we want to go tomorrow.

It is time to take genuine global action to enable people, mar-

53

kets, and governments to make sustainable choices. The more influence we have in society, the greater is our potential impact on the planet and our responsibility to behave sustainably–never more so than today, when globalization and the constraints of our natural resources mean that individual choices can have global consequences.

For too many of us, the problem is not unsustainable choices, but a fundamental lack of choices. Real choice is possible only once basic needs and human security are assured. They must include

- **international commitments** to eradicate poverty, promote human rights and human security, and advance gender equality;
- **education for sustainable development**, including secondary and vocational education, and building of skills to help ensure that all of society can contribute to solutions that address today's challenges and capitalize on opportunities;
- **employment opportunities**, especially for women and youth to drive green and sustainable growth;
- enabling consumers to make **sustainable choices** and advance responsible behavior individually and collectively;
- **managing resources** and enabling a 21st Century Green Revolution in agriculture, oceans and coastal systems, and energy and technology;
- **building resilience** through sound safety nets, disaster risk reduction, and adaptation planning.

The opportunities for change are vast. We are not passive, helpless victims of the impersonal, determinist forces of history. We have the exciting prospect of choosing for the future.

The challenges we face are great, but so are the new possibilities that appear when we look at old problems with fresh eyes.

Solutions include, for example, unleashing technologies capable of pulling us back from the planetary brink; new markets, new growth, and new jobs emanating from game-changing products and services; new approaches to public and private finance that can truly lift people out of the poverty trap.

The truth is that sustainable development is fundamentally a question of people's opportunities to influence their future, claim their rights, and voice their concerns.
Democratic governance and full respect for human rights are key prerequisites for empowering people to make sustainable choices.

The Panel calls for a new approach to the political economy of sustainable development to be implemented to address the sustainable development challenge in a fresh and operational way. That sustainable development is the right approach is self-evident. Our challenge is to demonstrate that it is also rational, and that the cost of inaction far outweighs the cost of action.

The Panel's report makes a range of concrete recommendations to implement our vision for a sustainable planet, a just society, and a growing economy:

- It is critical that we embrace a new nexus between food, water, and energy rather than treating them in different silos. All three must be fully integrated, not treated separately if we are to deal with the global food security crisis. It is time to embrace a second green revolution – an evergreen revolution – that doubles yields but builds on sustainability principles.

- It is time for bold global efforts, including launching a major global scientific initiative, to strengthen the interface between science and policy. We must define, through science, what scientists call "planetary boundaries," "environmental thresholds," and "tipping points." We should give highest priority to challenges now facing the marine environment and the "blue economy."

- Most goods and services sold today fail to bear the full environmental and social costs of production and consumption. On the basis of the science, we must reach consensus, over time, on methodologies to price them properly. Costing environmental externalities could open new opportunities for green growth and green jobs.

Addressing social exclusion and widening social inequity, too, requires that we measure them, cost them, and take responsibility for them. The next step is exploring how we can deal with these critical issues to create better outcomes for all.

Equity needs to be at the forefront. Developing countries need time, as well as financial and technological support, to transition to sustainable development. All of society must be empowered – particularly women, young people, the unemployed, the most vulnerable, and weakest sections of society. Properly reaping the demographic dividend requires us to include young people in society, politics, the labor market, and business development.

Any serious shift toward sustainable development requires gender equality and an end to persistent discrimination against women. The next increment of global growth could well come from the full economic empowerment of women.

The scale of investment, innovation, technological development, and employment creation required for sustainable development and poverty eradication is beyond the range of the public sector. Therefore, the Panel supports using the power of the economy to forge inclusive and sustainable growth and create value beyond narrow concepts of wealth. Markets and entrepreneurship will be a prime driver of decision making and economic change.

Therefore, the Panel presents a challenge for our governments and international institutions: to work better together in solving common problems and advancing shared interests. Quantum change is possible when willing actors join hands in forward-looking coalitions and lead the contribution to sustainable development.

The Panel argues that by embracing a new approach to the political economy of sustainable development, we will bring the sustainable development paradigm from the margins to the mainstream of the global economic debate. Thus, the cost of both action and inaction would become transparent. Only then would the political process be able to summon both the arguments and the political will necessary to act for a sustainable future.

Achieving sustainability requires us to transform the global economy. Tinkering at the edges will not do the job. The current global economic crisis, which has led many to question the performance of existing global economic governance, offers an opportunity for root-and-branch reform. It gives us a chance to shift decisively toward green growth, not only in the financial system but also in the real economy. Policy action is needed in a number of key areas:

- **incorporating social and environmental costs** in regulating and pricing of goods and services, as well as addressing market failures;
- creating an **incentive roadmap** that increasingly values long-term sustainable development criteria in investment and financial transactions;
- increasing **finance for sustainable development**, including public and private funding and partnerships to mobilize large volumes of new financing;
- changing **how we measure progress** in sustainable development by creating sustainable development indicators.

To achieve sustainable development, we must clearly build a more effective framework of institutions and decision-making processes at the local, national, regional, and global levels.

We must overcome the legacy of fragmented institutions established around single-issue silos, deficits of both leadership and political space, lack of flexibility in adapting to new kinds of challenges and crises, and a failure to anticipate and plan for both challenges and opportunities, all of which undermine both policymaking and delivery on the ground.

To build better governance, coherence, and accountability for sustainable development at the national and global levels, these are priority areas:

- **coherence at sub-national, national, and international** levels;
- a set of **Sustainable Development Goals**;

- a periodic **Global Sustainable Development Outlook report** that brings together information and assessments currently dispersed across institutions and analyzes them in an integrated manner;
- a new commitment to revitalize and reform the international institutional framework, including considering the creation of a **Global Sustainable Development Council**.

The Panel believes it is within the wit and will of our common humanity to choose for the future. We are on the side of hope.

All great achievements in human history began as a vision before becoming a reality. The vision for global sustainability, producing both resilient people and a resilient planet, is no different.

In the year 2030, a child born in 2012 will turn 18. Will we have done enough in the intervening years to give her the sustainable, fair, and resilient future that all of our children deserve? We all must join forces to give her an answer.

Our Unrecognized Emergency

Paul R. Ehrlich and Anne H. Ehrlich

Humanity has stumbled into an unprecedented yet scarcely recognized global emergency. Suddenly, in ecological time, the global community faces a desperate predicament, requiring it to quickly design and implement new global governance and economic systems that are at once more equitable and able to supply prosperity to billions more people. This task is more than daunting; however, with the additional requirement that those systems must put humanity on track to become sustainable on a finite planet – in effect, to "resize" the entire human enterprise – the challenge becomes truly monumental.

Yet, humanity's corporate behavior remains utterly inappropriate for dealing with a series of increasingly urgent problems such as resource constraints, environmental degradation, and climate disruption. The world community faces the potentially lethal fallout from a combination of increasingly rapid technological evolution matched with very slow ethical–social evolution. The human ability to do has vastly outstripped the ability to understand. Both genetically and culturally, people have always been small-group animals; evolution shaped us to deal with at most a few hundred other individuals who were genetically closely related to us. Although, over centuries, we have progressed far enough to manage national entities with shared languages and cultures, contending successfully with a global population of billions has so far largely eluded us. As a result, humanity faces a perfect storm of problems driven by overpopulation, overconsumption by the rich, the use of environmentally damaging technologies, and gross inequalities.

Earth is now so overpopulated that it would require about five additional planets to support in the long term today's global population at the lifestyle of the average citizen of the United States. In fact, even with today's consumption patterns, leaving billions in poverty, Earth is insufficient to sustain the present population over the long term. Nonetheless, as many as two and a half billion more people are scheduled to be added to that population by mid-century.

Powerful technologies that benefit people in many ways have a dark side in that they have facilitated the rapid depletion of humanity's natural capital: deep agricultural soils, fossil groundwater, the biodiversity that runs its life-support systems, and natural sinks to absorb its dangerous effluents. Civilization is disrupting the global climate, spreading toxic chemicals from pole to pole, increasing the chances of vast epidemics, and risking nuclear war over resources, particularly water, and nuclear terrorism over political and religious differences. A significant portion of the scientific community fears that, at most, a decade or two remain to undertake seriously revolutionizing our energy-mobilizing systems, which are still extremely dependent on fossil fuels, and make substantial progress in revising the global agriculture system to meet future needs flexibly. If leading climatologists are correct,[1] Earth's temperature and precipitation patterns will probably be changing continually for a millennium or more. Any chance of maintaining a level of food production adequate to provide a decent diet to all of today's population would require success in both increasing food production and upgrading water-handling systems as well as improving food distribution. Doing the same for 9.5 billion people by 2050 without further destruction of agriculture's underpinnings may prove impossible in the face of global change.

Today more than a billion people are inadequately nourished, even though the planet produces enough food to provide everyone an adequate diet. The inequity of this situation is underlined by several hundred million other people being overweight in industrialized nations. That fact alone suggests that improving equity could make a major contribution to re-solving the human predicament. For such improvement to oc-cur in a world faced with the possible addition of 2–3 billion more people in the next half-century, equity of access to food supplies must be high on the global agenda, as must be assur-ing that food production per capita does not continue to fall.[2]

On the demand side, more gender equity could help limit population growth and thus improve the chances of maintain-ing an adequate food supply. Total fertility rates correlate highly with measures of women's rights and opportunities; as women gain autonomy, their fertility tends to fall. A more gender, ra-cially, and economically equitable world could do more than greatly reduce both hunger and total fertility rates. In addition, it would allow for a better educated global population, where more people could focus on problems beyond those inherent in their personal situations. In turn, one hopes they would be able to deal more sensibly and cooperatively with both the environ-mental aspects of the current emergency and with the need for further efforts to reduce inequities.

The importance of reducing inequity to increase the chances of resolving the human predicament is obvious from only the differences in access to food and other resources caused by the tremendous power gap between the rich and the poor. The lack of funds for such activities as provision of family planning ser-vices and desperately needed agricultural research contrasts sharply with the expenditures by the United States and other rich nations to assure their supplies of oil.[3] The central geo-political role of oil continues unabated despite the dangerous conflicts that oil-seeking has already generated and the prob-able catastrophic consequences its continued burning portends for climate disruption. The international wars associated with oil and other resources will undoubtedly continue to be accom-panied by struggles within developing nations. Indeed, as long ago as 1993, a group of distinguished scientists warned, before Rwanda, Darfur, Somalia, and the Arab Spring, of coming vio-lence "especially in poor countries where shortages of water, forests, and, especially, fertile land, coupled with rapidly expanding populations, already cause great hardship."[4]

The recent shift of the United States and some other nations toward becoming corporate plutocracies, with wealth transferred in large quantities from the poor and middle classes to the very rich, has clearly done enormous environmental damage. The Citizens United decision of the U.S. Supreme Court in 2010 essentially made corporations the legal equivalent of human beings with all their rights and privileges, in effect equating money with speech. It was only the latest step of the rich to increase their own power to buy the votes of lawmakers, control the media, and pursue campaigns designed to put their profits above the social good.[5]

This malign corporate influence is particularly visible in the way the corporate–government complex in the United States and elsewhere promotes the impossible idea that economic growth is the cure for all the problems of the world. Actually, it is the disease. As economist Kenneth Boulding famously said in 1966, "Anyone who believes that exponential growth can go on forever in a finite world is either a madman or an economist."[6]

Unfortunately, many people fail to realize that the "standard" economists' goal of a 3.5% perpetual annual economic growth implies an impossibility–an economy more than 30 times as large as today's in a century. Even in the short term, it is a recipe for catastrophe; considering non-linearities, it would likely mean much more than doubling humanity's destructive impact on its life-support systems in just 20 years. Ehrlich and Holden pointed out long ago that population size and per capita environmental impact are not independent variables.[7]

Homo sapiens is a brilliant animal, greatly inclined to pick the low-hanging fruit first, and particularly in industrial societies, its activities are largely far past the point of diminishing marginal returns–a possible sign of impending social collapse.[8] For instance, the history of oil has been one of exploiting resources that were ever more remote and difficult and dangerous to extract, a history that has included rising prices on the world market. One of the worst recent environmental "events" was the Deepwater Horizon oil disaster that began in late April 2010. News coverage eventually explained that the wellhead was under a mile of ocean, the well itself was planned to extend nearly another three miles beneath the sea floor, that the high-tech devices protecting against disaster were faulty, and that the behavior of the corporations primarily involved was criminal. However, reports made little mention of the overall resource situation that necessitated such deep drilling. The first commercial oil well, drilled in 1859 in Pennsylvania, penetrated a mere 70 feet. That difference certainly suggests diminishing marginal returns.

Moreover, in the United States the "cost" of oil is not calculated by including the roughly 35% of the military budget dedicated to such things as invading other nations to get access to or control of oil fields. Nor does it include most of the tremendous external costs involved in the use of the oil, particularly those associated with climate disruption–a risk that major oil interests have blatantly attempted to discredit.[9]

One prominent analyst claims that international agreements for dealing with the latter costs are basically hopeless, and that instead, carbon taxes within nations offer the best hope of avoiding disaster.[10] However, in the United States, such a course seems unlikely. The odds are low because of the successful corporate campaign preventing the United States government from taking any action on climate disruption.[11] Given the important world position of the United States, this successful campaign may have been the most serious policy blow against global sustainability so far. It would probably have been impossible without the growing inequity in wealth and power within the nation, allowing money from corporations to block the necessary regulatory policies.

Diminishing returns in the global system of human support are now ubiquitous; the story of oil now applies to coal and natural gas, where the costs and environmental penalties of extraction are rising in the long term. Diminishing returns can also be seen in the fading ability of antibiotics to combat diseases and of pesticides to protect crops against insects and other pests. In addition, efforts to develop new land for agriculture have long since been superseded by intensified use of existing land, a process that itself faces limits. Consequently, each one of the approximately 2.5 billion people expected to be added to the world population in the next 40 years will, on average, have to be fed from crops grown on more marginal land, supplied with water requiring more energy to transport and/or purify, and supported with materials obtained from ever-poorer ores.

It has become increasingly obvious that conventional economic/cultural systems, be they capitalist, socialist, or communist, have simply proven inadequate. They have not provided the necessary development among the poor. They have not encouraged the development of societies that understand the environmental constraints imposed by the biospheric complex adaptive system within which the human socioeconomic complex adaptive system must function. As a result, the world community has not produced the sustainable redistribution and shrinkage of populations and equitable distribution of material wealth required to create an environmentally sound and equitable global society.

Homo sapiens' negative impact on the planet's life-support systems can be approximated by the I = PAT equation, in which the size of the *population* (P) is multiplied by the average *affluence*, or consumption, per capita (A), and that in turn is multiplied by a measure of the impacts of *technology* and socio-political-economic arrangements (T) used to supply the consumption. The product is *impact* (I), a rough index of how much humanity is assaulting its environment, threatening human health, and degrading the natural ecosystems upon whose services it depends. The factors in the equation, of course, are not independent, but that complication does not seriously lessen I = PAT's value as a heuristic tool.

The technological/economic/political dimensions of our predicament, such as the need to deploy alternatives to fossil fuel energy quickly, are frequently discussed in the academic community, but clearly not well understood by decision makers in business, government, or the media. To the degree that environmental problems are recognized in those communities, it is widely believed that they can be solved by minor technological "fixes." As ecologist William Rees put it, "most sustainability campaigns, corporate responses, and government policies emphasize 'simple and painless' (read "marginal and ineffective") actions that require only modest adjustments to personal lifestyles and none at all to the economic growth ethic or other key beliefs, values, and assumptions of techno-industrial society."[12] The frequent use of the oxymoronic phrase "sustainable growth" suggests that too many people view sustainability as involving only slight deviations from business as usual.

The complexity involved in revolutions such as converting from fossil fuels to wind, solar, and geothermal energy in industrial societies appears to be largely underappreciated by political leaders, leading to a lack of urgency or progress. Ironically, initiating the revolution in the poorest developing countries may be far easier than many leaders believe, stuck as they are in thinking that such countries must first create a 20th century energy infrastructure. However, the wildfire spread of cell phones in Africa and India in the last decade shows another path, as the cell phones are now becoming the infrastructure and credit mechanism for the spread of small-scale solar power in rural villages far from any grid.

Any visitor to the climate negotiations in Cancun or Durban quickly became aware that it is the developing countries, principally the poorest, who most feel the urgency to address climate disruption. They are keenly aware of their own vulnerability. In contrast, it is the richest and most powerful nations, the principal emitters of greenhouse gases, that are laggards in implementing their energy revolutions. The International Energy Agency (IEA) sent a message relevant to this situation to the participants at the 2011 climate negotiations in Durban by concluding that the world is "locking itself into an insecure, inefficient, and high-carbon energy system. If bold policy actions are not put in place over the next several years, it will become increasingly difficult and costly to meet the goal set at last year's talks of limiting a global temperature increase to 2 degrees C."[13] They might have added to "costly" "and likely impossible."

Silence on the overconsumption (Affluence) factor in the I = PAT equation is readily explained. Consumption is still viewed as an unalloyed good by many economists, along with business leaders and politicians, who tend to see increasing consumption, even among the super-rich, as a cure-all for economic ills. Hardly a day goes by without the spectacle of some economic "expert" in the U.S. mass media discussing the degree of success in getting the economy growing. Most people do not realize that expanding consumption among the already rich is a recipe for drastic environmental deterioration. Yet, it is a sad fact that providing today's seven billion people the consumption patterns of western Europe is a biophysical impossibility–to say nothing of supplying such a lifestyle to more than nine billion people by the middle of this century.

Indeed, the interactions among factors in our predicament are daunting. The need to expand agricultural production some 70–100% by 2050 to meet expected demand from a growing population, an increasing desire in emerging economies for meat-rich diets, and demand for biofuels will require further intensification of agricultural production and, among other things, increasing the oil subsidy to agriculture. Without significant progress in curbing greenhouse gas emissions, that demand will, in turn, raise oil prices and enlarge flows of greenhouse gases into the atmosphere on top of the increases traceable to the other activities of an additional 2.5 billion people. That situation, of course, will almost certainly cause further disruption of the climate, altering precipitation patterns further, and likely make more problematic supplying the needed water to farms. Furthermore, the difficulties of increasing yields and total food production will be exacerbated by other likely ecological effects of moving to more intensive and extensive agriculture, such as loss of biodiversity, erosion of soils, and further toxification of both land and oceans. Even the normally conservative UN realizes that the situation is extremely serious,[14] and that "environmental damage will undermine food productivity growth." Furthermore, the threat of famines is not, of course, the only negative effect of overpopulation; density-dependent factors range from the increased chances of epidemics and resource wars to higher death rates from violent climatic events.[15]

The rapidly deteriorating biophysical situation we face today is more than worse enough; however, it is still scarcely recognized by a global society afflicted by gross inequality and infected by the irrational belief that physical economies can grow forever – a myth enthusiastically embraced by politicians and economists as an excuse to avoid the tough decisions facing civilization.[16] Indeed, those who recognize the inequity portion of the human predicament usually call for more growth as a solution, unaware that growth demonstrably cannot do the job. Of course, focusing whatever physical growth we can afford on relieving the plight of the human beings most desperately in need must be one of the main tasks of a future social movement. However, that is not enough unless we ensure that such growth is biophysically safe, in part by compensating for it by sustainable material shrinkage among the rich. There is no escaping the need for redistribution of access to resources; meeting the extraordinary global emergency requires it. The most immediate threats are to poor people and poor nations; however, in the end, and possibly even in the beginning, the rich will fall further.

Against a grim background of corruption and ignorance, can we create a just society, in which caring for each other and our life-support systems moves to the top of the political agenda? Given that the UN Rio+20 conference will be attended by representatives of present governments whose leaders are probably happy with the status quo, it seems unlikely to us that it will stimulate the necessary urgent action. The human future may instead depend on the success of social movements such as Occupy Wall Street and its surrogates around the world, and the Millennium Alliance for Humanity and the Biosphere (MAHB – http://mahb.stanford.edu/). Both require us to step back and ask, "What are people for?" and consider whether the society we have built is indeed the one we want. In the face of an absolutely unprecedented emergency, the world community has no choice but to take dramatic action to avert a collapse of civilization. Either humanity will change its ways, or they will be changed for us.

1. Solomon S, Plattner G-K, Knutti R, Friedlingstein P. 2009. Irreversible climate change due to carbon dioxide emissions. *Proceedings of the National Academy of Sciences* 106: 1704–1709.

2. http://www.fao.org/docrep/006/Y5160E/y5160e15.htm

3. Klare MT. 2008. *Rising Powers, Shrinking Planet: The New Geopolitics of Energy*. New York, NY: Henry Holt and Company.

4. Homer-Dixon T, Boutwell J, Rathgens G. 1993. Environmental change and violent conflict. *Scientific American*: 38–45.

5. http://thepoliticalcarnival.net/2012/02/01/thank-you-citizens-united-for-the-outsized-influence-wealthy-individuals-are-having-on-the-2012-race-gop-super-pacs-way-ahead-of-dems/

6. Boulding KE. 1966. The economics of the coming Spaceship Earth. Pages 3–14 in Jarrett H, ed. *Environmental Quality in a Growing Economy*. Baltimore: Johns Hopkin University Press, p. 3.

7. Ehrlich PR, Holdren J. 1971. Impact of population growth. *Science* 171: 1212–1217.

8. Tainter JA. 1988. *The Collapse of Complex Societies*. Cambridge, UK: Cambridge University Press.

9. Oreskes N, Conway EM. 2010. *Merchants of Doubt: How a Handful of Scientists Obscured the Truth on Issues from Tobacco Smoke to Global Warming*. New York, NY: Bloomsbury Press.

10. Giddens A. 2011. *The Politics of Climate Change*. Cambridge, UK: Polity Press.

11. Antonio RJ, Brulle RJ. 2011. The unbearable lightness of politics. *The Sociological Quarterly* 52: 195–202.

12. Rees W. 2010. What's blocking sustainability? Human nature, cognition, and denial. Sustainability: *Science, Practice, & Policy* 6: 13–25.

13. http://www.iea.org/press/pressdetail.asp?PRESS_REL_ID=429

14. UN Department of Economic and Social Affairs. 2011. World Economic and Social Survey 2011: The Great Green Technological Transformation. New York, NY: United Nations.

15. Andrewartha HG, Birch LC. 1954. *The Distribution and Abundance of Animals*. Chicago: University of Chicago Press.

16. Spence M. 2011. *The Next Convergence: The Future of Economic Growth in a Multispeed World*. New York, NY: Farrar, Straus, and Giroux.

Emergence of BRICS and Climate Change

José Goldemberg

One outstanding characteristic of the world's economic development in the last 60 years is the decline of the proportion of GDP of the OECD countries and the emergence of non-OECD countries, particularly the BRICS*, as Table I indicates.

Table I   Fraction of GDP (%)

	1950	1980	2008
OECD	57	53	41
BRICS	21	21	31.5

Source: BRICS Policy Center[1]

The GDP proportion of OECD countries declined from 57% to 41% between 1950 and 2008 while the proportion of the BRICS increased almost from 21% to 31.5%.

The BRICS represented half of the GDP of all non-OECD countries. In 2008, China accounted for 60% of the BRICS GDP. (Appendix I)

According to Gilpin,[2] the emergence of the BRICS in the world economy results from two conflicting pressures: on the one hand, the development of industry and other economic activities in the advanced industrialized countries (the "center"); on the other hand, the diffusion of such activities and wealth from the "center" to the "periphery" (developing countries).

The initial advantage of the center over the periphery is technical and organizational superiority. In the short term, innova-

---

* BRICS are Brazil, Russia, India, China, and South Africa

Figure 1

GDP

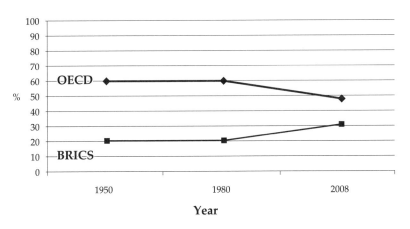

Year

tion and increased efficiency give the center greater profits and faster growth. However, in the long term, the center's growth rate tends to decelerate, and new economic activities migrate to the periphery, which, in the words of Gerschenkron,[3] benefit from the "advantages of latecomers." These countries initiate their industrialization process benefiting from the lessons learned from the advanced countries' earlier industrialization, and therefore can leapfrog over certain stages of development.[4]

Figure 2 illustrates such behavior by the evolution of the energy intensity (E/GDP) of the economy, which measures the amount of energy required to generate one unit of GDP measured in tons of oil equivalent per thousand dollars.

In the United States and other industrialized countries, the energy intensity increased as the infrastructure and heavy industry developed, going through a peak and then a steady decline. Latecomers in the industrialization process in other industrialized countries such as the United Kingdom, Germany, and India peaked later and at lower energy intensities than their predecessors, indicating early adoption of modern, more energy-efficient industrial processes and technologies; Figure 3 depicts such evolution.

Figure 2

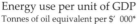

Energy use per unit of GDP
Tonnes of oil equivalent per $' 000*

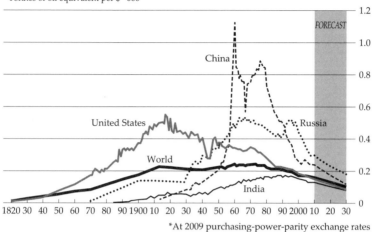

*At 2009 purchasing-power-parity exchange rates

Source: BP Energy Outlook 2030 London 2011[5]

Figure 3

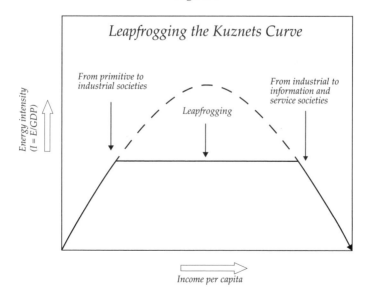

China and Russia industrialized very rapidly in the 20th century, basically in a "brute force" pattern based on the use of less efficient technologies.

The observed decline of countries' energy intensity results from the decoupling of energy consumption (E) originating largely from fossil fuel use and GDP caused by energy efficiency measures and shifts in the economic structure of these countries, from manufacturing to services. As an example, Figure 4 depicts the evolution of energy consumption in the OECD between 1973 and 1998, demonstrating that without energy efficient measures, energy consumption would be 49% higher than it actually was.

Figure 4

Energy Savings in the OECD (1973–1998)

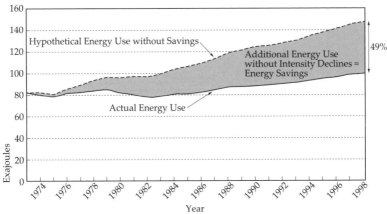

Source.[6]

In developing countries with low per capita consumption and a large fraction of the population still lacking access to many modern services, energy efficiency in itself might lead to deprivation, and therefore is not readily accepted. The rapid growth of industrialization in these countries, particularly in China, Russia, and the other BRICS countries—except Brazil— occurred by using fossil fuels, particularly coal.

Figure 5 depicts the 2010 sources of energy in the BRICS countries.

Figure 5

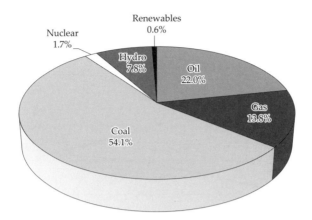

Fossil fuels represent 90% of the BRICS total, whereas such energy sources represent 83% of OECD usage because renewable energy sources such as biomass, hydro, wind, geothermal, and direct solar energy have grown in the aggregate at a higher rate than fossil fuel consumption, which has remained practically constant during the last 30 years in OECD countries.

Therefore, it is not surprising that the BRICSs economic growth is reflected in an increase in their greenhouse gas emissions, particularly CO_2 (Table II; Appendix II).

Table II Fraction of CO_2 emissions (%)

	1950	1980	2008
OECD	70	48	32
BRICS	15	29	35

The OECD proportion of CO_2 emissions declined from 70% in 1950 to 32% in 2008, while BRICS increased their proportion from 15 to 35% (Figure 6).

However, more recently, all the BRICS countries have made great efforts to decrease their energy intensity, and consequently carbon intensity as Figure 7 illustrates.

Figure 6

OECD and BRICS CO_2 Emissions

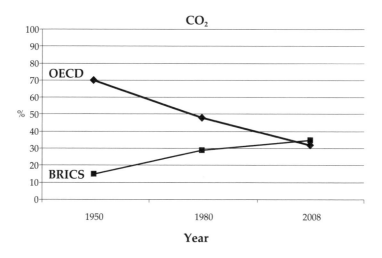

China and Russia, which are very dependent on coal, are making great progress in reducing their carbon intensity (CO_2/GDP) rapidly although it remains significantly higher than that of OECD countries. South Africa is making slight progress. India, a less industrialized country, has a rather low carbon intensity. Brazil, excluding deforestation in Amazonia, has a very low carbon intensity, primarily because it produces electricity almost entirely from hydroelectric plants. When the contribution to CO_2 emissions because of the deforestation in Amazonia is included, its carbon intensity increases considerably although it has been declining significantly in recent years.

However, data has indicated that the BRICS countries' significant growth of CO_2 emissions in recent years does not yet represent a large fraction of the accumulated emissions that have occurred since the 19th century and changed the composition of the atmosphere.

This argument is one of the strongest used by developing countries to refuse limitations on their emissions in the Climate Convention and Kyoto Protocol. They argue that to accept limitations on their emissions would be equivalent to accepting a

Figure 7

CO$_2$/GDP PPP
kg CO$_2$ per 2000 USD PPP

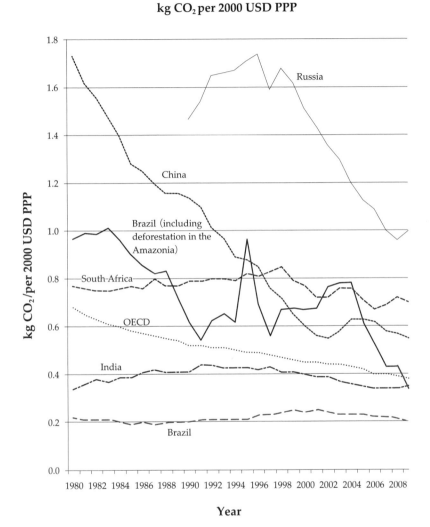

policy that keeps them poor and undeveloped now that it was their return to develop. Such reasoning relies on the false assumption that developing countries will grow and develop using the traditional fuels and technologies.

Table III and Figure 8 report the contribution of BRICS to accumulated emissions since 1850.

Table III   Accumulated CO₂ emissions (%)

	1850–1950	1850–2007	1850–2020
BRICS	16	22	28
Rest of the world	84	78	72

Figure 8

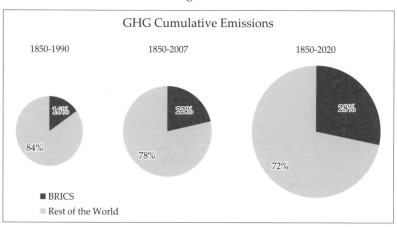

The BRICS contribution increased from 16% during 1850–1990 and 22% during 1850 to 2007 and will probably represent 28% in 2020. Considering that a fraction of the CO_2 emissions that occurred more than a century ago (largely from industrialized countries) have already been reabsorbed by the oceans, the size of recent BRICS emissions becomes more significant. This current emissions status is the main reason for the 17th Conference of the Parties, which met in Durban, South Africa in December 2011, deciding to initiate a new negotiating process to be concluded by 2015, which will incorporate mandatory reduction commitments of GHG for all countries and replace the Kyoto Protocol, which established such mandatory reduction only for industrialized countries.

Appendix I

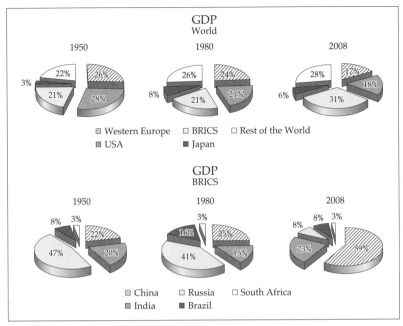

Source.[6]

Appendix II

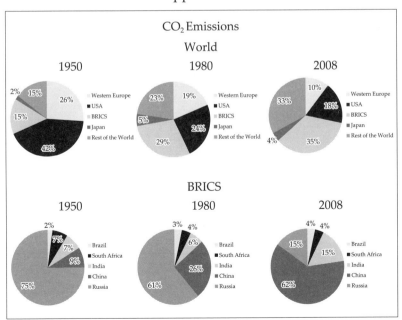

References

1. BRICS Policy Center 2011—The evolution of the participation of the BRICS in the global GDP from 1950 to 2008 (in Portuguese) Catholic University, Rio de Janeiro, Brazil.
2. Gilpin, R.—*The Political Economy of International Relations.* Princeton University Press, Princeton, USA (1987).
3. Geischenkron, A.—*Economic Backwardness in Historical Perspective.* Cambridge, Becknap, UK (1962).
4. Goldemberg, J.—*Georgetown Journal International Affairs*, Winter/ Spring 2011, pp. 135–141.
5. BP Energy Outlook 2030 London 2011.
6. Madison, A. Statistics on World Population, GDP and "per capita" GDP, 1 2008 AD (http://www.ggdc.net/MADISON/oriindex.htm

Environment and Development Challenges
Imperative of a Carbon Fee and Dividend

James E. Hansen

Most governments have paid little attention to the threat of human-made climate change. They have acknowledged its likely existence, notably in the Framework Convention on Climate Change (1), in which 195 nations agreed to avoid "dangerous anthropogenic interference" with climate. However, the instrument chosen to implement the Framework Convention, the Kyoto Protocol, is so ineffectual that global fossil fuel CO_2 emissions have increased by about 3% per year since its adoption in 1997, as opposed to a growth rate of 1.5% per year in the decades preceding the Kyoto Protocol (http://www.columbia.edu/~mhs119/Emissions/, which is an update of a graph in (2)).

This feckless path cannot continue much longer if we hope to preserve a planet resembling the one on which civilization developed—a world that avoids the economic devastation of continually receding shorelines and the moral nightmare of having exterminated a large fraction of the species on Earth. The science is clear enough: burning most fossil fuels would invoke such consequences (3).

At least a moderate overshoot of climate change into the dangerous zone is unavoidable now; however, fortunately, prompt actions initiating a change of directions in this decade could minimize the impacts on humanity and nature. The policies needed to produce a rapid phase-out of fossil fuel emissions would have a wide range of other benefits for the public, particularly in those nations that recognize the advantages of being early adopters of effective policies. Therefore, there is some basis for optimism that we could marshal the political will necessary to enact effective policies.

However, to achieve this goal, the next approach must not repeat the fundamental mistakes that doomed the Kyoto Protocol. If leaders waste another 15 years on an ineffectual approach, it will be too late to avoid catastrophic consequences for today's young people and future generations. Therefore, we must clarify the principal flaws in the Kyoto approach from the standpoint of climate science.

Kyoto Protocol

A fundamental flaw of the Kyoto approach is that it was based on a "cap" mechanism. This approach embodies two unavoidable problems. First, it made it impossible to develop a formula for emission caps that nations found equitable and that also reduced carbon emissions at the rate required to stabilize climate. Second, it failed to provide clear price signals that would reward businesses, individuals, and nations that led the way in reducing emissions.

The validity of the first assertion can be proven by comparing national responsibilities for climate change, which are proportional to cumulative historical emissions (4, 5). The United Kingdom, the United States, and Germany have per capita responsibilities exceeding those of China and India by a factor of nearly ten (Hansen, 4). Even if the United Kingdom, the United States, and Germany terminated emissions tomorrow, by the time China, India, and other developing nations reach comparable responsibility for climate change, the world would be on a course toward unavoidable climate disasters.

Key Points:
Why a Carbon Fee and Dividend Structure is Imperative

> 1. There is a limit on fossil fuel carbon dioxide that we can release into the atmosphere without guaranteeing unacceptably tragic and unethical climatic consequences for young people and nature.

2. It is clear that we will soon exceed the limit on carbon emissions because it requires decades to replace fossil fuel energy infrastructure with carbon-neutral and carbon-negative energies.

3. Climate system inertia, which delays full climate response to human-made changes in atmospheric composition, is both our friend and foe. The delay not only allows moderate overshoot of the sustainable carbon load but also risks passing a climatic point of no return that triggers a series of catastrophic events beyond human control.

4. The ineffectual paradigm of prior efforts to reign in carbon emissions must be replaced by one in which an across-the-board rising carbon fee is collected from fossil fuel companies at the place where the fossil fuel enters a domestic market, that is, at the domestic mine or port of entry.

5. All funds collected from fossil fuel companies should be distributed to the public. This measure motivates the public to endorse a substantial continually rising carbon price and provides individuals the resources to phase in needed changes in energy-use choices.

It is unrealistic to think that a "cap" approach can be made global or near-global. Nations less responsible for the world's climate predicament believe, with considerable justification, that they should not have to adhere to caps on CO_2 emissions (much less steadily shrinking caps) similar to those adhered to by industrialized countries. At the same time, some industrialized countries, including the United States, refuse to bind themselves to caps that are more stringent than those imposed on developing countries. A cap approach cannot resolve this impasse. Indeed, the targets adopted to date with a cap approach have been but a drop in the bucket compared to the reductions required to stabilize climate.

A secondary but critical flaw of the Kyoto approach is its introduction of "offsets." Nations are allowed to limit reduction of fossil fuel emissions by means of alternative actions such as tree planting or reduced emissions of non-CO_2 climate forcings such as methane or chlorofluorocarbons. However, these offsets are not equivalent to fossil fuel emissions because the fossil fuel carbon will remain in surface carbon reservoirs (atmosphere, ocean, soil, and biosphere) for millennia. Rapid phase-out of fossil fuel emissions, as required to stabilize climate, becomes implausible if leakage is permitted via offsets. The flat across-the-board carbon fee on fossil fuels in the fee-and-dividend approach avoids leakage. Incentives to reduce non-CO_2 climate forcings will be useful; however, such programs should not be allowed to interfere with the more fundamental requirement of phasing out fossil fuel CO_2 emissions.

Fee and Dividend

Fee-and-dividend (5) features a flat fee (a single number specified in \$/ton of CO_2) collected from fossil fuel companies covering domestic sales of all fossil fuels. Collection cost is trivial because there are only a small number of collection points: the first sale at domestic mines and at the port of entry for imported fossil fuels. All funds collected from the fee are distributed electronically (to bank accounts or debit cards) monthly to legal residents of the country in equal per capita amounts. Citizens using less than average fossil fuels (more than 60% of the public with current distribution of energy use) will receive more in their monthly dividend than they pay in increased prices. However, all individuals will have a strong incentive to reduce their carbon footprint to stay on the positive side of the ledger or improve their position.

The carbon fee would start small and rise at a rate that sows economic stimulation benefits while minimizing economic disruptions from sudden change. Economic efficiency requires the price of fossil fuels to rise toward a level that matches their cost to society. Presently, fossil fuels are the dominant energy only because the environmental and social costs are externalized onto society as a whole rather than being internalized into their prices (6). Human health costs because of air and water pollution from mining and burning of fossil fuels are borne by the public, as are costs of climate change estimated at $100–1000/tCO$_2$ (7).

International Implementation

When the reality and consequences of the climate threat become sufficiently clear, the international community should recognize that all nations are in the same boat, and that the fruitless cap-and-trade-with-offsets approach must be abandoned. The reality is that the Kyoto Protocol and proposed replacements are "indulgence" schemes (5) that allow aggressive development of fossil fuels to continue worldwide. Developing countries acquiesce if they will receive sufficient payments for offsets and adaptation. This approach works well for adults in developed and developing countries today. However, this abuse of the welfare of young people and future generations must eventually end as the facts become widely apparent.

A fundamental fact is that as long as fossil fuels are allowed to be cheap via subsidies and failure to pay their costs to society, people will burn them. Even ostensibly successful caps have no significant benefit. They simply reduce demand for the fuel, thus lowering its price and creating incentives for somebody to burn it somewhere. We require an approach that results in economically efficient phase-out of fossil fuels, with replacement by energy efficiency and carbon-free energy sources such as renewable energy and nuclear power.

In particular, such a system requires a flat (across-the-board) rising fee (tax) on carbon emissions. Such a flat fee, collected by the energy-using nation at its domestic mines and ports of entry, eliminates the need for trading carbon permits or financial derivatives based on them. Indeed, the price oscillations inherent in carbon trading drown out the price signals. The required rapid phase-out of fossil fuels and phase-in of alternatives requires that businesses and consumers be confident that the fee will continue to rise. Another flaw of trading is that it necessarily involves major banks into the matter, and all of the bank profits are extracted from the public via increased energy prices.

A carbon fee (tax) approach can be globalized much more readily than cap-and-trade (8). For example, say a substantial economic block (e.g., Europe and the United States or Europe and China) agrees to have a carbon tax. They would levy border duties on products from nations without an equivalent carbon tax on the basis of a standard estimate of fossil fuels used in production of the product. Such a border tax is permitted by the World Trade Organization's rules, with the proviso that exporters who can document that their production uses less fossil fuels than the standard will be assigned an appropriately adjusted border duty. Border duties will create a strong incentive for exporting nations to impose their own carbon tax, so they can collect the funds rather than have the importing country collect them.

Once nations recognize the inevitability of a rising carbon price, the economic advantages of being an early adopter of the fee-and-dividend approach will spur its implementation. These include improved economic efficiency of honest energy pricing and a head start in development of energy-efficient and low-carbon products. The potential economic gains to middle- and lower-income citizens who minimize their carbon footprint will address concerns of people in many nations where citizens are becoming impatient with growing wealth disparities. Note that the effect of a carbon price on upper class citizens is modest and non-threatening, except for a handful of fossil fuel moguls who extract obscene profits from the public's dependence on fossil fuels. An added social benefit of fee-and-dividend is its impact on illegal immigration—by providing a strong economic incentive for immigrants to become legal citizens, it provides an approach for slowing and even reversing illegal immigration that will be more effective than border patrols.

National Implementation

The greatest barriers to eliminating fossil fuel addiction in most nations are the influence of the fossil fuel industry on politicians and the media and the short-term view of politicians. Thus, it is possible that the leadership that leads the world to sustainable energy policies may arise in China (9), where the leaders are rich in technical and scientific training and rule a nation with a history of taking the long-term view. Although China's CO_2 emissions have skyrocketed above those of other nations, China has reasons to move off the fossil fuel track as rapidly as possible. China has several hundred million people living within a 25-m elevation of sea level, and the country stands to suffer grievously from the intensification of droughts, floods, and storms that will accompany continued global warming (3, 5, 10). In addition, China recognizes the merits of avoiding a fossil fuel addiction compared to that of the United States. Thus, China has already become the global leader in development of energy efficiency, renewable energies, and nuclear power.

Conceivably, the threat of impending second-class economic status could stir the United States into action; however, that action must contain no remnants of prior cap-and-trade fiascos, which were loaded with giveaways to big banks, utilities, coal, and oil. The approach must be simple and clear, with the fee rising steadily and 100% of the collected revenue distributed to legal residents on a per capita basis.

The fee-and-dividend approach allows the market to select technology winners. The government should not choose favorites; that is, subsidies should be eliminated for all energies, not only fossil fuels. This approach will spur innovation, stimulating the economy as price signals encourage the public to adopt energy efficiency and clean energies. All materials and services will naturally incorporate fossil fuel costs. For example, sustainable food products from nearby farms will gain an advantage over highly fertilized products from halfway around the world.

The carbon price must start small, growing as the public gains confidence that they are receiving 100% of the proceeds. If the fee begins at $15/tCO_2$ and rises $10 per year, the rate after 10 years would be equivalent to about $1 per gallon of gasoline. Given the current fossil fuel use in the United States, that tax rate would generate about $600B per year, thus providing dividends of about $2000 per legal adult resident or about $6000 per year for a family with two or more children, with half a share for each child up to two children per family.

In the United States, the policy director of Republicans for Environmental Protection (11) praised the proposal for a gradually rising fee on carbon emissions collected from fossil fuel companies with proceeds fully distributed to the public as "Transparent. Market-based. Does not enlarge government. Leaves energy decisions to individual choices.... Sounds like a conservative climate plan."

A grassroots organization, Citizens Climate Lobby (12), has been formed in the United States and Canada with the objective of promoting fee-and-dividend. My advice to this organization is adoption of a motto "100% or fight" because politicians will certainly try to tap such a large revenue stream. Already, there are suggestions that part of the proceeds should be used "to pay down the national debt"—a euphemism for the fact that it would become just another tax thrown into the pot. Supporters of youth and climate stabilization must exercise the determination and discipline shown by the Tea Party movement if they are to successfully overcome the forces for fossil fuel business-as-usual.

Global Strategic Situation

Europe is the region where citizens and political leaders have been most aware of the urgency of slowing fossil fuel emissions. Given the stranglehold that the fossil fuel industry has achieved on energy policies in the United States, it is natural to look to Europe for leadership. Yet, despite its dismal experience with cap-and-trade-with-offsets, Europe continues to push this feckless approach, perhaps because of bureaucratic inertia and individual vested interests. China, at least in the short run, would probably be only too happy to continue such a framework because the offsets have proven to be a cash cow for China.

The cap-and-trade-with-offsets framework, set up with the best of intentions, fails to make fossil fuels pay their costs to society, thus allowing fossil fuel addiction to continue and encouraging "drill, baby, drill" policies to extract every fossil fuel that can be found. There is a desperate need for global political leaders who can see through special financial interests and understand the actions required to achieve a bright future for the youth and the planet. Perhaps, such leaders exist—the problem is really not that difficult.

Acknowledgements. I thank Shi-Ling Hsu and Charles Komanoff for useful reviews and suggestions.

References

1. United Nations Framework Convention on Climate Change (FCCC), 1992: United Nations, http://www.unfccc.int.
2. Hansen, J. and Sato, M., 2001: Trends of measured climate forcing agents. *Proc Nat Acad Sci USA*, 98, 14778–14783.
3. Hansen, J., et al., 2012 (submitted): Scientific case for avoiding dangerous climate change to protect young people and nature. *Proc Natl Acad Sci USA*.
4. Hansen, J., et al., 2007: Dangerous human-made interference with climate: a GISS modelE study. *Atmos Chem Phys*, 7, 2287–2312.
5. Hansen, J., 2009: *Storms of My Grandchildren. Bloomsbury*, New York, 304 pp.
6. G20 Summit Team, 2010: *Analysis of the Scope of Energy Subsidies and Suggestions for the G-20 Initiative.*
7. Ackerman, F., DeCanio, S., Howarth, R., and Sheeran, K., 2009: Limitations of integrated assessment models of climate change. *Climatic Change*, 95, 297–315.
8. Hsu, S.-L., 2011: *The Case for a Carbon Tax.* Island Press, Washington.
9. Hansen, J.E., 2010: China and the Barbarians: Part 1: http://www.columbia.edu/~jeh1/mailings/20101124_ChinaBarbarians1.pdf accessed
10. Intergovernmental Panel on Climate Change (IPCC), 2007: *Climate*

Change 2007, Impacts, Adaptation and Vulnerability, Parry, M. L., Canziani, O. F., Palutikof, J. P., Van Der Linden, P. J., and Hanson, C. E. eds., Cambridge Univ Press, 996 pp.

11. Dipeso, J., 2010: Jim Hansen's conservative climate plan, blog post at Republican's for Environmental Protection, October 11, 2010: http://www.rep.org/opinions/weblog/weblog10-10-11.html accessed August 26, 2011.

12. Citizens Climate Lobby: http://citizensclimatelobby.org/ accessed

The Global Transition beyond Fossil Fuels

Amory B. Lovins and José Goldemberg

About 78% of the primary energy use by humans—nearly 90%, excluding traditionally scavenged biomass such as wood and dung—comes from ancient sunlight concentrated into the rotted remains of primeval swamp goo. Burning this annual ~17 cubic kilometers of oil, gas, coal, and related fossil fuels is the main threat to the Earth's climate. In addition, it is costly, particularly for poor people and nations; its extraction, transport, and combustion threaten public and environmental health; its uneven geological distribution fans tensions and inequities; its volatile prices (particularly for oil) destabilize economies and political systems; its revenues (again, particularly for oil), with some notable exceptions, often promote unsound development patterns, corruption, and tyranny; and even without these side-effects, its gradual economic and physical depletion, despite stunning technological progress by the world's most powerful industries, makes a transition beyond fossil fuels inevitable (Fig. 1).

Many numerical details of these issues are disputed. However, their general direction is clear: whether for reasons of economy (profits, jobs, competitive advantage, global development), security (dependence, reliable supplies, geopolitical stability, durability), or environmental stewardship, climate, and public health, the world has begun a gradual, historic, and immensely consequential shift from the anomalous few-centuries-long fossil-fuel "blip" shown at the bottom of Fig. 1 to an unbounded future of more efficient use and durable supply. This transition is the "master key" to solving or avoiding many

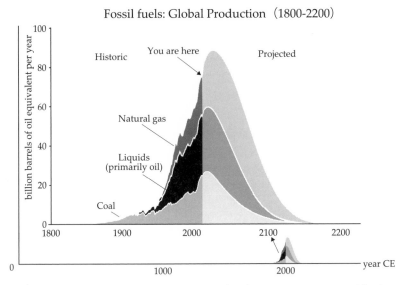

Fig. 1. Actual (historic) global output of the three major classes of hydrocarbons through 2010, with projections of the remaining amounts of each believed likely to be recovered if there are no aboveground constraints. The historic data are accurate; however, the smoothed illustrative projections are estimates, reflecting leading resource experts' knowledge in early 2011 but subject to many uncertainties. The projections include unconventional resources such as shale gas, heavy oil, tar sands, and shale oil, but not methane hydrates, potential Arctic and Antarctic resources, or Alaskan North Slope and central Siberian coal.[1]

of humanity's other most pressing problems.

Most policymakers and analysts assert that this shift will raise costs on the basis of two theoretical assumptions: markets govern transactions worldwide, and markets are essentially perfect, so market failures are minor and unimportant. The first assumption is obviously wrong; though market mechanisms are important and widespread, many economies are actually planned or mixed. An enormous body of scholarly and practical experience also contradicts the second assumption that if there were a cheaper way to meet the world's energy needs than burning fossil fuels, it would already have been fully adopted. Scores of well-known market failures[2] often make it difficult to use energy in a way that makes money, or prevent full and fair competition between savings and supply or even between

90

different sources of supply. (For example, only in a few countries and three-fifths of the United States are electricity savings allowed to bid against new supply; indeed, in 35 states and nearly all other countries, utilities are rewarded for selling more electricity and penalized for selling less.) Moreover, efficiency and renewable energy are rapidly becoming cheaper, as their impressive market performance attests.

An important obstacle to economically energy efficient use is that many users lack access to the cheap capital available to energy suppliers; most low-income users cannot obtain any financing. However, this capital gap can be bridged by such innovations as "feebates"[3] (like the five European "bonus/ malus" systems that enable automobile buyers to approach or apply societal discount rates) and long-term financing (like the US PACE bonds; on-bill utility financing; long-term Power Purchase Agreements for efficiency and renewables; and residential photovoltaic financing packages).

Such proven policy and business innovations can stimulate remarkable energy shifts. For example, an independent, detailed, documented, and peer-reviewed 2011 synthesis of the United States' vibrant and market-orientated economy[4] found a feasible potential to produce a 2.58 times bigger GDP in 2050 than in 2010, using no oil, no coal, no nuclear energy, and one-third less natural gas—all at $5 trillion lower net-present-valued cost than business-as-usual despite valuing all externalities at zero. This transformation requires no new inventions and no Act of Congress; rather, it could be led by business for profit.

Current market failures are so important that U.S. buildings could triple or quadruple their energy productivity with a 33% average Internal Rate of Return (IRR), industry could double its energy productivity with a 21% IRR,[5] and transportation could eliminate oil use through radical efficiency and supply substitutions averaging a 17% IRR. The average 14% IRR across all sectors for the resultant > 80% fossil-carbon reduction includes an 80% renewable electricity system, re-architected to be so resilient as to prevent major failures. All the same services as in the official forecasts would still be provided, often with higher quality. All the investments assumed meet commercial hurdle rates appropriate to each sector. These U.S.-specific findings suggest important analogies elsewhere because the proposed shifts appear highly fungible (many are already driven by global competition) and widely adaptable or adoptable in diverse locations, climates, and economic and social conditions. Indeed, in 2013 its authors entered a major collaboration with the Chinese government to inform that nation's strategic planning.

These astonishing, even seemingly impossible, findings result from combining four types of related innovations—in technology, policy, design, and strategy (the latter two normally omitted)—and from integrating all four energy-using sectors (transport, buildings, industry including primary production, and electricity) because, for example, the automotive and electricity problems are more easily solved together than separately. Superefficient autos[6] offering strong competitive advantage can be affordably electrified, such as those entering volume production in 2013 from two German automakers; their intelligent linkage with smart buildings and smart grids far from burdening the electricity system adds to it valuable flexibility and storage resources that make wind and solar power easier to integrate. This approach shows promise in a wide range of societies.

People can adopt these four types of widely transferable innovations for any reason. Thus, focusing on outcomes, not motives, bridges partisan divisions and makes the potential transideological. In the United States, congressional dysfunction currently blocks most actions on most issues, but can be end-run by the most effective institutions—private enterprise, coevolving with civil society, sped by military innovation. The new policies needed to unlock or hasten the transition can be implemented administratively or at a sub-national level where gridlock is less serious and more strategies to evade it exist. Societies with more coherent, stable, and farsighted governance can of course adapt and adopt similar innovations in their own distinctive ways, perhaps even faster.

This is far from a uniquely U.S. finding. The European Climate Foundation proposed a similarly ambitious EU transition in 2010[7], as have many of its member nations. McKinsey and Company found in 2009[8] that roughly 70% of projected global greenhouse gas (GHG) emissions in 2030 could be abated at an average cost of only $6/ton of CO_2, without including many of the newer technologies nor any of the integrative designs[9] that made the later U.S. findings so dramatic. In addition, McKinsey has published similar GHG-abatement-potential supply curves for a dozen nations including Brazil, China, India, and Russia.[10] Although the McKinsey studies are somewhat opaque regarding data sources (often based on proprietary client work) and sketchy on implementation, other detailed national analyses have been reporting such findings over the past three decades,[11] many deeply rooted in practical experience.

Practice is even overtaking theory. Non-hydroelectric renewable generating technologies have attracted $1 trillion of global investment since 2004.[12] Governments of all sizes, from California (the world's 8th largest economy) to Denmark and from Germany (4th largest) to Sweden, are successfully implementing aggressive efficiency-and-renewables strategies. In 1990–2006, California shrank GHG emissions per dollar of GDP by 30% (and has now held per-capita electricity use flat for three decades while real income per capita grew by four-fifths). Denmark's GDP grew by two-thirds during 1980–2009 while energy use returned to its 1980 level, and carbon emissions fell 21%. All new Danish power plants are renewable or combined-heat-and-power (CHP)—categories able by 2010 to produce 36% of electricity in an average wind year. Of all 2010 Danish electricity, 53% was CHP and 30% renewable. The average Dane released 52% less fossil carbon than the average American; yet, Danes have an excellent quality of life, with the second-most reliable electricity in Europe (after Germany) and at some of the lowest pretax prices.

Places as disparate as Sweden[13] and the Indian state of Karnataka[14] found in 1989 that renewable energy's modest extra cost could be repaid or turned to profit by savings from efficient end-use. Two decades later, renewables worldwide had actually achieved explosive growth and plummeting costs, each feeding on the other. China now leads the world in five renewable energy technologies and intends to do so in all.[15] In 2005–2010, Portugal soared from 17% to 45% renewable electricity (while the United States crawled from 9% to 10%). China in 2010 out-invested the United States by 60% in clean energy—139% per unit of GDP—and doubled its wind capacity for the fifth year running, blowing past its 2020 target, while Congressional wrangling halved U.S. wind power additions. India's clean-energy sector out-invested Japan's and Britain's. India recently quadrupled its renewable target and intends to add 20 GW of coal-displacing solar power by 2022. China is rapidly forming the world's largest carbon-trading zone and, unlike the United States, has laid the foundation for stabilizing its carbon emissions before 2030, consistent with a 450-ppm world. China is still building coal plants, but at less than half its 2006 pace, and its 2010 net capacity additions were 38% renewable, only 59% coal, emphasizing the world's most efficient plants and thereby raising its average coal-plant efficiency past America's.

Half the world's new electric generating capacity added during 2008–2012 was renewable, the majority now in developing countries. Global 2010 renewable capacity additions, excluding the $40–45 billion spent on large hydro dams, received $151 billion of private investment (by a broader measure, $195 billion)[16] and added ~66 GW, thereby overtaking nuclear power's total global installed capacity, and are projected to reach 34% of global power production by 2030 on a $5.4-trillion investment.[17] To be sure, the past century's cumulative fossil fuel and nuclear power investments (and subsidies) dwarf these figures, making total renewable power only one-fifth of the world's total, mostly big hydro. By the end of 2012, one-fourth of global installed capacity and one-fifth of global generation were renewable, often running fewer hours per year than traditional thermal power stations. However, in new orders, the shift from old to new technologies is unprecedented and exciting. For example, EU electric capacity additions were over 55% renewable in 2008–12, rising in 2012 to nearly 70% and pushing gas into third place after solar and wind. In 2012, China added more new electricity generation from non-hydro renewables than from fossil-fueled and nuclear plants combined, and generated slightly more wind than nuclear electricity.

The world can now manufacture about 75 GW of photovoltaic capacity each year—a capability that averaged 65% annual growth during 2005–2010. PVs, typically the costliest renewable, are at or near grid parity in many places, as wind power was years ago. In 2010, four German states obtained 43–52% of their electricity from wind power, and some regions of several European countries were at certain times over 100% wind powered. In 2012, Denmark was 41% and Germany 23% renewable-powered; in the first half of 2013, Spain's electricity averaged 48% renewable and Portugal's 70%. Such local examples rely on embedding such resources within a larger grid with flexible hydroelectric and fossil-fueled generators. However, even in large countries or entire continents, power generation coming 80+% from wind power and PVs (the two variable renewable sources) can sustain grid reliability with little or no bulk storage when a portfolio diversified by technology and location is properly forecasted and then integrated with flexible demand- and supply-side resources.[18]

Two-fifths of humanity lives in energy poverty. Yet, in Kenya, more households get their first electricity from PVs sold by local entrepreneurs than from the grid. Across Africa and Asia, a social revolution driven by solar-powered lighting and telecommunications is underway as vital services start to reach 1.6 billion people who lack electricity.[19]

These achievements reflect various mixtures of top-down policy, bottom-up entrepreneurship, and disaggregated market pull. They reflect a powerful trend toward decentralized electricity production. Economic reasons partly explain this phenomenon: 207 documented "distributed benefits" can often raise economic value by an order of magnitude.[20] In addition, led by the U.S. military,[21] security concerns are important: diverse and renewable supplies linked by netted and islandable microgrids can make power grids inherently resilient.[22] Right-sized electricity production can include industrial or building-scale CHP as well as many renewables: in 2008, "micropower" (CHP plus renewables minus big hydro) produced about 91% of the world's new electricity, and during 2000–12, micropower and nuclear power more than reversed their respective shares of global electricity generation. Distributed renewables can not only help create a decent life in rural villages, slowing urbanization, but also help poor urban and peri-urban dwellers obtain affordable and reliable energy services, using electricity generators as well as thermal (e.g., solar water heating) and sustainable biofuel technologies.

In short, the energy revolution now underway is making many policy and political debates moot or irrelevant. Since the Kyoto conference in 1977, most efforts to hedge climate risks have assumed that solutions will be costly rather than (at least mainly) profitable; insisted they be motivated by climate concerns rather than profit, economic development, or security; assumed they require a global treaty; and claimed that little can be done without U.S. carbon pricing. These ideas look increasingly dubious and outmoded in view of the following developments.

- Climate protection is generally not costly but profitable—a very convenient truth heretical to economic theorists but known to all practitioners—mainly because saving fuel costs less than buying it.[23] (Competitive renewables strengthen this point.) International climate discussions would become easier if focused on profits, jobs, and competitiveness rather than cost, burden, and sacrifice. While political leaders debate theoretical costs, smart corporate leaders are racing to pocket the profits before their rivals do: For example, Dow Chemical Company has already earned a $9-billion return on a $1-billion efficiency investment. The U.S. synthesis cited at the beginning of this paper found a $5-trillion net saving from cutting U.S. fossil carbon emissions by 82–86% below their year-2000 level, consistent with a < 450-ppm world.

- One can protect the climate without believing any of the climate science if one likes profit, development, or security. Any of those worthy motives, or several others, suffices; therefore, accepting the climate-science consensus, though correct, is not essential for effective climate protection.

- In 2005, China made energy efficiency its top strategic priority for national development, not because a treaty made them do it, but because leaders like Wen Jiabao understood that otherwise China cannot afford to develop; energy's supply-side investments would devour the national budget. That's why China's 1980–2001 growth in energy demand was already cut ~70% by deliberately reduced energy intensity. Enlightened self-interest can thus supplant treaties.

- Although U.S. carbon pricing (now blocked by the political party that once favored market solutions and applied emissions trading to SO_x and NO_x with stunning success) would be appropriate and helpful, it is not essential or sufficient—nor probably, in the long run, very important—because efficient carbon markets will clear at low prices. Strategies that do not depend on carbon pricing, such as those in Ref. 1, are far more robust. Fortunately, because almost all major economies do price carbon or are moving to do so, most multinational firms price or shadow-price carbon in their investment and strategic choices. Thus, U.S. non-pricing distorts decisions mainly within U.S. or non-Annex-B-country firms that sell only or mainly in their home markets.

Climate protection is thus changing course:

It will be led more by countries and companies than by international treaties and organizations, more by the private sector and civil society than by governments, more by leading developing economies than by mature developed ones, and more by efficiency and clean energy's economic fundamentals than by possible future carbon pricing of unknown (but not zero) likelihood and price. Furthermore, these benefits will be augmented by carbon and trace-gas savings from biologically informed agriculture, ranging from perennial polyculture to beef-system reforms to new ways to restore devastated tropical rainforests and their impoverished rural communities while reversing the huge greenhouse gas emissions of countries like Indonesia and producing abundant biofuel. In short, there is as much good news about advantageous ways to abate non-fossil (GHG) emissions as fossil-fuel ones.[24]

Cutting global carbon emissions quickly enough, without waiting for an elusive global agreement on vexing historical grievances and future divergent interests, is challenging but manageable. For example, in 1977–1985, the United States cut its oil intensity by an average of 5.2% per year. (GDP rose 27%, oil use fell 17%, oil imports fell 50%, and oil imports from the Persian Gulf fell 87%; they would have reached zero the following year had the policy continued.) Today, standard economic and decarbonization forecasts suggest, approximately, that cutting global primary energy intensity by about 3–4% per year, vs. the historic ~1% per year, could more than offset secular net growth in carbon emissions and thus abate further climate damage.

This appears feasible: the United States has long achieved 2–4% per year lower primary energy intensity (and cut its electric intensity in 2012 by an unprecedented weather-adjusted 3.4%) without national focus or concerted effort, while China beat 5% per year for a quarter-century through 2001 and returned to 4–5% per year in the past few years. Some firms have even achieved 6–16% per year. Why, then should 3–4% per year be difficult—particularly when most of the growth is in countries such as China and India that are building most of their infrastructure in the next few decades, and building it right is easier than fixing it later? Furthermore, because virtually everyone who invests in energy efficiency earns an attractive return at low risk, why should this activity be costly?

Profitable climate protection, economic growth and development, and energy security require sustained effort, relentless patience, and meticulous attention to detail. They're not easy—only easier than not doing them.

Such a strategy is even more vital for developing countries,[25] which typically use severalfold more energy to deliver a given service (regardless of how deprived of services their poorer citizens may be). The poor use little energy, but waste far more of what they do use and can afford the waste less; the poorest quintile can pay a sixfold or larger fraction of disposal income than people in developed countries. Reversing that waste and its opportunity costs yields stunning results. When a South Indian village switched from kerosene to fluorescent lamps (let alone today's far better LEDs), illumination rose 19-fold, energy input fell ninefold, and household lighting costs were halved. The indirect benefits of using saved kerosene costs to buy bed nets, clean water, and drip irrigation, let alone of girls' learning to read at night, are incalculable.

Saving energy, particularly electricity (the most capital-intensive sector), offers the greatest—yet unpulled and largely unnoticed—macroeconomic lever for development. For example, a standard Brazilian electric showerhead costing R$20 requires Eletrobras to invest about R$1,800–3,000; therefore, eliminating those chuveiros elétricos would leverage huge capital savings. Investing to make super-windows in Bangkok or LED lights in Mumbai, rather than building power plants and grids to deliver the same increased cooling and light, needs nearly a thousandfold less capital[26] and recycles it about tenfold faster. That approximately 10,000-fold lower capital requirement (intensity × velocity) could even turn the power sector, which devours one-fourth of global development capital, into a net exporter of capital for other development needs and even faster leapfrog development.[27]

The first trillion-plus dollars' savings could come from the 2011 Super-Efficient Equipment and Appliance Deployment (SEAD) initiative. By 2030, its full execution could save 1.8

PWh/y from 300 coal plants. The four appliances that SEAD targets use ~60% of residential electricity in China and India (which together burn half the world's coal) as also in the United States and the European Union. Together, these four places use nearly three-fourths of those key appliances' electricity, and only 15 firms make three-fourths of them.

Although developing countries often lag in technical capabilities, their people are no less intelligent, entrepreneurial, hardworking, resourceful, and determined.[28] Brains, as Gifford and Elizabeth Pinchot remind us, are evenly distributed, one per person, so they are mostly in the South and half in women. Thus, the flow of innovation is already reversing from South to North, sped by the emerging global nervous system: Facebook has more members than America has people, political revolutions happen on Twitter and YouTube, and for each person on the planet there are more than a billion transistors.

As central institutions become gridlocked and even moribund, vitality emerging at the grassroots is starting to pervade business and civil society, even where governments may be the last to know. As this quiet bottom-up energy revolution continues and expands, its global flowering could create for the world a new fire that, if efficiently used, can do our work without working our undoing.

References

1. A.B. Lovins & Rocky Mountain Institute, *Reinventing Fire: Bold Business Solutions for the New Energy Era* (Chelsea Green, 2011; www.reinventingfire.com), at p. 7; p. 268, note 237; and http://rmi.org/RFGraph-Fossil_fuels_global_production.
2. A simple summary is on pp. 11–20 of A.B. & L.H. Lovins, "Climate: Making Sense and Making Money," RMI (Snowmass CO), 1977, www.rmi.org/images/other/Climate/C97-13_ClimateMSMM.pdf.
3. N. Mims & H. Hauenstein, "Feebates: A Legislative Option to Encourage Continuous Improvements to Automobile Efficiency," RMI, 2008, www.rmi.org/rmi/Library%2FT08-09_FeebatesLegislativeOption.
4. Lovins & RMI, Ref. 1.
5. These buildings and industry findings draw heavily on U.S. National Research Council, *America's Energy Future*, 2009, www.nap.edu.

catalog/12098.html.

6. A.B. Lovins & D.R. Cramer, "Hypercars, hydrogen, and the automotive transition," *Intl. J. Veh. Design* 35(1/2):50–85 (2004), www.rmi.org/rmi/Library/T04-01_HypercarsHydrogenAutomotiveTransition.

7. European Climate Foundation, *Roadmap 2050: A Practical Guide to a Prosperous, Low Carbon Europe*. ECF, www.roadmap2050.eu/.

8. McKinsey Solutions, "Climate Desk for Governments," http://solutions.mckinsey.com/climatedesk/default/en-us/governments/mckinsey_on_climate_change/mckinsey_on_climate_change.aspx.

9. A.B. Lovins, "Integrative Design: A Disruptive Source of Expanding Returns to Investments in Energy Efficiency," RMI, 2010, www.rmi.org/Knowledge-Center/Library/2010–09_IntegrativeDesign;-, "Factor Ten Engineering Design Principles," RMI, 2010, www.rmi.org/Knowledge-Center/Library/2010-10-10xEPrinciples; -, "Advanced Energy Efficiency," Stanford Engineering School lectures, 2007, www.rmi.org/stanford.

10. This work is frequently updated at www.mckinsey.com/Client_Service/Sustainability/Latest_thinking/Costcurves.

11. Many are cited in A.B. Lovins & L.H. Lovins, "Least-cost climatic stabilization," *Ann. Rev. En. Envt.* 16:433–531 (1991), www.rmi.org/images/other/Energy/E91-33_LstCostClimateStabli.pdf, and in A.B. & L.H. Lovins, F. Krause & W. Bach, *Least-Cost Energy: Solving the CO_2 Problem*, Brick House (Andover MA), 1981 (summarized in *Clim. Chg.* 4:217–220 (1982)). Outstanding early examples include W. Feist, *Stromsparpotentiale bei den privaten Haushalten in der Bundesrepublik Deutschland*, Institut Wohnen und Umwelt (Darmstadt), 1987; D. Olivier & H. Miall, *Energy-efficient futures: Opening the solar option*, Earth Resources Research Ltd (London), 1983; and J.S. Nørgård, *Husholdninger og Energi*, Polyteknisk Forlag (København), 1979.

12. Bloomberg New Energy Finance, "Clean energy attracts its trillionth dollar," Dec 6, 2011, http://bnef.com/PressReleases/view/176.

13. B. Bodlund, E. Mills, T. Karlsson, & T.B. Johansson, "The Challenge of Choices," in T.B. Johansson, B. Bodlund, & R.H. Williams, eds., *Electricity*, Lund U. Press, 1989, at pp. 883–947, http://evanmills.lbl.gov/pubs/pdf/challenge-of-choices.pdf.

14. A.K.N. Reddy, A.D'Sa & G.D. Sumithra, "Integrated energy planning: Part II. Examples of DEFENDUS scenarios," *En. Sust. Develt.* II(4):12–26 (1995), repository.ias.ac.in/34367/1/34367.pdf.

15. Renewable Energy Policy Network for the 21st Century, *Renewables Global Status Report*, 2013, www.ren21.net.

16. Id.; *G-20 Clean Energy Factbook: Who's Winning the Clean Energy Race?*, Pew Charitable Trusts, 2011, www.pewtrusts.org/uploadFiles/wwwpewtrustorg/Reports/Global_warming/G-20%20Report.pdf.

17. Bloomberg New Energy Finance, "Global Renewable Energy Market Outlook," Nov 16, 2011, http://bnef.com/WhitePapers/download/53.

18. A.B.Lovins & RMI, op. cit.; US National Renewable Energy Laboratory,

Renewable Energy Futures Study, 2012, www.nrel.gov/analysis/re_futures/.

19. R. Kleinfeld & A. Sloan, *Let There Be Light*, Truman National Security Project (Washington, D.C.), 2011, in press; The Lumina Project, light.lbl.gov.

20. A.B. Lovins, E.K. Datta, T. Feiler, K.R. Rábago, J.N. Swisher, A. Lehmann, & K. Wicker, *Small Is Profitable: The Hidden Economic Benefits of Making Electrical Resources the Right Size* (Rocky Mountain Institute, Snowmass, CO, USA, 2002), www.smallisprofitable.org.

21. A.B. Lovins, "DoD's Energy Challenge as Strategic Opportunity, *Joint Force Quarterly* 57:33–42 (2010), www.ndu.edu/press/jfq-57.html; A.B. Lovins, "Efficiency and Micropower for Reliable and Resilient Electricity Service: An Intriguing Case-Study from Cuba," RMI, 2010, www.rmi.org/Knowledge-Center/Library/2010-23_CubaElectricity.

22. P. Stockton (Assistant Secretary of Defense), Testimony to Subcommittee on Energy and Power, Committee on Energy and Commerce, U.S. House of Representatives, May 31, 2011, http://republicans.energycommerce.house.gov/Media/file/Hearings/Energy/053111/Stockton.pdf.

23. A.B. Lovins, "Energy end-use efficiency, "InterAcademy Council (Amsterdam) white paper commissioned by S.Chu, 2005, www.rmi.org/rmi/Library/E05-16_EnergyEndUseEfficiency; - "More profit with less carbon," *Sci. Amer.* 293(III):7482, www.sciam.com/media/pdf/Lovinsforweb.pdf; - "Profitable Solutions to Climate, Oil and Proliferation," *Ambio* 39:236–248 (2010), doi:10.1007/s13280-010-0031-6, 2010, www.rmi.org/Knowledge-Center/Library/2010-18_ProfitableSolutionsClimateOil.

24. Ref. 1, p. 239, with endnotes omitted.

25. J. Goldemberg, T.B. Johansson, A.K.N. Reddy, & R.H. Williams, *Energy for a Sustainable World*, Wiley, 1989; A.K.N. Reddy, R.H. Williams, & T.B. Johansson, *Energy after Rio: Prospects and Challenges*, 1997, UNDP (NY).

26. A. Gadgil, A.H. Rosenfeld, D. Arasteh, & E. Ward, "Advanced Lighting and Window Technologies for Reducing Electricity Consumption and Peak Demand: Overseas Manufacturing and Marketing Opportunities," LBL-30389 Revised, Lawrence Berkeley National Laboratory (Berkeley CA), at pp.4-5 in *Procs. IEA/ENEL Conf. Adv. Technol. El. DSM*, April 1991.

27. J. Goldemberg, "Technological Leapfrogging in the Developing World," *Science & Technology*, pp. 135–141, Winter/Spring 2011.

28. C.K. Prahalad, *The Fortune at the Bottom of the Pyramid*, Pearson, 2005.

The Ecosystem Approach for Understanding and Resolving Environmental Problems

Gene E. Likens

The ecosystem approach, embracing complexity and inclusiveness rather than avoiding them, provides an important ecological tool for identifying, describing, and addressing multifaceted environmental problems (e.g., Likens 1998, 2001). Using the required inclusiveness of the ecosystem approach provides a powerful framework for identifying new environmental problems or reshaping existing ones and then tackling their complexity, particularly when ecosystem processes are coupled with social and economic considerations (e.g., Currie 2011). In the upcoming decades, we must deal with many existing environmental issues; however, new problems will emerge, requiring new knowledge and the need for new and more innovative solutions to those problems at all levels of consideration (e.g., Likens 2001; http://ecohusky.uconn.edu/docs/news - Sustainability Newsletter Fall–Winter 2011-2012.pdf). We are indeed "shooting at a moving target" (Wiens 2011), and if we do not look into the future and attempt to anticipate problems and "surprises" (Lindenmayer, Likens, Krebs, and Hobbs 2010), our chances of success will be dim. A comprehensive, integrated ecosystem approach provides an important window for doing that. Ecosystem scientists have helped to understand the ramifications of environmental deterioration by raising large-scale, realistic questions about impacts on Earth's systems from the onset of a problem's detection. This approach is crucial for finding management-relevant scientific results. Because of the magnitude and increased prevalence of environmental problems worldwide, Hobbs et al. (2011) have called for humans to intervene "...in ecosystems to restore ecosystem services and biodiversity." However, this time, our intervention must be positive, ethical, informed, broad-scaled, comprehensive, and not focused only on restoration.

Environmental change results from a complex mix of powerful factors called "human-accelerated environmental change" (Likens 1991), which includes such problems as climate change, loss of stratospheric ozone, loss of species, invasion of alien species, toxification of the biosphere, infectious disease, and land-use changes caused and accelerated by humans (Figure 1). Even more important are the linkages and feedbacks among these various human-accelerated environmental changes, with their significant, incongruent legacies (e.g., Likens 1994, 2001, 2004). Ecosystem ecology is one of the best ways to involve humans in more than mere single-topic issues. Unless humans unite toward taking action that solves ecosystem-level problems, efforts will remain piecemeal and ultimately ineffective. Even if humans choose to work on a single issue, they must see clearly how that issue fits within the larger picture. Seeing how it all comes together is indeed the only way to resolve environmental issues. The complexity of ecosystems is daunting but the only way to know what is important in attempts to integrate the whole picture in resolving environmental problems.

Regardless of the misrepresentation and hype currently associated with the concept of ecosystem management, the holistic consideration and management of entire ecosystems are extremely valuable goals in attempts to make lasting progress on environmental problems. In particular, the evaluation of ecosystem inputs and outputs are extremely critical measures in this regard for defining and reducing the effects of pollution, conservation of habitat and biodiversity, quantitatively evaluating the effects of disturbances such as forestry and agriculture or human development on watershed-ecosystems, and intelligently managing landscapes or regions (e.g., Likens

1998). Resolving large-scale biogeochemical cycles quantitatively is critical, not only for understanding how ecosystems are changing because of factors such as climate change but also for managing these changes in the face of feedbacks between climate change and element cycles (e.g., Mitchell and Likens 2011; Mitchell et al. 2011; Likens et al. 2011; Fig. 1).

Delineation of ecosystem boundaries is critical for quantitative measures of input and output fluxes for ecosystems (Bormann and Likens 1967, Likens 1998). Ecosystem boundaries are usually determined for the convenience of the investigator to measure quantitavely flux, rather than on the basis of some known functional discontinuity with an adjacent ecosystem, and this has attracted criticism from some quarters (e.g., Fitzsimmons 1996; Currie 2011). However, the theoretical and methodological constraints for boundary establishment are described in Bormann and Likens (1967), Likens (1972, 1975, 1992), Bormann and Likens (1979), Likens and Bormann (1985), and Wiens et al. (1985). Boundaries are required for quantitative measurements of flux (e.g., Likens 1998, pp. 264–265), and indeed, such delineation of boundaries normally provides a powerful advantage in conducting the necessary quantitative analyses of ecosystems, such as mass-balances. Inputs and outputs for individual ecosystems are the functional connection among all ecosystems of the planet, comprising the "pulse" of the planet, and have major management relevance in resolving environmental problems.

Although ecosystem ecology is a relatively young science (Tansley 1935, Odum 1959), the ecosystem approach has become a powerful integrating tool for unraveling the complexity of major environmental problems, such as acid rain and eutrophication. Many exciting changes, such as the increased availability of large data sets, opportunities to study major regional and global changes ("experiments"), longer-term financial support facilitating long-term research and monitoring, and powerful new tools such as isotopes and molecular/genetic approaches facilitate a greater unraveling of the enormous complexity comprising diverse ecosystems and, in turn, suggest management solutions to vexing environmental problems (e.g., Pace and Groffman 1998).

The environmental problem of acid rain gives a clear example of how the ecosystem approach can be effective throughout the continuum, from problem detection to comprehensive study and analysis, to management intervention (Likens 2010). This environmental problem continues to be one of the most urgent environmental issues related to long-term effects of human impacts on aquatic and terrestrial ecosystems (Likens et al. 2011).

Despite its ecological importance, the acid rain issue is very difficult to address experimentally, especially at small spatial scales, particularly with regional and international transboundary components regarding emission and transport of sulfur and nitrogen oxides. Short-term observations and experiments are relatively easy, but only through long-term, large-scale (ecosystem) observations and experiments can we understand and resolve the interaction with other drivers, such as the complex effects of changing climate. Identifying and interpreting the interactions among climate change and other human influences on targeted environmental problems, such as major disturbances in the global flux and cycling of nitrogen (e.g., Galloway et al. 2008; Vitousek et al. 1997; Tae-Wook Kim 2011; Bernal et al. 2012), remain extremely challenging. When long-term data from watershed-ecosystems are available, such as from the Hubbard Brook Experimental Forest (HBEF) in New Hampshire, USA (approaching 50 continuous years of the most complete, coordinated record in existence for precipitation and stream-water amount and chemistry (Likens 2004)), we can gain new insights into the workings of complicated ecosystems (Lindenmayer and Likens 2010).

As Likens (2001) has argued, never before have ecosystem ecologists needed to be as creative, innovative, proactive, and aggressive to meet the environmental challenges of the next fifty years (e.g., Lubchenco 1998; Ayensu et al. 1999; Vörösmarty 2000; Estes et al. 2011; Tae-Wook Kim 2011). Similarly, never before has a holistic, comprehensive ecosystem approach

Figure 1

A conceptual model for human-accelerated environmental change

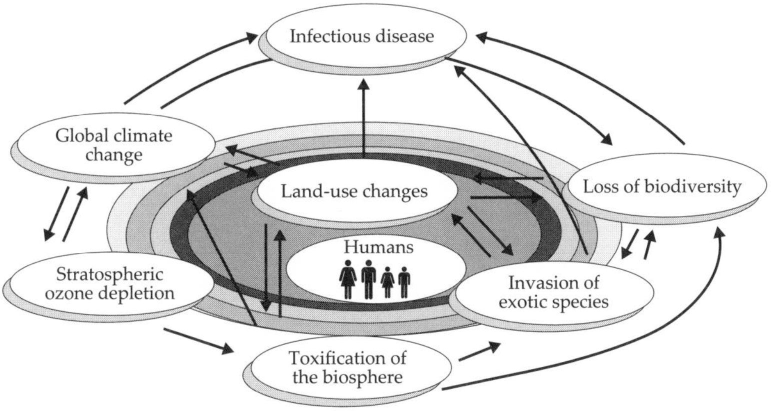

Source: Likens(2003).

(incorporating information from across the spectrum of ecology from more biotic-centric evolutionary ecology to more abiotic-centric biogeochemistry) been more needed to address these challenges. In particular, there is a need for holistic, ecosystem thinking, not necessarily holistic modeling that usually becomes excessively complex and thus unmanageable. Nevertheless, because of its integrative and comprehensive nature, the ecosystem approach offers hope in dealing with current and future large-scale environmental problems such as acidification of oceans and the widespread pollution following earthquake and tsunami damage during March 2011 in Japan (www.telegraph.co.uk/news/picture galleries). Not only are these problems catastrophic and profound for people in the local areas affected but they also involve the contamination and interaction of pollutants through air, land, and water on massive scales (not only atmospheric transport of radioactive materials).

Hopefully, "ecosystem thinking" (Likens and Franklin 2009) will become the overriding paradigm as we struggle to resolve increasingly large and more complex environmental problems in the future. The piecemeal approaches of the past will no longer serve our densely populated planet—for example, managing the environmental problems of a river, but not integrating this management approach with the management of the river's airshed, drainage basin, and the receiving estuary. Ecosystem thinking and a comprehensive, integrated ecosystem approach will be crucial for evaluating and reducing the ecological footprints of environmental problems.

References

1. Ayensu, E., D. van R. Claasen, M. Collins, A. Dearing, L. Fresco, M. Gadgil, H. Gitay, G. Glaser, C. Juma, J. Krebs, R. Lenton, J. Lubchenco, J. McNeeley, H. Mooney, P. Pinstrup-Andersen, M. Ramos, P. Raven, W. Reid, C. Samper, J. Sarukhán, P. Schei, J. Galizia Tundisi, R. Watson, Xu Guanhua and A. Zakri. 1999. International Ecosystem Assessment. *Science* 286:685–686.

2. Bernal, S., L. O. Hedin, G. E. Likens, S. Gerber and D. C. Buso. 2012. Complex response of the forest nitrogen cycle to climate change. *Proc. National Academy Sci.* doi/10.1073/pnas.1121448109

3. Bormann, F. H. and G. E. Likens. 1967. Nutrient cycling. *Science* 155(3761):424–429.

4. Bormann, F. H. and G. E. Likens. 1979. *Pattern and Process in a Forested Ecosystem.* Springer-Verlag New York Inc., pp. 253.

5. Currie, W. S. 2011. Units of nature or processes across scales? The ecosystem concept at age 75. *New Phytologist* 190:21–34.

6. Estes, J. A. et al. 2011. Trophic downgrading of planet Earth. *Science* 333:301–306.

7. Fitzsimmons, A. K. 1996. Sound policy or smoke and mirrors: does ecosystem management make sense? *Water Resources Bulletin* 32(2):217–227.

8. Galloway, J. N., A. R. Townsend, J. W. Erisman, M. Bekunda, Z. Cai, J. R. Freney, L. A. Martinelli, S. P. Seitzinger and M. A. Sutton. 2008. Transformation of the nitrogen cycle: recent trends, questions, and potential solutions. *Science* 320:889–892.

9. Hobbs, R. J., L. M. Hallett, P. R. Ehrlich and H. A. Mooney. 2011. Intervention Ecology: Applying ecological science in the Twenty-First Century. *BioScience* 61(6):442–450.

10. Likens, G. E. 1975. Nutrient flux and cycling in freshwater ecosystems. pp. 314–348. In: F. G. Howell, J. B. Gentry and M. H. Smith (eds.). *Mineral Cycling in Southeastern Ecosystems.* ERDA Symp. Series CONF-740513. May 1974, Augusta, Georgia.

11. Likens, G. E. 1991. Human-accelerated environmental change. *BioScience* 41(3):130.

12. Likens, G. E. 1992. The Ecosystem Approach: Its Use and Abuse. Excellence in Ecology, Vol. 3. Ecology Institute, Oldendorf/Luhe, Germany. 167 pp.

13. Likens, G. E. 1994. Human-Accelerated Environmental Change–An Ecologist's View. 1994 Australia Prize Winner Presentation. Murdoch University, Perth, Australia. 16 pp.

14. Likens, G. E. 1998. Limitations to intellectual progress in ecosystem science. pp. 247–271. In: M. L. Pace and P. M. Groffman (eds.)., Successes, Limitations and Frontiers in Ecosystem Science. 7th Cary Conference, Institute of Ecosystem Studies, Millbrook, New York. Springer-Verlag New York Inc.

15. Likens, G. E. 2001. Ecosystems: Energetics and Biogeochemistry. pp. 53–88. In: W. J. Kress and G. Barrett (eds.). *A New Century of Biology.* Smithsonian Institution Press, Washington and London.

16. Likens, G. E. 2003. Use of long-term data, mass balances and stable isotopes in watershed biogeochemistry: The Hubbard Brook model. *Gayana Botanica* 60(1):3–7.

17. Likens, G. E. 2004. Some perspectives on long-term biogeochemical research from the Hubbard Brook Ecosystem Study. *Ecology* 85(9):2355–2362.

18. Likens, G. E. 2010. The role of science in decision making: does evidence-based science drive environmental policy? *Frontiers of Ecology and the Environment* 8(6):e1-e8. doi:10.1890/090132

19. Likens, G. E. and F. H. Bormann. 1972. Nutrient cycling in ecosystems. *pp. 25–67. In:* J. Wiens (ed.). *Ecosystem Structure and Function.* Oregon State University Press, Corvallis.

20. Likens, G. E. and F. H. Bormann. 1985. An ecosystem approach. *pp. 1–8. In:* G. E. Likens (ed.). *An Ecosystem Approach to Aquatic Ecology: Mirror Lake and its Environment.* Springer-Verlag New York Inc.

21. Likens, G. E. and J. F. Franklin. 2009. Ecosystem Thinking in the Northern Forest–and Beyond. *BioScience* 59(6):511–513.

22. Likens, G. E., T. J. Butler and M. A. Rury. 2011. Acid rain. *Encyclopedia of Global Studies.*

23. Lindenmayer, D. B., G. E. Likens, C. J. Krebs and R. J. Hobbs. 2010. Improved probability of detection of ecological "surprises." *Proc. National Acad. Sci.* 107(51):21957–21962. doi: 10.1073/pnas.1015696107.

24. Lubchenco, J. 1998. Entering the century of the environment : a new social contract with science. *Science* 279:491–497.

25. Mitchell, M. J. and G. E. Likens. 2011. Watershed sulfur biogeochemistry: shift from atmospheric deposition dominance to climatic regulation. *Environ. Sci. Tech.* 45:5267–5271. dx.doi.org/10.1021/es200844n

26. Mitchell, M. J., G. Lovett, S. Bailey, F. Beall, D. Burns, D. Buso, T. A. Clair, F. Courchesne, L. Duchesne, C. Eimers, I. Fernandez, D. Houle,

D. S. Jeffries, G. E. Likens, M. D. Moran, C. Rogers, D. Schwede, J. Shanley, K. C. Weathers and R. Vet. 2011. Comparisons of watershed sulfur budgets in southeast Canada and northeast US: new approaches and implications. *Biogeochemistry* 103:181–207, doi:10.1007/s10533-010-9455-0.

27. Odum, E.P. 1959. (second edition). *Fundamentals of Ecology.* W.B. Saunders, Philadelphia, pp 546.
28. Pace, M. L. and P. M. Groffman (eds.). 1998. *Successes, Limitations, and Frontiers in Ecosystem Science.* Springer-Verlag New York, Inc. 499 pp.
29. Tae-Wook Kim, Kitack Lee, R. G. Najjar, Hee-Dong Jeong and Hae Jin Jeong. 2011. Increasing N abundance in the Northwestern Pacific Ocean due to atmospheric nitrogen deposition. *Science* 334:505–509.
30. Tansley, A. G. 1935. The use and abuse of vegetational concepts and terms. *Ecology* 16(3):284–307.
31. Vitousek, P.M., J. D. Aber, R. W. Howarth, G. E. Likens, P. A. Matson, D. W. Schindler, W. H. Schlesinger and D. G. Tilman. 1997. Human alteration of the global nitrogen cycle: sources and consequences. *Ecological Applications* 7(3):737–750.
32. Vörösmarty, C. J. 2000. Global water resources : vulnerability from climate change and population growth. *Science* 289:284–288.
33. Wiens, J. A., C. S. Crawford and J. R. Gosz. 1985. Boundary dynamics: a conceptual framework for studying landscape ecosystems. *Oikos* 45:421–427.
34. Wiens, J. 2011. Essay: Shooting at a moving target. *The Bulletin, British Ecol. Soc.* (December) 42(4):55–56.

Global Warming and Water Resources

Syukuro Manabe

When we talk about global warming, we usually think about temperature. However, it affects profoundly the exchange of moisture between the Earth's surface and the atmosphere through evaporation and precipitation (Manabe and Wetherald, 1975). The changes in precipitation and evaporation in turn alter the rate of river discharge and soil moisture, affecting the availability of water at continental surface. Let me elaborate further on the processes involved.

According to the law of thermodynamics, saturation vapor pressure of air increases almost exponentially with increasing temperature. Thus, the warmer the temperature of the Earth's surface, the higher is the saturation vapor pressure at the Earth's surface. This is the main reason why the rate of evaporation increases due to global warming. In response to the increase in the rate of evaporation, precipitation also increases, thereby satisfying the water balance of the atmosphere as a whole. If the change in the rate of evaporation were equal to that of evaporation at all locations, they would have no effect on the amount of water available for river discharge and soil moisture at the continental surface. In reality, however, the rate of precipitation changes differently from that of evaporation because of the change in the horizontal transport of water vapor in the atmosphere as explained below.

In middle latitudes, extra-tropical cyclones bring warm, moist air pole-ward and cold dry air equator-ward, thereby transporting water vapor from the subtropics toward the middle and high latitudes. In low latitudes, trade winds transport moisture-rich air from the subtropics toward the tropical rain-belt. When temperature increases due to global warming, absolute humidity also increases in the troposphere, accompanying the increase in saturation vapor pressure (i.e., moisture-holding capacity) of air. The increase in absolute humidity in turn increases the transport of water vapor in the troposphere. For example, the poleward transport of water vapor by extra-tropical cycloes increases, increasing precipitation between middle and high latitudes. Meanwhile, the equator-ward transport of water vapor also increases, thereby increasing precipitation in the tropics. In contrast, because of the increase in the export of moisture toward both high and low latitudes, precipitation decreases in the subtropical continents despite the increase in evaporation from oceanic region. It is therefore expected that the rate of river discharge increases not only between middle and high latitudes but also in the tropics. In contrast, soil moisture is expected to decrease in many semiarid regions of the world (e.g., grassland of Africa and Australia, southwestern part of North America) as indicated in many modeling studies (e.g., Wetherald and Manabe, 2002; Manabe et al., 2004a; Manabe et al. 2004b; Kundezewicz et al., 2007; Meehl et al., 2007; Manabe, 2013).

According to many modeling studies, global warming will induce large-scale change in water availability. For example, water will become more plentiful in those regions of the world that are already water-rich, whereas water stresses will increase in water-poor regions that are already relatively dry. Observational studies have found that the frequencies of both flood and drought have increased around the world. As we know, many semi-arid regions have already experienced serious water shortages due mainly to rapidly increasing population, per capita consumption of water, demographic shift, and other factors. Unfortunately, it is quite likely that global warming will aggravate this situation, worsening the existing contrast between water-rich and water-poor regions of the world.

To manage this large-scale change in water availability,

increasing emphasis should be placed on water management through

- Desalinization
- Filtering/recycling
- Storage (dams, artificial lakes)
- Conservation
- Transport through pipelines and canals
- Changes in agricultural practice
- Applying biotechnology to agriculture.

Reference

1. Kundzewicz, Z.W. et al., 2007: Freshwater resources and their management. Climate Change 2007: Impact, Adaptation and Vulnerability. Contribution of Working Group II to the Fourth Assessment Report of the IPCC, M.L. Parry et al. Eds., Cambridge University Press, Cambridge, UK, 173–210.
2. Manabe, S. and R.T. Wetherald, 1975: The effect of doubling CO_2 concentration on the climate of a general circulation model. *Journal of Atmospheric Sciences*, 32, 3-15.
3. Manabe, S. 2013: Global warming and "water" (in Japanese). *Transaction of Japan Academy*, 67, 51-60.
4. Manabe, S., R.T. Wetherald, P.C.D. Milly, T.L. Delworth, and R.J. Stouffer, 2004a: Century-scale change in water availability: CO_2-quadrupling experiment. *Climatic Change*, 64, 59–76.
5. Manabe, S. P.C.D. Milly, and R.T. Wetherald, 2004b: Simulated long-term changes in river discharge and soil moisture due to global warming. *Hydrological Sciences-Journal*, 49, 625–642.
6. Meehl, G.A. et al., 2007: Global Climate Projections. In: Climate Change 2007: The Physical Science Basis. Contribution of Working Group I to the Fourth Assessment Report of the IPCC [Solomon, S. et al. Eds.]. Cambridge University Press, Cambridge, Cambridge, UK, and New York, NY, USA.
7. Wetherald, R.T., and S. Manabe, 2002: Simulation of hydrologic changes associated with global warming. *Journal of Geophysical Research*, 107 (D19), 4379–4393.

Underlying Drivers of Change and their Inter-relationships
Demographic Changes

Robert May

The growth of the population of *Homo sapiens* has been far from merely exponential. For most of our approximately 200,000-year tenancy of our planet, we were bands of hunter–gatherers, whose total population has been estimated at roughly 5–20 million.

With the commencement of settled agriculture in several places about 10,000 years ago, things began to change. Towns and cities began to grow, and recorded history began. The first few thousand years of this growth are estimated to have seen numbers increase faster than in later millennia, as infectious diseases that could not be maintained within low-density populations were acquired from domestic animals, and began to spread. Some 300 such infections, including smallpox, measles, and others, can be identified; endemic measles, for example, requires population aggregations of 300,000 or more.

The next great acceleration in population growth rates, beginning in the seventeenth century mainly in Western Europe, resulted from the increasingly systematic understanding of how the natural world works, based on experimental science. Even so, mortality rates in industrial cities such as Liverpool in the mid-1800's were not much better than those for hunter–gatherers, with roughly half of the children dying before the age of five.

The past 70 years have been markedly different, as increasing basic scientific understanding of the transmission and treatment of infectious diseases has been applied in simple measures of primary health care. Furthermore, these benefits have, to a degree, been more equitably distributed. In summary, global average life expectancy at birth 50 years ago was 46 years; today, it is about 68. The main factor in this change is that the difference in life expectancy between developed and developing countries 50 years ago was 26 years; today, it is a still disgraceful 12 years. Even so, as a result of enlightenment science, the average child born in a poor country today is – at least in terms of life expectancy – better off than one born 150 years ago in the industrializing centers of the Western World.

To summarize, it took several hundred thousand years for human populations to reach one billion around 1830. It took a century for that total to double, and only 40 years to double again to four billion in 1970. Forty years on, in 2011, the total is seven billion. Recently, however, higher average living standards in both developed and developing worlds have seen fertility rates decrease to about replacement levels: around the globe, women are having on average one female child who will survive to adulthood. This replacement rate corresponds to a Total Fertility Rate (TFR) of roughly 2.3 children, allowing for non-survivors (or slightly less than 2.1 otherwise; a boy baby is slightly more probable than a girl).

On average, today's women are having only half as many children as their mothers did. Overall, TFR has dropped from 4.9 children per woman in 1950 to about 2.5 in 2011 (consisting of 4.1 in the least developed countries and 1.65 in more developed regions) and is expected to reach 2.2 by 2025. These trends are seen even in some of the poorest countries, such as Bangladesh, and in some of the more repressive Muslim countries (Iran had a TFR of 5.5 in 1988, which had reduced to 2.1 in 2000 and 1.9 in 2006; this figure of 1.9 comprises 1.7 for urban and 2.1 for rural regions).

Figure 1 strikingly depicts these changes in total population and in the annual increase, from 1750 and projected forward, assuming current trends continue, to 2050. The past century exhibits an extraordinary singularity.

These trends of smaller families indeed vary somewhat among regions. They correlate highly with education of women,

Figure 1

Estimated world population growth: 1750-2050 (McDevitt 1999)

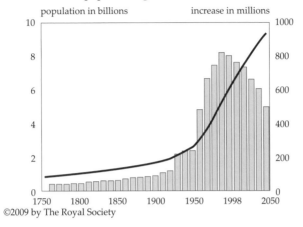

©2009 by The Royal Society

Source: Speidel, J. J. et al. Phil. Trans. R. Soc. B 2009; 364: 3049-3065.

along with availability of non-coercive fertility control. Recent studies in diverse developing countries (Niger, Guatemala, Yemen, Haiti, Kenya, and the Philippines) report that girls completing primary education have on average 1.5 fewer children than those not so educated. Girls completing secondary education have an additional 2.0 fewer children (i.e., 3.5 fewer than those denied education). In Iran in recent decades, more women are obtaining higher education and marrying later, resulting in the odds of having only one child increasing by a factor of 2.64 with progression from school diploma to undergraduate degree. In addition, investing in sexual and reproductive health and rights is cost effective, significantly improving individual lives and contributing to slowing population growth. Unfortunately, however, more than 200 million women in developing countries still have unmet family planning needs. Although the need is increasing, it is estimated that funding decreased by 30% between 1995 and 2008 (largely as a result of legislative pressure from the religious right in the USA). In view of the correlation between education and TFR, Figure 2 interestingly depicts the proportion of the world's males and

117

Figure 2

World population by age, sex, and four levels of educational attainment in (*a*) 1970, (*b*) 2010 and (*c*) projected to 2050 under the GET scenario.

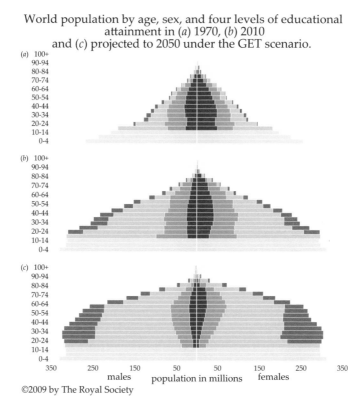

©2009 by The Royal Society

Source: Lutz, W. Phil. Trans. R. Soc. B 2009; 364: 3031-3047.

females by age and level of educational attainment (none, primary, secondary, and tertiary) in 1970, 2010, and projected to 2050.

Despite these encouraging trends, the world population continues to grow, albeit at a diminishing rate, as a result of the "momentum of population growth." This momentum results from there being many more young than old people in many, if not most, developing countries. Even though they seem very likely to have fewer children than their mothers, their number means that populations will continue to increase. Populations will not attain steady levels until "age pyramids" become "age rectangles." Looking ahead to 2050, and assuming that current fertility trends continue, we expect 9.1 billion people. If each woman has 0.5 children fewer than the median projection, this number would be 7.7; with 0.5 children more, 10.6. In addition, if we assumed that the already diminished 2005 fertility levels simply persisted, we would have 11.7 billion.

Some, arguably many, of the population growth problems are compounded by the fact that 95% of the build-out of human numbers will occur in developing countries' urban areas. In 1700, fewer than 10% of the world's population lived in cities. By 1900, the proportion was 25%; today, it is 50%; and by 2050, it will be 67%. In 1950, there were 86 cities with populations in excess of 1 million; today, there are well over 400; and by 2015, there will be at least 550.

We can illustrate the truly unprecedented nature of our current situation by deconstructing a phrase of Walt Whitman's: "row upon row rise the phantoms behind us." One dramatic way of conveying our present situation is to ask, if indeed all our predecessors were lined up behind the phalanx of those alive today, how deep would these rows be? Demographic guesstimates put this total in the 80–100 billion range, which roughly implies only 11–14 shadows–reaching back to the first humans in Africa–behind you.

In summary, over the past 150 years, human numbers have increased sevenfold. At the same time, the average per capita amount of energy subsidizing daily activities (derived mostly from burning fossil fuels) has increased sevenfold. Thus, our species' ecological footprint has grown by a factor of about 50 in this 150-year interval. This footprint consists of demands for food, water, and myriad other resources. WWF has estimated the average per capita such footprint for each of the world's nations in 2009, along with the corresponding footprint each country could support sustainably, given its population size and resources. Fascinating ethical questions arise. For example, who are more virtuous: Egyptians, with an average footprint of 1.7 ha (but this is not important for the comparison) in a country whose corresponding biological capacity is 0.4, or Australians, with a footprint of 7.8 but a biological capacity estimated at 15.4. The average Egyptian treads more lightly on the planet, but nevertheless exceeds the country's sustainable capacity; Australians are more profligate but arguably can live sustainably, given their greater resource base.

Broadly, today's growing populations require resources whose supplies are decreasing relative to demands. More food requires both more water and more land. However, demands for water (70% of it for agriculture) are estimated to exceed sustainable supplies around 2040. Our impacts on terrestrial ecosystems for food and other purposes have already caused plant and animal extinction rates to climb to rates last seen in the Big Five mass extinctions in the fossil record. Furthermore, our understanding of the services that ecosystems deliver to us remains such that we cannot say how serious the impacts of such extinctions will be (never mind the ethical or esthetic aspects of these questions).

Most importantly, our demand for energy causes us to burn fossil fuels at such a rate that we emit one million years' deposits of such sequestered carbon into the atmosphere each year, thickening the greenhouse gas blanket and changing the climate. Ultimately, of course, the problem is a product of both ever more people and each one stamping a larger ecological footprint.

Ecosystem Services
Protecting our Heritage and Life Support System:
Key Issues and Ways Forward

Harold Mooney

In a relatively short amount of time, the concept of ecosystem services has penetrated deeply into research agendas and policy decisions at all levels, from international agreements to national and local priorities for agencies, both public and private. The term "ecosystem services" is beginning to appear in the popular press. Why is this so? Quite simply, the concept resonates with so many sectors of society because ecosystem services provide benefits to people. Politicians serve society, and therefore, they are interested in protecting and enhancing these benefits. Conservationists are attracted to the concept because ecosystem services are built on the diversity of organisms in a habitat, and thus speak to the preservation of diversity. Businesses are interested because some of these services are vital to their enterprises, as is also the case with agriculturalists. Development agencies are embracing the concept because of the strong links with ecosystem delivery and poverty alleviation (Barrett, Travis et al. 2011). All sectors of society benefit from the inspiration of nature and the clean water that vegetated watersheds provide. Therefore, we are all beneficiaries of these services, and indeed, our very life depends on them.

What we can do? Although the ecosystem concept is penetrating many sectors, it still needs a campaign to build societal awareness. Introducing the concept in secondary school education would be a good pathway to accomplish this goal, along with a campaign for the general public.

A large number of the services that nature provides are abundant and free for all. That is both good and bad news. Because they are free and have been so abundant, people have not paid much attention to protecting these resources. Consider the statement of the famous English biologist, Thomas Huxley, at the opening of a Fisheries Exhibition in London in 1883 (Huxley 1883) "I believe….that the cod fishery, the herring fishery, the pilchard fishery, the mackerel fishery, and probably all the great sea fisheries, are inexhaustible; that is to say, that nothing we do seriously affects the number of the fish. And any attempt to regulate these fisheries seems consequently, from the nature of the case, to be useless."

Since that optimistic statement not so long ago in human history, we have seen many of these fisheries collapse from overfishing, enabled by technological advances in harvest technology and the lack of a regulatory framework for the harvest of this "free" resource. More generally, a global survey involving over a thousand scientists concluded that, in fact, over 60% of these services had declined in availability to society, mostly during the past half century (MA 2005).

What can we do? We must support the developing Intergovernmental Platform on Biodiversity and Ecosystem Services (IPBES) that will provide periodic assessments of ecosystem service delivery and the status of the delivery system including the biophysical and social drivers of change.

The Earth contains a vast array of living things, no doubt numbering in millions. However, even these large numbers do not capture the true richness of our biological heritage. Each member of a population of virtually all species will be, to varying degrees, genetically distinct, possessing individual or combinations of traits that determine their distinctive interaction with members of their own species and other interacting species (Whitham, Gehring et al. 2012). Yet, certain keystone species exert a predominant influence on the functioning of any ecosystem. These may be a tree species or even a microbe (Power, Tilman et al. 1996). However, these keystones in turn depend upon other species for their survival. Nature contains apex species, such as top predators, that control the nature of the entire community or food chain. Throughout history, humans have hunted these apex species both on land and in the oceans. Their extinction has resulted in modification, and sometimes collapse, of the entire ecosystem to a new state, often less favorable to humans (Estes, Terborgh et al. 2011).

The breakdown of the historical barriers to intercontinental movement of species among continents has resulted in the movement of species into new environments where they are generally free of the co-existing species that had regulated their populations in their native habitats. Without such control, the invader may have explosive growth and even occupy greater climatic limits than they had at home. In many cases, successful invaders will not provide benefits but rather do great harm to the ecosystem that they invaded and to the benefits society derives from it. Examples include diseases that can decimate crops and forests as well as directly affect human health. They can adversely affect water availability and increase ecosystem flammability. The numbers of invading species are increasing in all continents coincident with increased global trade (Mooney, Mack et al. 2005). Unwanted invaders are being transported by ships and airplanes in increasing numbers, generally inadvertently. The ecosystem disruptions of rapid climate change will exacerbate this problem (Mooney and Hobbs 2000).

Perrings et al. (Perrings, Mooney et al. 2010) note a number of issues that we can address, in particular, bringing international agreements into conformity such as the International Health Regulations (IHR) and the WTO's Sanitary and Phytosanitary Agreement (SPS). The WTO's mandate to foster global trade must consider, and address, to a much greater extent those potential negative impacts of global commerce. It is clear that the costs of adequate border protection from potential pests associated with imports are less than those of controlling established invaders. There is very uneven border inspection capacity globally, and without it the invasive species problem will continue to grow.

What can we do? Align policy instruments regulating global trade and enhance national border inspection capacity.

We face an enormous challenge in the protection,

management, and design of ecosystem services that are critical for our well-being. Although the general features and broad results from our knowledge of the relationship between the multiple elements of the variety of life and ecosystem services are well articulated (MA 2005; Leadley, Pereira et al. 2010), the details of the relationships between species diversity and ecosystem functioning and service provisioning remain rudimentary. We know a good deal about particular systems and places; however, this knowledge needs expansion on the basis of more broadly practiced experimentation so we can apply this knowledge more generally. Such information is invaluable not only for managing optimal utilization of resources but also for preparing for the changing nature of our ecosystems resulting from multiple global changes, including climate. The structure and functioning of the ecosystems at any given location will undoubtedly change its character in the future. We will see the development of new climatic systems and the corresponding disruption of what we see today as well as the development of novel environments and ecosystem types (Hobbs, Higgs et al. 2009). We need more basic information to manage what we have now and predict the future so we can inform managers and policymakers of the challenges and opportunities of intervention versus restoration to some former state.

What can we do? Develop a global and comprehensive experimental network that probes the nature of diversity and ecosystem process and services under present and anticipated future environments, thus accelerating our future scenario development capacity.

In recent years, a flurry of research has explored the economic valuation of ecosystem services. These efforts provide decision makers the information needed to determine the economic consequences of specific development decisions. Many policy frameworks require a cost–benefit analysis for planning. In the past, the economic value of biodiversity and the related ecosystem services were not part of the process because there was little understanding that ecosystem services could have very high monetary value. The Millennium Ecosystem Assessment

(MA 2005) provided a stimulus for such analyses; however, the information base was slim at the time of the study in the early 2000s. To remedy this lack, UNEP launched The Economics of Ecosystems and Biodiversity (TEEB; TEEB 2010), and nations executed or stimulated their own assessments or built the capacity to do so (EPA 2009, UK 2011). The Natural Capital Project led by a consortium of universities and NGOs has produced an array of software tools for developing spatially explicit valuations of the services on a given landscape. This information provides the base for understanding the full economic consequences of any particular development scenario (Kareiva, Tallis et al. 2011).

Many services are not amenable to economic valuation, particularly cultural services with local importance. However, these non-economic services can be critical and should be evaluated because they can play an important role in final decision making.

What can we do? Provide the tools with which decision makers can balance the tradeoffs in choosing among ecosystem services in land use decisions at multiple spatial scales and that include both economic and non-economic valuation.

Although progress is being made in economic valuation of ecosystem services, the markets for these services have been slow to develop comprehensively. There are well-established markets for provisioning services, such as food, fiber, and fuel. In addition, there are developing markets for carbon sequestration and, to a more limited extent, biological diversity. However, much more is needed and soon. As noted by Kinzig, Perrings et al (Kinzig, Perrings et al. 2011), "we get what we pay for" illustrates that the losses we have seen in ecosystem service delivery globally is predominately on those services that are not in the market place – public goods such a watershed protection, pest regulation, climate, and erosion control.

We find an example of the urgency for a more comprehensive market development in the multi-use or "working landscapes" of the world that are storehouses of both natural and cultural diversity. These are the landscapes highlighted in the

125

recent adoption of the Satoyama Initiative of the Convention on Biological Diversity. As human populations shift to cities, landscapes that were utilized in a manner that provided multiple services are being abandoned or developed to large-scale industrial agriculture. To give another example, the oak woodlands of California have been traditionally used for cattle grazing. The grazing practices on these landscapes actually enhance biological diversity, both directly and indirectly, by preserving the oak trees as a major habitat for a broad spectrum of species. The ranchers have become the guardians of the landscape beauty, its biological diversity, its storehouse of carbon, and its watersheds. The ranchers receive no reward for protecting and maintaining these services. They get little economic return on their cattle operations, although they do gain the amenity value of a traditional way of life enjoyed by their forebears. Inheritance taxes can result from the loss of the lands and a conversion to industrial agriculture or dispersed housing projects as a current major development pathway. A full payment for ecosystem service system could help maintain the traditional systems and the vital sources of ecosystem cultural and biotic services they provide.

At the scale of nations, researchers have noted that such metrics as GDP are not a full measure of human well-being and national wealth (Dasgupta 2002). Countries that appear by traditional metrics to be gaining wealth can in fact be losing wealth because their natural capital, and its depletion, is not taken into account. Efforts now underway utilize metrics of inclusive wealth that incorporate not only manufactured and human capital but also natural capital (World Bank 2006). This approach represents a very large step forward in correcting society's perception of the value of the services that we are losing because of essentially faulty or at least incomplete accounting systems.

Literature Cited

1. Barrett, C. B., A. J. Travis, et al. (2011). "On biodiversity conservation

and poverty traps." *Proceedings of the National Academy of Sciences of the United States of America* 108(34): 13907–13912.

2. Dasgupta, P. (2002). *Human Well-Being and the Natural Environment.* Oxford, Oxford University Press.

3. EPA (2009). Valuing the Protection of Ecological Systems and Services. A Report of the EPA Science Advisory Board. Washington, D.C., US Environmental Protection Agency.

4. Estes, J. A., J. Terborgh, et al. (2011). "Trophic Downgrading of Planet Earth." *Science* 333(6040): 301–306.

5. Hobbs, R. J., E. Higgs, et al. (2009). "Novel ecosystems: implications for conservation and restoration." *Trends in Ecology & Evolution* 24(11): 599–605.

6. Huxley, T. H. (1883) *Inagural Address.* International Fisheries Exhibition, London.

7. Kareiva, P., H. Tallis, et al., Eds. (2011). *Natural Capital. Theory and Practice of Mapping Ecosystem Services.* Oxford, Oxford University Press.

8. Kinzig, A. P., C. Perrings, et al. (2011). "Paying for Ecosystem Services-Promise and Peril." *Science* 334(6056): 603–604.

9. Leadley, P., H. M. Pereira, et al. (2010). Biodiversity Scenarios: Projections of 21st century change in biodiversity and associated eco-system services. Montreal, Canada, Secretariat of the Convention on Biological Diversity.

10. MA (2005). *Ecosystems and Human Well-being:Synthesis.* Washington, DC, Island Press.

11. Mooney, H. A. and R. J. Hobbs, Eds. (2000). *Invasive Species in a Changing World.* Washington, D.C., Island Press.

12. Mooney, H. A., R. N. Mack, et al., Eds. (2005). *Invasive Alien Species: A New Synthesis.* Washington, D.C., Island Press.

13. Perrings, C., H. Mooney, et al., Eds. (2010). *Bioinvasions and Globalization. Ecology, Economics, and Policy.* Oxford, Oxford University Press.

14. Power, M. E., D. Tilman, et al. (1996). "Challenges in the quest for key-stones." *Bioscience* 46(8): 609–620.

15. TEEB (2010). *The Economics of Ecosystems and Biodiversity: Mainstreaming the Economics of Nature: A synthesis of the approach, conclusions and recommendations of TEEB.* Nairobi, United Nations Environmental Report.

16. UK, N. (2011). *The UK National Ecosystem Assessment Technical Report.* Cambridge, UNEP-WCMC.

17. Whitham, T. G., C. A. Gehring, et al. (2012). "Community specificity: life and afterlife effects of genes." *Trends in Plant Science.* r7(5): 271-281.

18. World Bank (2006). *Where is the Wealth of Nations: Measuring Capital for the 21st Century.* Washington, D.C., World Bank.

The Policy-Science Nexus
An Area for Improved Competence in Leadership

Karl-Henrik Robèrt

Abstract

It is a fantastic experience to understand basic principles for worthy goals together – across disciplinary, professional, and ideological boundaries – and to realize that we need each other to attain those goals. Conversely, it is sobering that so few of our leaders know how to incorporate full sustainability into their decision making and shape their analyses, debates, action programs, stakeholder alliances, economies, and summit meetings accordingly. That deficiency is reflected in the questions put to scientists who are often caught in the middle of conflicting policy proposals. On such occasions, empirical facts may be presented out of context and applied as arguments for alternative solutions: for or against the rapid phase-out of fossil fuels, for or against nuclear power, and so on. This results in attempts to deal with one issue at a time, often creating a new sustainability problem while "solving" another. Strategic planning toward sustainability is not something that you simply pick up as you go along, only if you are sufficiently engaged in public debate, have a certain field of expertise, or remain faithful to a certain ideology. What we need today are decision makers who are open to learning the crucial competence of strategic planning and the language that goes with it – a language that facilitates multi-sectoral collaboration at the scale required for success. Only then can leaders make their leadership relevant and cooperate effectively across discipline and sector boundaries, and only then can they ask the relevant questions of scientists and other experts. This approach is neither incompatible with a strong economy nor with competitiveness. It is merely the opposite. We are now experiencing increasing costs and lost opportunities because of a lack of competence in strategic sustainable development. Such competence is neither incompatible with the freedom to embrace different values and ideologies nor with the creative tensions that may arise from conflicts between such values and ideologies. On the contrary, the potential value of creative tensions increases when they are not rooted in lack of knowledge and misunderstandings.

*   *   *

There is a major problem with the current sustainability discourse between scientists and policymakers, such as the summit meetings in Rio, Kyoto, Copenhagen, Durban and Warsaw, which nearly always involve attempts to move directly from scientific data to policymaking without any agreed-upon framework for sustainable decision making in the process. First-rate natural and social scientists in the fields of climatology, ecology, chemistry, economy, and other sciences typically provide data on negative developments in the socio-ecological system and on various possible means to deal with each of them. Policymakers are expected to devise strategies and agreements directly from this information. This does not work well, and this chapter describes how the flawed thinking results in lost opportunities, and outlines basic constituents of a framework that facilitates better use of empirical science.

Absence of a generic framework for organizing data in a comprehensive decision-making process increases complexity as more problems inevitably evolve and models become unmanageable. This situation leads to serious risks of misunderstanding each other's frameworks for organizing data, with corresponding risks of also failing to satisfy both common and individual interests relating to sustainable development (1). Examples of the resulting shortcomings include the following:

1. Failing to see the individual benefits of sustainable development over and above the collective benefits.
2. Failing to deal effectively with system boundaries and trade-offs.
3. Failing to estimate sustainable resource potentials.
4. Creating a new problem in attempting to solve another.
5. Sub-optimizations.
6. Running into expensive blind alleys, i.e., employing expensive measures to improve the current situation without ensuring that the chosen measures can serve as platforms for further progress later on.

The question thus arises: Is it possible to link sciences to policy in a more effective manner, so that policymakers can make better use of empirical data during decision making?

There are two key elements missing from the current discourse on sustainable development. First, there is a poor grasp of the obvious benefits of taking the initiative rather than waiting for others to act (2). Second, once the benefits of being ahead of the game are understood, there is a lack of competence in how to act strategically to exploit opportunities in a spirit of enlightened self-interest (for references, see (3)).

A new framework for leadership and decision making for sustainability

This chapter supplies those two missing elements mentioned above by outlining a framework for making policy decisions on the basis of the valuable empirical data provided in the other chapters of this book. This framework has been developed in a scientific consensus process that has continued for over 20 years. The process is peer-reviewed and has been practically applied by political and business leaders in diverse real-life situations in many different parts of the world.

First missing element:
The benefits of strategic sustainable development
in a dynamically changing world

The benefits to an organization, region, or country in moving gradually toward sustainable practices and lifestyles are typically not understood. Heads of state, mayors, and business executives act as though they would lose a competitive edge if all entities involved do not share the initial costs of developing new and sustainable paradigms and technologies. However, has this ever been a winning strategy in a changing world? Who wins – the last to abandon obsolete paradigms and practices or those who proactively take the lead in adapting to the inevitable needs of change?

Many leaders may feel intuitively that the assumption of lost competitive edge may be flawed, and that it might be a good idea instead to be a bit ahead of the game and part of the solution – to act in a spirit of enlightened self-interest. That would be the optimal approach for any business or political entity, that is, acting as a role model for others and not only saying the right things and taking the right actions but also improving on bottom-line financial success in the process. The benefits occur at two levels.

Common good. The benefits of sustainable development now seem to be gradually becoming better appreciated, and lack of understanding is perhaps a declining obstacle to international agreements. As noted in other chapters of this book, there will be a shared cost to everyone if we continue to lose biodiversity, natural resources, purity of ecosystems and climate stability; the same principle applies to loss of trust between people and their leaders and institutions. That part of the discourse is more or less complete, particularly in the European Union and China. Clearly, it is in everyone's benefit to develop technologies and policies for the inevitably and abruptly changing conditions in global markets that we can already foresee. By the same token, we must find ways of financing the transfer of clean technology to developing countries to help them avoid repeating our mistakes.

Self-interest. However, the corollary regarding self-interest is not as widely appreciated or understood. Leaders continue to anxiously watch "competitors," including other nations, to ensure that all share the costs for sustainable practices. This attitude ignores the fact that the declining resource potential to sustain civilization means that it is a good idea for the bottom line of individual organizations or actors to be comparatively proactive (2).

The gradual loss of social and environmental systems' capacity can be conceptualized as those systems moving deeper and deeper into a funnel whose narrowing circumference represents increasingly harsher constraints and smaller degrees of freedom. It follows that the risk of being hit financially by the narrowing walls of the funnel are relatively higher for those organizations whose contribution to the global problem is relatively large, and that those organizations' risk is accelerating.

Any organization that requires more resources and/or creates more toxic waste per added value, or relies more on unsustainable energy systems with fuel-cycles based on larger resource flows (fossil, nuclear, and biofuels), thereby becoming increasingly irrelevant in markets that evolve as a consequence of the funnel, is subject to increasingly larger financial risks than its competitors. Such organizations will increasingly, and in abrupt ways that will be increasingly difficult to foresee, experience harsh financial impacts because of the narrowing "funnel." They will encounter higher and higher relative costs for resources, waste management, and insurance, as well as lost market opportunities, lower creativity, and other consequences. The opposite is true for those organizations that are skillfully and gradually becoming part of the solution, developing their practices so that they move toward the opening of the funnel, i.e., being ahead of the game.

This emphasis on dynamic aspects is quite different from the traditional approach of sustainable development proponents, who typically stress the public relations value of sustainable development messages for return on investments. However, gains from improved PR are merely the icing on the cake. In purely financial terms, it corresponds merely to how much extra customers are prepared to pay for products or services provided by "nice" organizations.

Again, the major benefits result from adapting at an early stage to future markets by providing products and services that are sustainably produced and that will help others to be sustainable, while decreasing waste production and saving resources, the costs of which will skyrocket as the "funnel" narrows.

"Cylinder" VS. "Funnel"

It is believed that ...   However, in reality ...

... SD is about fixing damage when income from this balance costs.

... the costs for damage move toward infinity. Therefore, SD is about strategic transitions at lowest needed cost.

Beyond that, S.D is about affordable ethics.

... ethics (PR) are merely the icing on the competitive cake.

Beyond that, competitive edge is lost ... unless summits, politicians, and international agreements can guarantee that others are forced to follow.

... clever role models win, regardless of what others do, and then pave the way for smart agreements and policies that will increase the pace and awaken up the latecomers.

©2011 The Natural Step

Unfortunately, top executives in business and governments around the world (not least in the U.S. Congress) have been laboring under the flawed assumption of a "cylinder paradigm" (see figure). That view of the world, one that assumes a basically unchanged system potential, is a crucial barrier to sustainable development and relevant international policies and agreements at summits. It has resulted in steadily deteriorating consequences for the world at large, and what is typically neglected is that the deterioration is greatest for those individual organizations, regions, and nations that are relatively larger parts of the problem. How much of the current financial problems confronting several nations actually result from previous decisions leading toward the narrow outlet of the funnel rather than to its opening?

For decision makers to get stuck in the "cylinder" paradigm or be obligated to congresses or parliaments back home that are stuck in the cylinder is counter-productive. It backfires collectively, and particularly on those organizations and nations that hold fast to obsolete mindsets, policies, technologies, and practices. The further civilization moves into the funnel, the less "free" it will be. To both Democrats and Republicans in the United States, for instance, the idea of freedom is a key policy component. However, neglecting the consequences of the "funnel" while waiting for others to take the lead to avoid its imperatives does not promote freedom.

Most likely, the problem is not a result of poor values. It is not about inferior intelligence. It is about incompetence in the face of a paradigm shift, even among very talented people.

Second missing element: A framework that strategically exploits the opportunities of sustainable development

The next hurdle to overcome is how to strategically manage the complex transition, that is, to gradually prepare for new demands in the dynamically changing markets and avoid skyrocketing costs for poor resource management or dependencies on inherently unsustainable technical systems for energy, forestry, fisheries, agriculture, transport, and others.

From the individual organization's viewpoint, it is necessary to strike a balance so that the transition is, first of all, not so slow that it misses the opportunities offered by the constraining funnel dynamics outlined above. Second, it must not be too fast for maintaining adequate return on investment. It is about surfing on the cutting edge. To do this systematically requires a very clear view of the endgame and logical guidelines to reach it.

We cannot continue sidestepping the key element of strategic planning, which is to define what we want to be heading toward, the goal, that is, toward the opening of the funnel. If sustainability is what we want, then we must have a powerful concept of what that looks like. Every leader responsible for investments must be able to clearly visualize sustainability, be free to improve upon it, and be engaged to "own" it as a personal and societal mission.

Furthermore, it must be a comprehensive vision. By piling up ad hoc projects piecemeal, each addressing a separate sustainability thread, we have not been weaving a tapestry that can inspire people everywhere. There should be a clear differentiation between studies of the system within which we act, our definition of the objective of the planning, and the process by which we approach the objective. This principle has long been known to both military (4) and civil (5) strategic planners. However, the dominant planning method is "forecasting" in many decision-making settings. Forecasting extrapolates current trends into the future as means of predicting and fixing problems (6–8). This method leads to "path-dependencies" (9,10) and is insufficient to proactively plan toward a novel future objective.

One way to deal with these problems and approach the more military method of heading toward clear objectives is called "backcasting." It is generally applied in the context of scenario planning, that is, envisioning a simplified picture of the desired future and then plan–"backwards in time"–to make it possible to get there. Scenario planning has at least four potential shortcomings (3). First, it may be difficult for large groups to agree on relatively detailed descriptions of a desirable distant future. Second, given technological and cultural evolutions, it is unwise to lock into overly specific assumptions about the future. Third, if basic principles for sustainability are not explicit, it is difficult to know whether any given scenario is really sustainable. Fourth, a lack of common principles for success also makes it difficult to relate one planning endeavor to another; the process may need to be reinvented from scratch each time.

Unifying Framework

A unifying sustainability framework is already being developed to take these four obstacles into consideration (for reference, see www.alliance-ssd.com). Through an ongoing consensus process between pioneering scientists of many sustainability related methods/tools and concepts (2, 3, 6, 11–23), policymakers (24–28), and business leaders (29–37), an overarching framework for strategic sustainable development is emerging. A rapidly growing group of decision makers, including hundreds of mayors, CEOs, and other high-level managers across the world, are using it to tackle the sustainability challenge.

The framework has been developed first in theoretical science, and then improved in action research with business and municipalities. It is designed to be unifying, by placing any organization or planning endeavor (regardless of scale) within a context of global sustainability. In addition, it has a unifying effect by making better use of various tools and concepts for sustainable development such as ecological footprinting, management systems, life-cycle assessments, product service systems, value-chain management, modeling and simulation, and development of indicators.

To serve such a unifying role, the framework had to comply with the following logical sequence:

1. If you want to be strategic, you must at least know the objective.
2. The objective can generally not be defined in detail when it comes to complex systems. "Nobody can look into the future." For complex endeavors in complex systems, we need basic principles as constraints for the design.
3. If a set of principles is to serve as a basic and operational definition of an objective, for example, sustainability, the principles must be

- necessary, but not more than that, to avoid imposing unnecessary restrictions and to avoid confusion over elements that may be debatable;
- sufficient, to avoid gaps in the thinking, that is, to allow elaboration into second and higher orders of principles from a complete base;
- general, to be applicable in any arena, at any scale, by any member in a team and all stakeholders, regardless of field of expertise, to allow for cross-disciplinary and cross-sector collaboration;
- concrete, to pragmatically guide problem solving and redesigning and a step-by-step approach in real-life planning;
- non-overlapping, to enable comprehension and facilitate development of indicators for monitoring progress.

4. When you have defined a goal by a set of principles that fulfill such criteria, only then, can you attain the following benefits:

- The resource potential becomes calculable. If you do not know how to define the objective, you cannot even attempt to calculate the resource potential and determine the degrees of freedom within the constraints of the objective. However, if you do, your planning and decision making can be supported by a scientific estimate of the resource potential (for example, using physics and ecology), rather than being based only on the constraints of current technologies and cultures.
- Trade-offs can be rationally managed. Advantages and disadvantages often relate to different variables and parameters and come in different units. "Is it better to risk polluting with mercury than to waste energy (as in the case of low-energy light bulbs)?" Analyzing the either/or of "snapshots" in the short term has limited strategic value. However, if you know the end goal, you can evaluate various options for their capacity to serve as stepping-stones to bringing the process to a

stage where the trade-off does not exist. You model optional routes to complete success, rather than evaluating snapshots at this moment as good vs. bad. If you frame a choice as between plague or cholera, you are likely to get one or the other.

- System-boundaries setting can be guided by the objectives. Science puts demands on clear and adequate boundaries when studying systems. Sustainability discourses in an organization often come with debates regarding where to draw the system boundaries. Trained scholars tend to ask: "Do you mean the factory with its walls, or do you include clients... supply chains... other stakeholders... the whole world?" The last alternative is often proposed with a little smile to demonstrate how unimaginable that would be. Yet, the truth is that when it comes to sustainability, the whole world does count to some extent. Again, basic principles of objectives provide a way forward. You put yourself in the shoes of the CEO or project manager and ask yourself what, in the whole world, needs to be taken into account to make the respective organization/planning region/topic support societal comply with sustainability principles, and you let this inform your decision on system boundaries, from geography to disciplines and beyond.

- Interdisciplinary cross-sector cooperation can be better facilitated. With a principled definition of the objective, each expert group becomes better in drawing the relevant knowledge from their respective silos. Again, each sector that must be taken into account to comply with the sustainability principles and the relevant data from each, following the same principles, are brought to the table.

- Unknown problems can be avoided. You can do much better than just fixing the impacts you already know. If you redesign your respective area of responsibility using basic principles that are robust for success, you

139

will not need to learn all the detailed consequences of not doing so. For instance, you can avoid contributing to increasing zinc or silver levels in natural systems, without knowing exactly what further increases in such concentrations may imply at certain (unknown) ecotoxic thresholds—for example, just as we should have done with CFCs from their very introduction, before we learned what they do to the ozone layer. They are relatively persistent and foreign to nature, and therefore, it was inevitable that they would gradually increase in concentrations in the biosphere for as long as they were used in consumer goods. It was clear from the beginning that, as such, they did not belong in a sustainable society.

- Selection, use, and development of other concepts, methods, and tools can be guided. A principled definition of the objective, fulfilling the listed criteria, makes it possible to make better use of other existing concepts, methods, and tools for sustainable development by guiding the selection of such concepts, methods, and tools necessary for reaching the objective. The framework is applied to reveal the gap of an organization to comply with the basic sustainability principles, then the participants propose action plans to bridge it, and they select the appropriate tools and concepts to monitor the bridging. The framework can also help identify a need for development, and then guide the development, of new concepts, methods, and tools.

A framework for strategic sustainable development (FSSD)– including sustainability principles fulfilling the above criteria, and thus capable of providing the aforementioned unique benefits (see Point 4) –has been developed, scrutinized, practically tested, refined, and scrutinized again in a peer-reviewed scientific consensus process that spanning over 20 years. The FSSD helps to merge seemingly impossible-to-merge polarities into unity: big picture with small picture, long term with short term, ethics with money, and sectors and disciplines with each other.

The FSSD is structured in five levels, each of which is "cut" along the dimension of what we want in the system, that is, the second level of the framework, the principled vision (including the sustainability principles). The five levels are described briefly as follows:

1. System. The global socio-ecological system (society within the biosphere) including laws of nature; the biogeochemical cycles of nature; and, integrated in this system, the global social system and, integrated in this system, the respective organization, region, or planning activity.

2. Success. Basic principles of sustainability for all of civilization, plus the organization/region/topic reaching its goals without contributing to violation of the basic sustainability principles.

3. Strategic Guidelines. Backcasting from the aforementioned image of success, that is, envisioning it, and then drawing the appropriate strategic conclusions backward in time from this image; logical guidelines for stepwise transitions between current challenges and future opportunities.

4. Actions. Actions put into a plan that help move the organization/region/topic toward its sustainable vision.

5. Tools. Tools used to help planners explore actions (4) to be strategic (3) in achieving the objectives (2) within the system (1).

The current formulation of the sustainability principles (level 2) is as follows:

In the sustainable society, nature is not subject to systematically increasing

1. concentrations of substances extracted from the Earth's crust;

2. concentrations of substances produced by society;

3. degradation by physical means, and

4. in that society, people are not subject to conditions that systematically undermine their capacity to meet their needs.

Furthermore, an organization can "translate" the sustainability principles to its own ultimate objectives to eliminate its contribution to

1. systematic increases in concentrations of substances from the Earth's crust,

2. systematic increases in concentrations of substancesproduced by society,

3. systematic physical degradation of nature, and

4. conditions that systematically undermine people's capacity to meet their needs.

Guidelines on how to put each of the basic principles into practice include the following:

1. Certain minerals that are scarce in nature can often be replaced by others that are more abundant. This principle includes using all mined materials efficiently, and systematically reducing dependence on fossil fuels and nuclear power.

2. Certain persistent and unnatural compounds can often be replaced by others that are normally abundant or break down more easily in nature. Use efficiently all substances produced by society.

3. Draw resources only from well-managed ecosystems. Systematically pursue the most productive and efficient use of both those resources and land. Exercise caution in all modifications of nature, including the introduction of new species.

4. Consider how our behavior has consequences for people, now and in the future, and how it can restrict their opportunities to lead fulfilling lives. The key question is whether we would like to be subjected to the conditions we create.

The major intellectual contribution of FSSD is not only the sustainability principles; those are under continuous scrutiny and refinement in peer review. The major contribution is the concept of "Backcasting from Principles." Because there are myriad possible sustainable designs of human society, sustainability must be defined by principles. Once that idea, that is, the rationale for "Backcasting from Principles," is understood, we need principles that are necessary, sufficient, general, concrete, and non-overlapping. It may be theoretically possible to create other principles that carry those characteristics; however, thus far, the aforementioned sustainability principles are the only ones designed for this purpose.

The economic imperative and lack of clear visions

The most urgent challenge is to arrive at a critical mass of leaders adhering to the FSSD principles, who master the logistics of putting basic principles of sustainability on the table and then asking questions about alternative routes toward that goal, including relevant economic questions.

This approach is opposed to believing that fixing the myriad problems one by one, such as climate change, outside the realm of all the other sustainability-related problems would be a feasible solution, or to believing that if only sufficiently knowledgeable people meet and share knowledge collected from their respective "silos," the big systems perspective will take care of itself. Beyond a robust framework for sustainable decision making, sufficiently comprehensive in time (backcasting) and scale (all of civilization), the big picture of sustainability and sustainable development has not, and will not, take care of itself.

One example of what may otherwise happen is that biofuels sourced from cropland to help curb fossil CO_2 emissions (first sustainability principle) may lead to increased food prices with serious implications for social sustainability (fourth principle), thereby delaying adequate system-level solutions to climate change. Another well-known example is the change from ammonia to CFCs to eliminate a highly irritating gas, only to discover that we had developed a life-threatening problem at the global level (violating the second sustainability principle). Yet another is believing that some "silver bullet" modification of the economy might ensure sustainability, over and above effective leadership with its demands for adequate means, of which the economic system is but one.

The common discourse of searching for silver bullets in the economic system is in itself an evidence of our era's lack of competent leadership. We have become so accustomed to the lack of clear and robust sustainability visions among our leaders, who have focused too strongly and too long on the short-term economy with its growth imperative, that the current costs of this strategy are already exploding, still without leaders drawing the right, systems-derived conclusions.

"Economic growth," that is, increased GNP, could be a good means of achieving some worthy goal, but is certainly not a goal in itself. We need scientific research and actions for completing/modifying our economic system. Relevant questions to ask include, "How can our present economic system be used more effectively to bridge the gap to sustainability?" and "How could we complete/modify the economic system such that it would even more effectively empower the proactive leaders to harvest all the sustainability driven opportunities and wake up the latecomers?"

A research alliance for strategic sustainable development

A research alliance has been established for more effective cooperation across silo boundaries. The objective of a new research alliance will be all about inspiring change, with examples set by competent and successful role models, and helping them cooperate effectively across value chains, sectors, regions, and nations (see www.alliance-ssd.com).

A model for such systematic cooperation has already been tested in cooperation with five Swedish agencies in a 3-year research program called Real Change (see three year report on www.alliance-ssd.org). The program is based on all scientists and practitioners sharing the framework for the approach outlined above, the FSSD. We have seen and published reports on several examples of how leaders, inspired by their acquired competences, first begin developing stepwise industrial and governance models toward the full scope of sustainability, and then turn to politicians to suggest higher taxes (e.g., Electrolux concerning heavy metals in batteries, and OK petroleum demanding higher tax on petroleum), tougher legislation (e.g., IKEA demanding harsher legislation than the EU Reach protocol on chemicals), or development of CO_2 labeling of their consumer goods, suggesting that this become the norm (e.g., Max Hamburgers).

The objective of the alliance is to scale up this model, that is, to increase the number of leaders in business and municipalities across the globe who share the FSSD, and empower them with the research they need to (a) create an arena for active modeling and problem-solving across borders of disciplines, sectors, value-chains, regions, and nations; (b) develop and test FSSD tools that are adequate for analyses, envisioning, planning, decision-support, monitoring, modeling, simulation, and communication in relation to global sustainability; (c) create a growing database of case studies of best practices; and (d) widely disseminate the results of those efforts to influence change through successful role models.

It is a fantastic experience to understand basic principles for worthy goals together – across disciplinary, professional, and ideological boundaries – and realize that we need each other to attain those goals. To make that happen, we must first understand that unsustainability is the greatest challenge that humanity has ever faced. Second, we must fully grasp the benefits to ourselves of being proactive. Third, the leaders of our era must learn that the competence of how to move strategically toward sustainability, step by step, while ensuring that each step is in the right direction, can be further developed later on and will generate enough income to sustain the transition. Effective policies, adaptations of the economic system, and constructive decisions made at summits rely on developing sufficient numbers of leaders with this competence in policy and business.

References

1. Kates, R. W., W. C. Clark, R. Corell, J. M. Hall, C., et al., 2001. Sustainability science, *Science*, Vol. 292, p. 641–642.
2. Holmberg, J. and K.-H. Robèrt. 2000. Backcasting - a framework for strategic planning. *International Journal of Sustainable Development and World Ecology* 7(4): 291–308.

3. Ny, H., J. P. MacDonald, G. Broman, R. Yamamoto, and K.-H. Robèrt. 2006. Sustainability constraints as system boundaries: an approach to making life-cycle management strategic. *Journal of Industrial Ecology* 10(1).

4. C. v. Clausewitz. 1832. *Vom kriege* (On war) (Dümmlers Verlag, Berlin, Germany, 1832).

5. Mintzberg, H., Lampel, J., Ahlstrand, B., 1998. *Strategy Safari: A Guided Tour Through the Wilds of Strategic Management.* Free Press, New York, USA, p. 416.

6. Robèrt, K.-H. 2000. Tools and concepts for sustainable development, how do they relate to a general framework for sustainable development, and to each other? *Journal of Cleaner Production* 8(3): 243–254.

7. Dreborg, K. H. 1996. Essence of backcasting. *Futures* 8.28(9): 813–828.

8. Robinson, J. B. 1990. Future under glass–A recipe for people who hate to predict. *Futures* 22(9): 820–843.

9. Holmberg, J. and K.-H. Robèrt. 2000. Backcasting–A framework for strategic planning. *International Journal of Sustainable Development and World Ecology* 7(4): 291–308.

10. Hukkinen, J. 2003. From groundless universalism to grounded generalism: Improving ecological economic indicators of human-environmental interaction. *Ecological Economics*, Vol. 44, No. 1, pp. 11–27.

11. Hukkinen, J. 2003. Sustainability indicators for anticipating the fickleness of human-environmental interaction. *Clean Technologies and Environmental Policy*, Vol. 5, No. 3-4, pp. 200–208.

12. Robèrt, K.-H., J. Holmberg, and E. U. v. Weizsacker. 2000. Factor X for subtle policy-making. *Greener Management International*(31): 25–38.

13. Holmberg, J.,U. Lundqvist, K.-H. Robèrt, and M. Wackernagel. 1999. The ecological footprint from a systems perspective of sustainability. *International Journal of Sustainable Development and World Ecology* 6: 17–33.

14. Robèrt, K.-H., B. Schmidt-Bleek, J. Aloisi de Larderel, G. Basile, J. L. Jansen, R. Kuehr, P. Price Thomas, M. Suzuki, P. Hawken, and M. Wackernagel. 2002. Strategic sustainable development - selection, design and synergies of applied tools. *Journal of Cleaner Production* 10(3): 197–214.

15. MacDonald, J. P. 2005. Strategic sustainable development using the ISO 14001 Standard. *Journal of Cleaner Production* 13(6): 631–644.

16. Byggeth, S. H. and E. Hochschorner. 2006. Handling trade-offs in ecodesign tools for sustainable product development and procurement. *Journal of Cleaner Production* 14(15-16): 1420–1430.

17. Robèrt, K.-H., H. E. Daly, P. A. Hawken, and J. Holmberg. 1997. A compass for sustainable development. *International Journal of Sustainable Development and World Ecology* 4: 79–92.

18. Byggeth, S. H., G. I. Broman, and K. H. Robèrt. 2006. A method for sustainable product development based on a modular system of guiding questions. *Journal of Cleaner Production*: 1–11.

19. Korhonen, J. 2004. Industrial ecology in the strategic sustainable

development model: strategic applications of industrial ecology. *Journal of Cleaner Production* 12(8–10): 809–823.

20. Byggeth, S., H. Ny, J. Wall, and G. Broman. 2007. Introductory Procedure for Sustainability-Driven Design Optimization. Paper presented at International Conference on Engineering Design (ICED'07), 28–31 August, Paris, France.

21. Ny, H., J. P. MacDonald, K.-H. Robèrt, and G. Broman. 2009. Sustainability constraints as system boundaries: introductory steps toward strategic life-cycle management. In Web-Based Green Products Life Cycle Management Systems: Reverse Supply Chain Utilization, edited by H.-F. Wang. Hershey, PA, USA: IGI Global.

22. Byggeth, S., H. Ny, J. Wall, and G. Broman. 2007. Introductory Procedure for Sustainability-Driven Design Optimization. Paper presented at International Conference on Engineering Design (ICED'07), 28–31 August, Paris, France.

23. Hallstedt, S., H. Ny, K.-H. Robèrt and G. Broman. 2010. An approach to assessing sustainability integration in strategic decision systems, *Journal of Cleaner Production* 18: 703–712.

24. Ny, H., S. Hallstedt, Å. Ericson. 2012. A Strategic Approach for Sustainable Product Service System Development. Accepted for the 22nd CIRP Design Conference (focus on Sustainable Product Development), 28–30 March, Bangalore India.

25. Rowland, E. and C. Sheldon. 1999. The Natural Step and ISO 14001: Guidance on the Integration of a Framework for Sustainable Development into Environmental Management Systems British Standards Institute (BSI).

26. Cook, D. 2004. *The Natural Step towards a Sustainable Society*. Dartington, UK: Green Books Ltd.

27. Robèrt, K.-H., D. Strauss-Kahn, M. Aelvoet, I. Aguilera, D. Bakoyannis, T. Boeri, B. Geremek, N. Notat, A. Peterle, J. Saramago, Lord Simon of Highbury, H. Tietmeyer, and O. Ferrand. 2004. Building a political Europe - 50 proposals for tomorrow's Europe. "A Sustainable project for tomorrow's Europe" Brussels: European Commission.

28. James, S. and T. Lahti. 2004. *The Natural Step for Communities: How Cities and Towns Can Change to Sustainable Practices*. Gabriola Island, British Columbia, Canada: New Society Publishers.

29. Electrolux. 1994. *Electrolux annual report* 1994. Stockholm, Sweden: Electrolux.

30. Anderson, R. C. 1998. *Mid Course Correction - Toward a Sustainable Enterprise: The Interface Model*. Atlanta, USA: The Peregrinzilla press.

31. Nattrass, B. 1999. The Natural Step: corporate learning and innovation for sustainability. Doctoral thesis, The California Institute of Integral Studies, San Francisco, California, USA.

32. Broman, G., J. Holmberg, and K.-H. Robèrt. 2000. Simplicity Without Reduction: Thinking Upstream Towards the Sustainable Society. *Interfaces* 30(3): 13–25.

33. Robèrt, K.-H. 2002b. *The Natural Step story - Seeding a Quiet Revolution*.

Gabriola Island, British Columbia, Canada: New Society Publishers.

34. Matsushita. 2002. *Environmental sustainability report 2002*. Osaka, Japan: Matsushita Electric Industrial Co., Ltd.

35. Leadbitter, J. 2002. PVC and sustainability. Progress in Polymer *Science* 27(10): 2197–2226.

36. Ny, H., S. Hallstedt, K.-H. Robèrt, and G. Broman. 2008. Introducing templates for sustainable product development through a case study of televisions at Matsushita Electric Group. *Journal of Industrial Ecology* 12(4): 600–623.

37. Ny, H., A. W. Thompson, P. Lindahl, G. Broman, O. Isaksson, R. Carlson, T. Larsson, and K.-H. Robèrt. 2008. Introducing strategic decision support systems for sustainable product-service innovation across value chains. Paper presented at Sustainable Innovation 08. Future Products, Technologies and Industries. 13th International Conference, October, 27–28, Malmö, Sweden.

In Search of
a Green Equitable Economy

Emil Salim

Global cooperation along the conventional pattern of development has failed to achieve the objectives of sustainable development. New modalities from building regional blocks have emerged to seek more effective cooperation. Established since 1968, the Association of South East Asia Nations (ASEAN) has become a vibrant force of regional cooperation between Brunei Darussalam, Cambodia, Indonesia, Lao PDR, Malaysia, Myanmar, the Philippines, Singapore, Thailand, and Vietnam. Except for Singapore, all are developing economies. ASEAN cooperation has now grown into "ASEAN Plus Three," which includes Japan, the People's Republic of China, and the Republic of Korea, and the "East Asia Summit," which includes Australia, India, and New Zealand. These regional cooperative arrangements with ASEAN as its core have proven helpful in overcoming the recent turbulent years of global crises.[1]

Asia—particularly China, India, and ASEAN—has strategic potentials for rapid development: first, large domestic markets supported by large labor forces with rising incomes; second, the revolution in information communication technologies strengthening regional integration within Asia; third, ample potential for growth from untapped natural resources; fourth, wide adherence to a lifestyle of "man in harmony with God the Creator, nature, and society," as revealed in *"Tri Hita Karana"* (Bali) and *"Hamemayu Hayuning Bawana"* (Java). In Bhutan, His Majesty the King has set "Gross National Happiness" as the goal of development to balance tradition and modernity on the basis of resource development with environmental and cultural preservation guided by good governance; fifth, all Asian nations cope with poverty eradication as the overriding goal of Asian development while maintaining that Asian nations must ensure the resiliency of the global common to cope with climate change and biodiversity erosion.

To accomplish this growth, Asia must address the most serious challenges of poverty eradication and social inequality, which, in countries with wide social diversities in ethnicity, culture, religion, and race, have serious implications for forging social cohesion in building one nation. During the past decade of development, income inequality as revealed by the *Gini Coefficient* in Indonesia has been increasing.[2] Similarly, disparities in economic capabilities among Asian countries have also widened.

Past processes of current industrialized countries have followed a path of natural resource exploitation along a single linear track of economic growth and have been successful in raising material wealth to an unprecedented high level. However, its negative impacts on social equity and poverty eradication have been huge. Most disturbing is that past development models have wrecked the equilibrium of ecological systems and eroded biological diversity that, combined with rising global warming, affects climate change.

Such an experience of the "creative destruction" approach to development has increased Asia's need to abandon this conventional economic single linear development model with its over-emphasis on material wealth, and instead explore different venues of growth that align more closely with the "Asian values" of seeking equilibrium in life between man and God, nature, and society. There is an implicit recognition of an interdependent relationship between man, society, and nature in a "web of life" created by the Almighty. Therefore, in many Asian cultures, the meaning of development has a triple content: creating material wealth, enhancing social cohesion, and preserving ecological equilibrium.

However, in pursuing such a development model today, Asia confronts the grim reality that the air, as the global common, is heavily polluted by greenhouse gas emissions caused by burning fossil fuels, mainly by industrialized economies, with its wide repercussions on global warming and climate change. This situation will change monsoons, with negative impacts on agricultural and food production. Sea level is expected to rise, increasing the frequency of floods affecting coastal populations. It increases weather related diseases that affect the vulnerable poor in particular. Therefore, Asia needs to conduct its development while conserving precious natural life supporting systems to preserve biological diversity, control greenhouse gas emissions, and strive for ecological sustainability. It is with these considerations that Asia must pursue a different model of development that is more green and equitable along a triple track of economic, social, and environmental development. Many models have already been developed since the concept of sustainable development was launched at the Rio Summit, Brazil, in June 1992, such as the Economic Social Sustainable Development(ESSD). It is now time, 20 years later, that Asia pursues more effective policies to meet the challenges of sustainable development.

Triple Fundamentals of Asian Development

On the basis of the lessons learned from most countries in crises, Asian development must first firmly establish *economic* fundamentals as prerequisites of development. It needs to maintain society's stable purchasing power by controlling inflation and maintaining a stable national currency properly managed by viable financial and banking institutions with foreign exchange reserves sufficient to support economic resiliency internationally, backed by the nation's productivity level capable of supporting its competitiveness.

In addition, Asia must establish *social* fundamentals. Most Asian nations must build a united nation from a foundation of diverse ethnic, cultural, and religious social groups. The enhancement of social equity and poverty eradication are most strategic to unite a nation with diverse races, ethnicities, and social entities. Poverty in Asia occurs not only in monetary value but also in non-monetary values such as poor physical connectivity because of inadequate infrastructure for transportation and communication services and lack of electricity, clean drinking water, sanitation, human settlement facilities, and other factors. In addition, poverty results from inadequate human resource development because of poor education and lack of accessibility to banking and other financial services. The poor require equal access to obtain productive natural resources and effective legal protection. All these multi-faceted shortages of accessibility trap the poor in poverty holes, and by ignoring the poor stuck in these poverty holes, development cannot achieve social equity.[3]

Asia must also establish *ecological* fundamentals recognizing that development occurs within a "web of life" that interconnects man and society with natural ecological systems that function as a life supporting system. In many parts of Asia, terrestrial and marine ecosystems are habitats for unique biological natural resources that are important for human survival. Many Asian countries close to the sea are vulnerable to rising sea levels and tsunamis. Surrounded by the "Ring of Fire," these countries are also vulnerable to natural disasters. Therefore, Asian developmental policies must explicitly include these ecological considerations.

The Asian Development Bank has predicted that Asia, growing in its recent trajectory, could by 2050 produce more than half the global GDP with per capita income potential increasing sixfold, equaling the global average of current European levels. However, this optimistic outcome is fraught with multiple risks and challenges such as growing inequality within countries, falling into the "Middle Income Trap," the impacts of global warming, climate change, erosion of biodiversity, and poor governance.

On the basis of the past economic performance of Asia since 1970, the Asian Development Bank has classified the Asian region's 49 economies into three groups of economic performance: (1) "High-Income developed economies," such as Japan, Brunei Darussalam, Hong Kong, Singapore, and three other similarly highly developed economies; (2) "Rapidly growing, converging economies," such as the People's Republic of China, India, Indonesia, and eight other economies; and (3) "Slow or modest growth aspiring countries," such as the Philippines, Sri Lanka, and 29 other countries.

From these three groupings, the "rapidly growing, converging countries" are now producing 52% of Asian GDP and comprise 77% of the Asian population.

As a representative of the "rapidly growing, converging countries," it is useful to explore the Indonesian sub-national development as a proxy of Asian countries to pursue sustainable development.

From the macroeconomic viewpoint, the Indonesian national economic growth rate has performed well despite the economic crisis of recent years. However, from the sub-national regional development perspective, the economic growth rate is unequally distributed among the islands. The 2010 national GDP came from Java (58%), Sumatra (23.1%), Borneo (9.2%), Celebes (4.6%), Bali and the Nusa Tenggara Islands (2.7%), and Moluccas and Papua (2.4%).

The Indonesian archipelago can be divided into two major island groups: West Indonesia, covering islands of Sumatra, Java, and Bali, and East Indonesia covering Borneo, Celebes, Nusa-Tenggara Islands, Moluccas, and Papua. The distance between the most western and the most eastern tip of Indonesia is equal to London–Teheran, with wide variations in climate, ecosystems, and the ethnicity, religion, and culture of social communities.

During 1980–2010, West Indonesia contributed to about 80% of GDP from approximately 80% of Indonesia's total population. The West Indonesian economy is more advanced than East Indonesia's. Although the total numbers of population living in poverty in East Indonesia is less than in West Indonesia, the former has a much higher percentage of poor people than the latter. This deviation of poverty percentage distribution also characterizes many Asian countries, such as between the Eastern (rich) and Western (poor) areas of China, South (rich) and North (poor) India, South (rich) and North (poor) Vietnam, North (rich) and South (poor) Thailand, West (rich) and East (poor) Malaysia, North (rich) and South (poor) Philippines.

Regional distribution of poverty in these countries shares the same fate as Indonesia, of suffering poor physical connectivity to sea, river, and land transportation; poor accessibility to education; lack of facilities for increasing human capabilities; lack of access to financial facilities; lack of access to productive natural resources, the rule of law, and government services, which are essential prerequisites for lifting the poor out of the poverty hole.[4]

Indonesian efforts in meeting the goals of "Pro Growth, Pro Job, Pro Poor, and Pro Environment" have taught us that macroeconomic policies are necessary but not sufficient. The high growth rate at the national macro-economy level may well be biased in favor of growth only for those already advanced sub-national regions and social groupings living primarily in Java (58%). These national macro-targets must be translated into sub-national targets in (a) economic sector targets with the required job absorption investments, (b) taking into account its impacts on raising the income of the poor, and (c) through the use of resources that sustain natural life-supporting systems.

Sub-national spatial planning creates the opportunity to link economic investments in real terms with job creation, poverty alleviation, and sustained natural resource management. The appropriate direct investment in the resource sector must not only sustain economic growth but also positively affect social development.[5]

Development at sub-national and district levels can practically apply the principles of (1) acquiring Total Factor Productivity, raising more output per unit of input; (2) raising value added per unit of natural (particularly biological) resources through the application of innovative technology; (3) renewable energy based decentralized grid-system and widespread public transportation enabling the creation of more manageably sized cities; (4) scientific aquaculture fisheries; (5) hydroponic agriculture, among others, on building roofs to optimize urban space and reduce heat along the Singaporean Model; and (6) merging economic with social and ecological considerations in the field by involving NGOs, as revealed by the development of markets for watershed services and improved livelihoods by NGOs as honest brokers in devising pseudo-markets to replace market failures.[6]

Environmental impact analysis; requirements of obtaining social licenses, particularly for extractive industries; and preferences for biological resource value added enrichment through science and technology, as well as post-mining non-renewable resource recovery requirements are useful tools to link economic with social and environmental considerations.

To link economic macro policies to poverty alleviation, it is important to trace the impacts of these policies on components of the poverty line and its impact on the size of the incomes of the poor. In this context, macro-economic policies must operate within the constraints of reducing values of components affecting the poverty line and also increase incomes of the poor.[7]

To cope with this unequal areal distribution of growth, Indonesia deems it necessary to complement the macro-model with layers of economic resource mapping, sub-national poverty mapping, and sustained natural resource mapping. As the *first layer*, the sub-national regional economic development plan in Indonesia is divided into six major corridors for major growth centers in each main island, to be linked with networks of transportation and communication covering the entire country. This layer is superimposed on the *second layer*, the sub-national regional social development plan revealing the location of the poor and striving for social cohesion among communities spread over all islands, districts, and provinces. A *third layer* is the sub-national regional natural resource management plan that identifies the location of unique natural resources with the potential for development in conjunction with the economic and poverty eradication plans.

These triple layers of sub-regional national development plans provide significant inputs in drawing the "dynamic general equilibrium model." In addition, it is useful to suggest a simplified 3-factor matrix consisting of economic growth, social development, and environmental development as the main factors and identify with relevant stakeholders the possible intensity of interdependency and linkages that this triple sector development may encounter.

Economic growth traces its impact on GDP (economic factor), job creation (social factor), and CO_2 emissions (environmental factors). Social development affects the growth factor through education, health, capacity building, poverty eradication (social factor), and local wisdom for resource enrichment (environmental factor). Environmental development affects growth through resource efficiency (economic factor), resource provision for job creation (social factor), and sustaining life-supporting systems (environmental factor). Through iterations among stakeholders in the field, the interdependency between economic, social, and environmental factors enables the creation of a working arrangement conducive to implementation of sustainable development.

There may be no "one size fits all" solution, and Asian nations are not growing simultaneously but moving in waves of different stages of development. The low-income nations can learn and avoid the mistakes made by the middle-income nations, who can also learn from the experiences of the high-income economies.

We recognize that the market is not fully efficient and has a built-in failure to capture social and environmental costs and benefits. Therefore, we must apply *social and environmental impact analysis* to identify and facilitate internalization of external social and environmental costs into economic cost/benefits calculation. In this context, a *social accounting matrix* approach can support the development of a multi-sector approach covering economic, social, and environmental sectors within an extended input–output analysis.

Superimposing these various development layers in geospatial mapping helps us to effectively follow these multiple, interactive impacts of economic, social, and environmental development. Thus, on a sub-regional scale, we can trace the interdependent linkages between economic growth factors, with the poor in specific locations with clear natural resource endowment information.

When economic development overshoots the constraints of the environment, it feeds back the need to devise a *different growth pattern*. When palm-oil plantation extensification hits the arable land constraints, the palm-oil plantation must shift toward resource enrichment, raising the value of palm oil among new products using science and technology along the vertical value chain. Product development must be identified to combine natural resource enrichment and raise its value added. The developments of rattan in numerous products through creative industries raise its value, and the same token rattans that grow on trees are saving the forests.

Biomimicry, the knowledge of mimicking nature and the behavior of biological natural resources opens the frontiers for applying nature's behavior in raising value added through science and technology. Local ethnic communities, such as those in Indonesia, have developed local medicine, cosmetics, food, horticulture, and products, and can continue to do so; they can provide their ethnic local wisdom to be enhanced by modern science and technology. This approach enables shifting the orientation of development from *resource exploitation* to *resource enrichment*, while maintaining the existence of natural resources and raising its value added. Development and conservation need not be considered as an either-or policy choice, they can go hand in hand through the use of science, technology, and local wisdom.

Economic policies must explicitly consider poverty eradication as an inherent goal of its development. It can be most influential in reducing factors affecting non-income poverty, such as improving the poor's accessibility to the market by building physical infrastructure and improving financial infrastructure, such as village banks, cooperatives, and credit unions. By raising human capacity through education, health, social insurance schemes, and the like, an economic and socially sound model of development that focuses on poverty eradication can be developed.

If this model is implementable on the national scale, to what extent can it be developed on the regional scale for Asia? In theory, the answer must be affirmative. However, it needs relevant and correct data to design the building blocks for a workable, sustainable development model for Asia.

The experiences thus far have indicated that it is a cumbersome and painful process. However, we can draw an ASEAN Regional Sustainable Development model and do the same for Asia, Africa, Latin America, and other regions. Regional cooperation is already increasing, currently driven by common interests in managing the same economic, social, and environmental challenges. Despite the fact that global cooperation has proven not to be effective thus far, we can perhaps more realistically strive for regional cooperation driven from below by the nations' respective interests that can become the pillars for future global cooperation to meet the challenges of sustainable development in the twenty-first century.

References

1. Asian Development Bank, *Institutions for Regional Integration*, Asian Development Bank, 2010.
2. (National Statistical Bureau, *Monthly Report of Social Economic Data*, Jakarta, 2011).
3. Juzhong Zhuang, editor, *Poverty, Inequality, and Inclusive Growth* in Asia, Part A, Asian Development Bank, 2010.
4. Essay "Out of the Poverty Hole in "A Better Feature for the Planet Earth Volume III, the Asahi Glass Foundation, 2007.
5. Iwan J. Aziz and Emil Salim, *Development Performance and Future Scenarios in the context of Sustainable Utilisation of Natural Resources*, Paper, Jakarta, 2004.
6. Munawir and Sonya Vermeulen, *Fair Deals for Watershed Services in Indonesia*," International Institute for Environment and Development, UK, 2007.
7. Iwan J. Aziz, *Macroeconomic Policy and Poverty*, ADB Institute Discussion Paper no.111, June 2008, Tokyo, Japan.

Seawater-based Carbon Sequestration
The Key to Climate Change Mitigation and Adaptation

Gordon H. Sato and Samuel N. Welderufael

The only hope of solving the CO_2 problem is to use photosynthetic organisms that can use seawater. Seawater contains all the elements of the Zarrouk algae medium, except for nitrogen, phosphorous, and iron. The elements of the Zarrouk algae medium are required for the growth of all plants including algae, various seaweeds, and giant redwood trees. Plants need no element that is not found in the Zarrouk algae medium. Exceptions to these generalizations are rare and exist only in plants that survive in extreme and rare environments. Therefore, adding nitrogen, phosphorous, and iron in seawater permits the growth of plants that can grow in seawater. Mangrove trees would be grown in the Sahara desert with irrigation using seawater supplemented with nitrogen, phosphorous, and iron.

A mature mangrove forest, which may only take up to four years to fully mature, should fix up to 10 tons of CO_2 per hectare per year. If the entire Sahara desert were planted with mangrove forests, it could fix all the CO_2 produced by the activities of man. Many deserts can serve to grow mangrove trees, such as those in Saudi Arabia, Iraq, Iran, and Mexico.

Furthermore, we believe that fertilizing the sea bottom across coastal waters could drastically reduce world poverty. The difficulty of fertilizing coastal waters is that it would encourage eutrophication and growth of toxic algae. Therefore, man has refrained from fertilizing coastal waters. Plants beneficial to coastal waters such as eelgrass and kelp have the same nutritional requirement as red tide algae. We have devised fertilization methods that encourage the growth of beneficial plants but not algae. We incorporate urea and diammonium phosphate in bricks (balls) of gypsum and a small amount of cement. Pieces of iron are also sprinkled in the soil. These are spread over the soil of coastal waters from the balls sinking into the mud, and the plants can access these fertilizers imbedded in the soil. Thus, we have seen great increase in the growth of eel grass and kelp with no visible growth of algae. These methods can be used to regenerate lost underwater vegetation such as seagrass and enhance easily accessible environments. Considering the size of the easily accessible shallow continental shelf, it is easy to imagine the impact of such initiatives in tackling climate change mitigation and adaptation issues. We strongly believe that we can greatly increase the wealth of coastal countries in this manner.

Furthermore, seawater irrigation in barren coastal deserts could contribute to solving global food security challenges exacerbated by the quest for alternative renewable energy resources using biofuels. Marine algae and halophytes such as salicornia bigelovii (which can be cultivated by seawater irrigation) are more sustainable biofuel sources, unlike conventional crop-based biofuels that compete with food and land use and pressurize other resources including freshwater, rain forests, and, in some cases, political stability.

Similarly, promoting mangrove forest and seagrass rehabilitation in degraded mangrove forests and seagrass beds and planting in new sites can deliver greater CO_2 reduction and positive ecological and sustainability outcomes in existing carbon market mechanisms.

Irreversibility of Climate Change because of Anthropogenic Carbon Dioxide Increases

Susan Solomon

As the world considers its next steps in the United Nations Framework Convention on Climate Change (UNFCCC) on the occasion of the 20th anniversary of the Rio conference, we should consider the breadth, depth, and role of inputs from scientific advances. The text of the convention includes Article 2: setting out the "ultimate objective" of "stabilization of greenhouse gas concentrations" that would "prevent dangerous interference with the climate system." Much has been written regarding the definition of what is dangerous, and the ways in which this represents the intersection of science, policy, economics, and other disciplines. Article 3 of the convention states the Parties should be guided by factors such as "threats of serious or irreversible damage."

The identification of what is likely to be irreversible is purely a scientific matter, quite different from the complexities of Article 2. In this contribution, I wish to highlight the substantially improved scientific understanding of the irreversibility of changes in climate driven by anthropogenic carbon dioxide increases that has resulted from research of the past several years. I will restrict my focus to the Earth's climate system and not consider human actions that may be proposed to "geoengineer" that system and reduce future warming.

As carbon dioxide increases, the Earth's energy budget is altered in such a way as to warm the planet. This warming is nearly irreversible (within about ±0.5°C) over timescales of at least a thousand years, even if emissions of carbon diaxide were to cease entirely. This result was first identified in one model of intermediate complexity (Matthews and Caldeira, 2008), subsequently confirmed in many different models of intermediate complexity (Plattner et al., 2008; Solomon et al., 2009), and has now also been simulated in a number of more detailed ocean-atmosphere general circulation models (Lowe et al., 2009; Gillett et al., 2011). This broad range of studies has demonstrated that the irreversibility of the warming because of anthropogenic increases in carbon diodide is a fundamental property of the climate system.

The persistence of warming arises largely from ocean heat uptake (Solomon et al., 2010). The deep ocean can be envisioned as a bath that can keep the entire planet warm over a long time, so the amount of anthropogenic heat transported to the deep ocean is important. In addition, carbon dioxide is a unique gas that does not have a single atmospheric decay process over time. If human emissions of carbon dioxide were to stop, the human increase in this gas to the atmosphere would decay over several different timescales, and though the surface ocean would remove some added carbon on a timescale of a few decades, some would remain in the atmosphere for many millennia, yet again because of the slow timescales of the deep ocean (Archer et al., 1997). The timescales for the removal of carbon and warming from the deep ocean combine to produce the near-irreversibility of the carbon dioxide-induced warming. Persistent warming for a long time will lead to a wide range of climate impacts, including rising sea levels through the ocean's thermal expansion, and could also slowly erode the mass of the Greenland or Antarctic ice sheets. Because the warming is nearly irreversible, the anthropogenic carbon dioxide added to the atmosphere in the 21st century will set the amount of sea level that should be expected in a thousand years, even if emissions were to cease. Therefore, the decisions made at this conference will be critical for determining how much the Earth's climate system will be altered, including whether low-lying regions will continue to exist in the far future on planet Earth.

References

1. Archer, D., H. Kheshgi, and E. Maier-Reimer, Multiple timescales for neutralization of fossil fuel CO_2. *Geophys. Res. Lett.*, 24 (4), 405–408, 1997.
2. Gillett, N. P., V. J. Arora, K. Zickfeld, S. J. Marshall, and W. J. Merryfield, Ongoing climate change following a complete cessation of carbon dioxide emissions. *Nature Geosci.* 4, 83–87, 2011.
3. Lowe, J. A., C. Huntingford, S. C. B. Raper, C. D. Jones, S. K. Liddicoat, and L. K. Gohar, How difficult is it to recover from dangerous levels of global warming?, *Env. Res. Lett.*, 4, 014,012, 2009.
4. Matthews, H. D., and K. Caldeira, Stabilizing climate requires near-zero emissions, *Geophys. Res. Lett.*, 35, L04,705, 2008.
5. Plattner, G.-K., et al., Long-term climate commitments projected with climate-carbon cycle models, *J. Clim.*, 21, 2721–2751, 2008.
6. Solomon, S., G. Kasper Plattner, R. Knutti, and P. Friedlingstein, Irreversible climate change due to carbon dioxide emissions, *Proc. Natl. Acad. Sci.*, 106, 1704–1709, 2009.
7. Solomon S et al., Persistence of climate changes due to a range of greenhouse gases, *Proc. Natl. Acad. Sci.*, 107,18354–18359, doi: 10.1073/pnas.1006282107, 2010.

Climate Change, Economics, and a New Energy-Industrial Revolution

Nicholas Stern*

Why is there a problem?

Science tells us that the problems created by the accumulation of greenhouse gas (GHG) emissions are potentially immense. Some climate models suggest a median temperature increase over the next one or two centuries in the region of 4°C or warmer, with substantial probabilities of well above 4°C. Global mean temperatures regularly exceeding 4°C above pre-industrial have likely not been seen for at least 10 million years, perhaps much more (see below). The potential climate change associated with such temperatures is likely to transform the lives and livelihoods of billions of people, including where hundreds of millions could live. Resulting population movements could lead to extended, severe, and widespread conflict. This is the scale of the stakes that follow from the science.

The potential effects are subject to major uncertainties–they appear with long lags, and the effect of a kilogram of GHG emissions is independent of who or where are the emitters are (emissions are "public bads" in the language of economics). The combination of the magnitude, uncertainty, lags in the consequences, and "'publicness'" of the causes, all of which follow from the science, makes the politics and economics of policy supremely difficult.

People have difficulty in understanding the scale of risk

* I am very grateful to James Rydge for his guidance and support.

165

from climate change. More generally, misunderstanding the meaning of uncertainty and how to respond are pervasive in both public and private decision making. In addition, the lags are compounded by ratchet effects and irreversibilities: once carbon -dioxide, the most important of the GHGs, is in the atmosphere, it is likely to stay for many decades. Furthermore, capital equipment and infrastructure can last for several decades, locking in high-carbon structures. Thus, if leaders postpone decisions until the effects are very clear and the scale is demonstrated, it may be difficult, extremely costly, or impossible to extricate ourselves. We may even have to consider very risky and, not fully explored alternatives, such as geoengineering, which themselves may carry immense and potentially damaging consequences. The publicness of the cause may tempt people to leave action to others on the articulated grounds that each individual contribution is small, or they may decline to act because they do not have confidence that others will act.

We have a problem of risk management and public action of immense importance whose scientific logic makes the formulation, decision making, and implementation of policy extremely difficult. However, the policy challenge is far from insoluble; indeed, if it were, it is likely that the future for our children and grandchildren would be dire.

The building of the political will to take the radical decisions necessary will require the widespread and shared understanding of two fundamental propositions. So far, we as scientists, social scientists, and communicators have not made sufficient progress in explaining and demonstrating these propositions. The two propositions concern 1) the scale of the risks and the urgency of action, and 2) the nature and attractiveness of the new energy-industrial revolution that is required. They are discussed in the second and third sections of this brief paper. The remainder of this first section is devoted to the key elements of economic policy for the management of climate change and broader issues of sustainability beyond climate change.

GHG emissions are not the only market failure relevant to the management of climate change. There are crucial market failures concerning research, development, and deployment; networks and grids; long-term risk and capital markets; property markets; and information. Furthermore, there are failures in the valuing and understanding of co-benefits of action on climate change (beyond the fundamental benefits of reducing the risks of climate change) and embedding these in policy. These arise particularly around the valuation of ecosystem services and biodiversity issues that require close attention in their own right as well as being profoundly affected by action or inaction on climate change.

Each of these requires careful attention: thus, the problems of market failure associated with promoting action on GHGs go beyond the fundamental market failure of the unpriced externality of emissions. That market failure is indeed fundamental and is a primary and crucial element of any policy foundation; however, policy will fail to generate the scale and urgency of the response required if it stops there. The demonstration of ideas and new techniques helps others, and thus should be fostered; networks depend on interaction and require government policy to work effectively and achieve desired outcomes. Policy, in relation to each of the failures described, should be based on careful analysis of the origins of the failure itself, and thus how best to tackle it.

Markets generally fail to recognize the economic and social value of much of the services of ecosystems and biodiversity that the associated activities affect. We urgently need to deepen our understanding and strengthen our practice for methods for valuing ecosystems and biodiversity. In many cases we need methods that allow us to calculate the social value of the services required, which can require some care and subtlety both in understanding the physical and biological effects of the ecosystem on say, rainfall water supply or the spread of disease or pests, as well as how to value those effects in terms of impacts on well-being. It is clear that great challenges exist in attempting to place a value on such a wide array of diverse and often only partially understood natural systems, many of which are public goods with no prices or markets. However, it would be a gross error, to suppose that because the challenges of valuation are difficult, we might as well assume that the costs are negligible or zero. Internalizing these costs into prices or regulations would change our economic and social relationship with the natural world. In too many cases, we currently behave as though ecosystem services and biodiversity have zero economic value. Consequently, their critical role in maintaining our well-being; economic activity; and environmental, natural, and social assets remains unaccounted for, leading to severe overuse, degradation, and destruction.

The benefits and uses of ecosystems and biodiversity are large and wide-ranging and are discussed elsewhere in this set of papers. Our purpose here is to emphasize the intimate links with climate change and the importance of measurement. It is a great mistake to attempt to separate climate change and ecosystems/biodiversity into distinct boxes and set them as competing priorities. For example, the degradation of ocean ecosystems, such as the observed rapid decline in phytoplankton biomass that produces around half of all atmospheric oxygen and absorbs large amounts of CO_2 from the atmosphere, may severely weaken the carbon cycle; and the loss of forests can lead to greater flooding and increased need for costly adaptation.

Crucial here is an urgent need to develop more widely accepted metrics for measuring ecosystem services and biodiversity. Without these tools, it will be difficult to develop more effective methods for valuing natural assets and engaging more constructively with policy makers. We can examine the costs of damage from neglect and the value of the use of these services by measuring the costs of damage prevention or repairs (e.g., flood control or recovery), at the costs of being forced to find different ways of doing things, or at the potential costs of forgoing options that might become available (what do we fail to learn because we destroy the book of life before reading it?)

The implications of such degradation and loss are uncertain. There may be complex feedback loops between ecosystem services, biodiversity, and climate change, and it could take a long

168

time, perhaps millennia, for ecosystems and biodiversity to recover, if at all. The valuation of the emissions market failure, though complex, perhaps embodies a more straightforward set of measurement questions than those for some of our natural assets; although, given how closely they are intertwined, we must be wary of this type of comparison. The potential magnitude of the value of ecosystems and their intimate relationship with the effects of climate change suggest that we should not make the mistake of focusing exclusively on climate change while examining the challenges and importance of sustainability more generally.

Scale of the risks and dangers of delay

Global GHG emissions are currently almost 50 billion metric tons of carbon dioxide-equivalent (CO_2e) per year and are growing strongly, mainly because of carbon-intensive growth in the developing world. As the carbon cycle is unable to absorb all of the world's annual emissions, concentrations (stocks) of GHG emissions in the atmosphere have increased to around 440 ppm of CO_2e today. Currently, the emissions are at a rate of around 2.5 ppm per year, and this rate is rising. Thus, if we continue with something like BAU over the course of this century, we would probably add at least 300 ppm, taking concentrations to around 750 ppm CO_2e or higher at the end of this century or early in the next. Some climate models suggest a median temperature increase over the next one or two centuries in the region of 4°C or warmer, with substantial probabilities of well above 4°C. Global mean temperatures regularly exceeding 4°C above pre-industrial have likely not been seen for at least 10 million years, perhaps much more.

The world's current commitments to reduce emissions, as pledged in the Appendices to the Copenhagen Accord and confirmed in the Cancun agreement and recently at Durban, are consistent with at least a 3°C rise (again with about 50-50 chance of higher or belower). The world has not seen an increase of 3°C for around three million years. *Homo sapiens* has experienced nothing like this, having been present for only around 200,000–250,000 years. In addition, and our civilizations, in terms of arable farming, villages, towns, and so on, have been here for only 8,000 or 9,000 years since the emergence from the last ice age, that is, during the Holocene period, when average temperatures have fluctuated in a quite narrow range of between ±1°C.

Such warming would likely cause disruption on a huge scale to local habitats and climates, for example, through flooding, desertification, and water scarcity. Hundreds of millions of people, perhaps billions, would probably have to move, with the associated risks of severe and extended conflict. The great advances in development of the last few decades, which have seen hundreds of millions of people in developing countries rise out of income poverty, substantial improvements in health and life expectancy, large reductions in fertility rates, and major advances in education and literacy, would likely be put at risk.

The scale of the risks and the inherent uncertainty around these projections clearly suggest that policy analysis of climate change must be framed in terms of risk-management. The potential risks are huge, and the associated probabilities are not small.

The uncertainty present in these projections may suggest to some that delay while we learn more is the best response, rather than early and strong action to reduce emissions. That would be a profound mistake. First, the flow-stock process, from emissions to increasing concentrations of GHGs in the atmosphere, particularly with CO_2, very long-lasting in the atmosphere, implies that we have a ratchet effect. Processes to remove emissions from the atmosphere or prevent solar energy from reaching the earth, known as geoengineering, are undeveloped, largely untested, and likely to involve significant risks. Second, much of infrastructure and capital investment can result in technological "lock-in". With little action, the long lifetimes of much of the relevant high-carbon infrastructure and network investment could imply that the lock-in could last for many decades. Delay is clearly very dangerous; we are

170

already at a difficult starting point in GHG concentrations, and weak action or inaction for a decade could make stabilization of concentrations at levels that reduce the risks to acceptable levels, in particular 2°C, very difficult.

To embark on strong action now, if the science turns out to be wrong and the risks are small, would leave us with a more energy-efficient and bio-diverse economy and new technologies even though ex post, we might have wished that there had been somewhat smaller investment in these areas. However, if the science turns out to be right, and we ignore the risks, we would be in an extremely difficult position from which it would be very hard to extricate ourselves. Given this logic, basic decision theory or common sense points to strong action, particularly because the science is very likely to be right. To argue for weak or delayed action involves claiming to be pretty sure the risks are small – an extraordinary position given 200 years of cumulative scientific analysis – and/or that delay has only modest downside.

The Stern Review (2006) makes the case for early action. Strong action, starting now, with the aim of stabilizing GHG concentrations, as it suggested, at between 500 ppm and 550 ppm would require extra global investments of around 1% (–1 to +3) of annual world GDP. Given rapidly rising emissions; advances in our knowledge of climate change science; which make inaction look ever more worrying, and rapid technological advance since the Stern Review, I and many others would now suggest a target of around 450 ppm. That means acting more strongly, particularly given delays since 2006, and that the extra global investment necessary may now be around 2% of world GDP. The Stern Review estimated that the costs and risks of unmanaged climate change may be equivalent to damages, in welfare terms, of between 5–20% of annual GDP, averaged appropriately over space, time, and possible outcomes. The likely damages from inaction do indeed appear very large; however, one need not follow the kind of approach of formal cost–benefit analysis and all the attendant particular assumptions to make the case for strong and urgent world action. As we have argued, it follows from a fairly basic approach to an analysis of risk.

Size of the response and the new energy-industrial revolution

As expressed in the current global negotiations (the agreement at Cancun at the UNFCCC meeting of December 2010), most nations now agree that limiting the rise in global temperature to 2°C is necessary in the sense that levels above this are (sensibly) regarded as dangerous. To achieve this goal with a 50-50 probability, global emissions would need to fall from current levels to pass well below 35 billion metric tons of CO_2e in 2030, and well below 20 billion metric tons of CO_2e in 2050. These "global constraints" should be at the heart of discussions and of the understanding of action.

Reducing absolute emissions levels by a factor of at least 2.5 in 40 years would require a reduction in emissions per unit of output by a factor of around 8 if the world economy grows over 40 years by a factor of around 3 (equivalent to an annual world GDP growth rate of around 2.8%). Emissions reductions on this scale should surely be regarded as a new energy-industrial revolution. The transition to low-carbon growth and the energy-industrial revolution represent a far more attractive path than the previous high-carbon, dirty, and environmentally destructive path. The transition is likely to be a period of innovation, creativity, and growth and will involve substantial investment across the economy. In addition, low-carbon growth is likely to be cleaner, safer, quieter, more energy secure, and more biodiverse. Low-carbon growth is the genuine growth option; an attempt at high-carbon growth will self-destruct.

The study of past periods of economic/technological transformation has much to teach us here. Past industrial revolutions, such as steam and the railways, and much more recently, the ongoing information, communications, and technology (ICT) revolution, involved a transformation that saw two or more decades of strong innovation and growth, with investment flowing to those pioneer countries and businesses that demonstrated leadership and embraced the transition. Such transformations involve periods of "creative destruction" (in the tradition of the economist Joseph Schumpeter), where new firms and ideas drive out the old, generating a dynamic period of innovation, opportunity, employment, and economic growth. Countries and states such as China, Korea, Germany, the Scandinavian countries, and California are leading the transition, with the size of their low-carbon markets growing strongly. The costs of low-carbon technologies, such as solar PV and offshore wind power, have declined rapidly over recent years, and similar cost reductions are expected in the future as their deployment accelerates.

The transition will require strong action to reduce emissions across all countries and all economic sectors. Energy efficiency will be central to the response, as will the introduction of new low-carbon technologies and strong and determined action to slow and halt deforestation. This action will involve the implementation of transparent, long-term, and credible public policies (to address the market failures) and public investments that create a positive environment for innovation and change. They should carefully consider, and be integrated with, policies to protect ecosystems and biodiversity.

As this transformation progresses, the world must also be prepared to adapt to the climate change to which we are already committed because of past and future emissions. We have to manage the unavoidable along with avoiding the unmanageable. We are already outside the temperature range of the Holocene period, when our societies developed. Another 1–1.5°C, which appears very likely, will require major adaptation to changing weather and climate patterns. There should be close intertwining with mitigation and development; indeed, it is a mistake to excessively separate their organization and implementation. Much of irrigation and water management should combine mitigation, adaptation, and development, and so should buildings, city management, power, and others. The stronger the emissions reduction, the less the necessary scale of adaptation however, our previous and current emissions performance will require the large-scale adaptation.

We are already starting to see many countries introduce emissions reduction policies. However, action must be stronger and more rapid, more coordinated, and extend more widely across the many relevant market failures if we are to achieve the level of investment and pace of change necessary to avoid dangerous climate change. Delay is dangerous, and now is the time to accelerate. The world economy risks a prolonged slow-down as a consequence of the financial and economic crises of the last few years. Low-carbon growth is the only sound basis for a sustainable recovery.

Rio +20
Green Economy with Inclusive Growth

M. S. Swaminathan

The Blue Planet Prize, first awarded at Rio de Janeiro in 1992, is a landmark in human efforts to keep our planet ever blue. Twenty years after Rio, we are struggling to find a pathway for development that concurrently integrates the principles of ecology, economics, equity, ethics, and employment. Green Economy can be defined as "Enhancing economic growth in perpetuity without associated ecological and/or social harm."

Green Economy ensures both economic growth and ecological and social sustainability. Because agriculture is the predominant occupation of a vast majority of the population of developing countries, I would like to deal with methods of achieving a paradigm shift from green to evergreen revolution. Evergreen revolution involves the enhancement of crop productivity in perpetuity without associated ecological harm. India has been chosen as a case study for understanding how green economy and inclusive growth can become mutually reinforcing.

While visiting the National Dairy Research Institute, Bangalore, on June 27, 1927, Mahatma Gandhi wrote "Farmer" in the Visitors' Book in the column titled "Occupation," thus emphasizing that farming is the most dignified profession of our country. Furthermore, he used to emphasize that Gram Swaraj is the pathway to Poorna Swaraj. Later, Lal Bahadur Shastri gave the slogan "Jai Jawan, Jai Kisan" to stress that "jawans" and "kisans" are the two pillars of our freedom. The extreme volatility of the price of food grains in the international market emphasizes that the future belongs to nations with grains and not guns.

For the youth to take up agriculture, farming must be both intellectually satisfying and economically rewarding. This quality necessitates technological and managerial upgrading of farm operations. We must harness the best in frontier science and marry it with the best in traditional knowledge and ecological prudence. Such a blend leads to the science of ecotechnology. In addition to ecotechnology, our agricultural universities should become leaders in biotechnology, information technology, space technology, nuclear technology, nanotechnology, renewable energy, and management technology. The university should enable every scholar to become an entrepreneur and help to achieve the technological transformation of agriculture.

During his 2010 visit to India, US President Barack Obama noted that India is fortunate to have over half of its total population of 1.2 billion under the age of 30. Of the 600 million young persons, over 60% live in villages. Most of them are educated. Mahatma Gandhi considered the migration of educated youth from villages to towns and cities as the most serious form of brain drain adversely affecting rural India's development. Therefore, he stressed that we should take steps to end the divorce between intellect and labor in rural professions.

The National Commission on Farmers (2004–2006) stressed the need for retaining and attracting educated youth in farming. The National Policy for Farmers, proposed in Parliament in November 2007, includes the goal, "to introduce measures that can help to attract and retain youth in farming and processing of farm products for higher value addition by making farming intellectually stimulating and economically rewarding." Presently, we are deriving very little demographic dividend in agriculture. However, the pressure of population on land is increasing, and the average size of a farm holding is decreasing to below one hectare. Farmers are becoming indebted and increasingly tempted to sell prime farmland for non-farm purposes. Over 45% of farmers interviewed by the

176

National Sample Survey Organization wanted to quit farming. Under these conditions, how are we going to persuade educated youth, including farm graduates, to stay in villages and adopt agriculture as a profession? How can the youth earn a decent living in villages and help shape the future of our agriculture? Furthermore, women scholars are outnumbering men in many Agricultural and Veterinary Colleges. How are we going to benefit from the large number of qualified women in crop and animal husbandry, fisheries, and forestry? This goal will require a four-pronged strategy.

(a) Improve the productivity and profitability of small holdings through appropriate land use policies, technologies, and market linkages; develop for this purpose a "4C approach": Conservation, Cultivation, Consumption, and Commerce as an integrated system

(b) Expand the scope for the growth of agro-processing, agro-industries, and agri-business and establish a "Farm to Home" chain in production, processing, and marketing

(c) Promote opportunities for the services sector to expand in a manner that will trigger the technological and economic farm operation upgrading

(d) Create opportunities for women professionals to adopt a career of self-employment, based on a flex-time, flex-duration, and flex-place approach to job creation (e.g., Women's Biotechnology Park in Chennai)

A few years ago, the Government of India launched a program to enable farm graduates to start agri-clinics and agri-business centers. This program has not yet attracted the interest of educated youth to the degree originally expected. Therefore, it is time to restructure the program on the basis of lessons learned. Ideally, a group of four to five farm graduates with specializations in agriculture, animal husbandry, fisheries, agri-business, and home science could jointly launch an agri-clinic-cum-agri-business center in every block of each state.

Agri-clinics will provide the services needed during the production phase of farming, and the agri-business center will cater to the needs of farm families during the post-harvest phase of agriculture. Thus, farm women and men can receive assistance during the entire crop cycle, from sowing and extending through value addition and marketing. The multi-disciplinary expertise available within the group of young entrepreneurs will help them to serve farm families in a holistic manner. The home science graduate can specialize in nutrition and food safety and processing and help a group of farm women to start a food processing park. In addition, the group can assist farm families to achieve economy and power of scale during both the production and post-harvest phases of farming. Such an integrated center can be called an "Agricultural Transformation Center."

Several opportunities exist for young entrepreneurs. Climate-resilient agriculture is another area that needs attention. In dry farming areas, methods of rainwater harvesting and storage, aquifer recharge, and watershed management, as well as the improvement of soil physics, chemistry, and microbiology must become widespread. The cultivation of fertilizer trees, which can enrich soil fertility and help to improve soil carbon sequestration and storage, can be promoted under the Green India Mission and the Mahatma Gandhi National Rural Employment Guarantee program. A few fertilizer trees, a *jal kund* (water harvesting pond), and a biogas plant in every farm will help to improve enormously the productivity and profitability of dryland farming and contribute to climate change mitigation.

Furthermore, the "yuva kisans," or young farmers, can help women's self-help groups to manufacture and sell the biological software essential for sustainable agriculture. These include biofertilizers, biopesticides, and vermiculture. The fisheries graduate can promote both inland and marine aquaculture using low external input sustainable aquaculture (LEISA) techniques. Feed and seed are important requirements for successful aquaculture, and trained youth can promote their production at the local level. They can train rural families in induced fish breeding and spread quality and food safety literacy.

Similar opportunities exist in the fields of animal husbandry. Improved technologies of small-scale poultry and dairy farming can be introduced. Codex alimentarius standards of food safety can be popularized for perishable commodities. For this purpose, the young farmers should establish Gyan Chaupals, or Village Knowledge Centers, based on the integrated use of the Internet, FM radio, and mobile telephony.

In the services sector designed to meet the demand driven needs of farming families, an important sector is soil and water quality testing. Young farmers can organize mobile soil-cum-water quality testing and go to each village in their area of operation and issue a Farm Health Passbook to every family. Farm Health Passbook will contain information on soil health, water quality, and crop and animal diseases, so that the farm family has access to integrated information on all aspects of Farm Health. Very effective and reliable soil and water quality testing kits are now available. This will help rural families to utilize in an effective manner the nutrient-based subsidy introduced by the government from April 1, 2010. Similarly, educated youth could help rural communities to organize gene-seed-grain-water banks, thereby linking conservation, cultivation, consumption and commerce in a mutually reinforcing manner.

Young farmers can also operate climate risk management centers, which will help farmers to maximize the benefits of a good monsoon and minimize the adverse impact of unfavorable weather. Educated youth can help to introduce the benefits of information, space, nuclear, bio- and eco-technologies. Ecotechnology involves the blend of traditional wisdom and frontier technology and is the pathway to sustainable agriculture and food security, as well as agrarian prosperity. If educated youth choose to live in villages and launch the new agriculture movement based on the integrated application of science and social wisdom, our untapped demographic dividend will become our greatest strength.

Mahila Kisans (Women Famers) and Yuva Kisans will determine the future of our agrarian and rural economy. In the central budget of 2010-2011, a Mahila Kisan Sashaktikaran Pariyojana was introduced by the Finance Minister on my suggestion. The Home Science graduates participating in the Agricultural Transformation Center movement should also organize a "Feeding Minds–First 1000 Days" program to ensure that there is no maternal and fetal undernutrition, and that every new born child has an opportunity for realizing its innate genetic potential for mental and physical development. Babies with low birth weight resulting from fetal undernutrition suffer from handicaps in brain development and cognitive ability. Our desire to become a knowledge and innovation superpower can be achieved only by paying attention to nutrition and education on a life-cycle basis, i.e., from conception to cremation.

Addressing the World Climate Conference held in Geneva in 1989 on the theme, "Climate Change and Agriculture" (Swaminathan (1990), "Agriculture and food systems" in Proceedings of the Second World Climate Conference, Geneva, World Meteorological Organization), I pointed out the serious implications of a rise of 1–2° C in mean temperature on crop productivity in South Asia and Sub-Saharan Africa. An Expert Team constituted by Food and Agriculture Organization (FAO) in its report submitted in September 2009 also concluded that for each 1° C rise in mean temperature, wheat yield losses in India are likely to be around six million tons per year or around $ 1.5 billion at current prices. There will be similar losses in other crops, and our impoverished farmers could lose the equivalent of over US $ 20 billion in income each year. Rural women will suffer more because they look after animals, fodder, feed, and water.

We are now in the midst of a steep rise in the prices of essential food items such as pulses, vegetables, and milk. The gap between demand and supply is high in pulses, oilseeds, sugar, and several vegetable crops including onion, tomato, and potato. Production and market intelligence as well as a demand–supply balance based an integrated import and export policy are lacking. The absence of a farmer-centric market system aggravates both food inflation and rural poverty. FAO estimates that a primary cause for the increase in the number of hungry persons, now exceeding over a billion, is the high cost of basic staples. Unfortunately, India has the unenviable reputation of being home to the largest number of undernourished children, women, and men in the world. The task of ensuring food security will be quite formidable in an era of increasing climate risks and diminishing farm productivity.

China has already built strong defenses against the adverse impact of climate change. During 2010, China produced over 500 million tons of food grains in a cultivated area similar to that of India. However, Chinese farm land is mostly irrigated unlike India's, where 60% of the area still remains rainfed. Food and drinking water are the first among our hierarchical needs. Therefore, while assessing the common and differentiated impacts of a 2° rise in temperature, agriculture and rural livelihoods should be prioritized.

The year 2010 was the International Year of Biodiversity. We can classify our crops into climate resilient and climate sensitive. For example, wheat is a climate-sensitive crop, while rice shows a wide range of adaptation in terms of growing conditions. We will have problems with reference to crops such as potato because a higher temperature will render raising disease free seed potatoes in the plains of Northwest India difficult. We will have to shift from planting tubers to cultivating potato from true sexual seed. The relative importance of different diseases and pests will be altered. The wheat crop may suffer more from stem rust, which normally occurs only in Peninsular India. Therefore, a search for new genes conferring climate resilience is urgent. We must build gene banks for a warming India.

Anticipatory analysis and action hold the key to climate risk management. The major components of an Action Plan for achieving a Climate-Resilient National Food Security System will be the following:

- Establish in each of the 127 agro-climatic sub-zones, identified by the Indian Council of Agricultural Research on
  the basis of cropping systems and weather patterns of
  the country, a Climate Risk Management Research and
  Extension Center.
- Organize a Content Consortium for each center, consisting
  of experts in different fields to provide guidance on alternative cropping patterns, contingency plans, and com-
  pensatory production programs when the area witnesses
  natural calamities such as drought, flood, high temperatures, and in case of coastal areas, a rise in sea level.
- Establish, with the help of the Indian Space Research
  Organization (ISRO), a Village Resource Center (VRC)
  with satellite connection at each of the 127 locations.
- Link the 127 agro-climate centers with the National
  Monsoon Mission to ensure better climate, crop, and market intelligence.
- Establish, with the help of the Ministry of Earth Sciences
  and the India Meteorological Department, an Agro-
  Meteorological Station at each Research and Extension
  Center to initiate a "Weather Information for All" program.
- Organize Seed and Grain Banks based on Computer
  Simulation Models of different weather probabilities and
  their impacts on the normal crops and crop seasons of the
  area.
- Develop Drought and Flood Codes indicating the anticipatory steps necessary to adapt to the impact of global
  warming.
- Strengthen the coastal defenses against rise in sea level
  and the more frequent occurrence of storms and tsunamis through the establishment of bioshields of mangroves
  and non-mangrove species. In addition, develop sea water
  farming and below-sea-level farming techniques. Establish
  major Research Centers for sea water and below-sea-level
  farming. Agri-aqua farms will have to be promoted along
  the coast. The year 2010 marked the 80th anniversary of

Gandhiji's salt satyagraha. Gandhiji emphasized that sea water, which forms 97% of the global water resources, is a social resource. There should be a major program to convert sea water into fresh water through halophytes.

- Train one woman and one male member of every Panchayat to become Climate Risk Managers. They should become well versed in the art and science of Climate Risk Management and help to blend traditional wisdom with modern science. The Climate Risk Managers should be supported with an internet connected Village Knowledge Center.

A Climate Literacy Movement and anticipatory action to safeguard the lives and livelihoods of all living in coastal areas and islands will have to be initiated. Integrated coastal zone management procedures involving concurrent attention to both the landward and seaward sites of the ocean and to coastal forestry and agro-forestry as well as capture and culture fisheries are urgently needed. A Genetic Garden for halophytes is being established at Vedaranyam in Tamil Nadu. Biodiversity is the feedstock for a climate-resilient agriculture and food security system.

Gandhiji pointed out long ago that the future of rural enterprises will depend upon our ability to marry intellect will labor. The Mahatma Gandhi National Rural Employment Guarantee Program, which prioritizes water harvesting, aquifer recharge, and watershed management, provides a unique opportunity for integrating brain and brawn. The Mahatma Gandhi National Rural Employment Guarantee Act (MGNREGA) workers should feel that they are working for the important cause of water security. Government should institute an "Environment Savior Award" to recognize and reward the best MGNREGA team in the areas of water harvesting and watershed management.

The challenging economic, environmental, and social problems that our country is facing can be solved only with the help of science and technology. Technology is the prime mover of change, as will be evident from the impact of mobile telephony in our everyday life. Jawaharlal Nehru, with his characteristic vision, said over 60 years ago, "The future belongs to science and to those who make friendship with science." Therefore, for the benefit of young scientists, I cite a few examples from the work of the M. S. Swaminathan Research Foundation (MSSRF), Chennai, on the translation of vision to impact.

From Vision to Impact

During the last 21 years, the scientists and scholars of the MSSRF have been working on the design and implementation of projects which could have a large extrapolation domain with respect to imparting a pro-nature, pro-poor, pro-women, and pro-sustainable livelihood orientation to technology development and dissemination. A few of the MSSRF initiatives, which have now become State, national, and global programs have been discussed below.

Mahila Kisan Sashaktikaran Pariyojana:
Strengthening women's role in agriculture

In 2007, the MSSRF initiated the Mahila Kisan Sashaktikaran Pariyojana in the Vidarbha region of Maharashtra for empowering women farmers, including the widows of farmers who had committed suicide, in areas related to enhancing the productivity, profitability, and sustainability of small-scale, rainfed farming. The empowerment measures incorporated access to technology, credit, inputs, and the market. Separately, it introduced an education program for children who had lost their fathers because of the agrarian crisis. Encouraged by the results of this small program, Finance Minister Shri Pranab Mukherjee included funds in the Union Budget for 2010-11 for initiating a national Mahila Kisan Sashaktikaran Pariyojana. India's Ministry of Rural Development, responsible for implementing this program, has made it an integral part of its Rural Livelihood Mission. Recently, the MSSRF was invited to launch the Mahila Kisan program in the Wardha and Yavatmal districts of Vidarbha from 2011 to 2014. This will include both

technological and organizational empowerment. It is anticipated that by 2014, a well-organized Mahila Kisan Federation
with a membership of over 3000 women farmers will emerge.
There is a growing feminization of agriculture in India, and it
is hoped that the Wardha–Yavatmal Mahila Kisan Federation
will be a forerunner of other federations at the state and national levels, capable of securing women farmers their entitlements. In addition to technology, inputs, and market, women
farmers also need services such as crèches and day care centers. The gender-specific needs of mahila kisans, both as wom-
en and as farmers, will have to be met if they are to play their
rightful role in India's agricultural progress.

In addition to action at the grassroots, the MSSRF organized
several consultations to draft a Women Farmers' Entitlements
Bill to be introduced in Parliament as a Private Member's Bill.
The draft bill is currently circulating among women parlia-
mentarians and gender specialists for their scrutiny and advice. This two pronged action—at the village and national
policy levels—is expected to help the over 350 million women
engaged in farming to contribute more effectively to agrarian
prosperity and sustainable food security.

Pulses Villages: Bridging the demand–supply gap

To illustrate how the gap between the demand and supply of
pulses, which is one of the factors contributing to food inflation
in the country, can be speedily bridged, the MSSRF organized
Pulses Villages in the Pudukottai and Ramanathapuram districts of Tamil Nadu over 15 years ago. In these Pulses Villages,
located in low rainfall areas, farmers undertook rainwater harvesting in farm ponds and cultivating pulses with appropriate
varieties, soil fertility, and agronomic management. On the basis of the success of this approach to accelerate the production
of pulses, a national program for the establishment of Pulses
Villages was recommended to the Union Finance Minister, who
announced financial support for starting 60,000 Pulses Villages
throughout the country. A sum of Rs. 300 crore was provided in
the 2011-12 Union Budget for organizing 60,000 Pulses Villages.

The impact of this integrated and concentrated approach had become evident from the increase observed in pulses production from 14.66 million tons in 2009-10 to 16.51 million tons in 2010-11. Under the umbrella of the Pulses Village program, special Arhar Villages (pigeon pea; Cajanus cajan) are being developed on the basis of hybrid arhar strains. High-yielding arhar hybrids have been developed at the International Crops Research Institute for the Semi-arid Tropics (ICRISAT) located in Hyderabad. Women's self-help groups will be trained to become hybrid-seed producers, and some of the pulses villages will be developed into Pulses Seed Villages for this purpose. This will enable the rapid spread of a yield revolution in pulses.

Nutri-cereals:
Role in strengthening food security and climate-resilient farming

Very early on, the MSSRF started working on underutilized or orphan crops such as a range of millets belonging to Panicum, Pennisetum, Paspalum, Setaria, Eleucine, and other genera. These crops, normally classified as coarse cereals, are very nutritious and rich both in macro- and micronutrients. In fact, a combination of millet and Moringa (drumstick) provides most of the macro- and micronutrients needed by the body. The widespread hidden hunger now prevailing in the country as a result of a deficiency of iron, iodine, zinc, vitamin A, vitamin B_{12}, and other necessary micronutrients in the diet can be overcome at a low cost through by consuming millets and vegetables.

In 1992, the MSSRF began work in the Kolli Hills in Tamil Nadu for the revitalization of culinary traditions involving a wide range of millets. It initiated a four-pronged strategy with concurrent attention to conservation, cultivation, consumption, and commerce. Commercialization proved to be a trigger in the area of conservation because farmers generally prefer to grow crops such as rice, wheat, or tapioca, for which there is a ready market. Similarly, in the Wayanad district of Kerala, tribal families were enabled to continue the conservation and consumption of tuber crops like Dioscorea. There is now a revival of interest in millets and other underutilized crops because of both their ability to help in overcoming chronic and hidden hunger and their role in the design of climate-resilient farming systems.

In partnership with Bioversity International and the Agricultural Universities of Bangalore and Dharwar, and with financial support from the International Fund for Agricultural Development (IFAD) and the Swiss Agency for Development Cooperation (SDC), the MSSRF has succeeded in introducing appropriate milling machines and markets for value-added products in a wide range of millets. Several Policy Makers' Workshops and efforts in nutritional literacy promoted an understanding of the role of millets, tubers, and other underutilized crops in improving rural nutrition and income in an era of climate change. Thus, Finance Minister Shri Pranab Mukherjee referred to jowar (sorghum), bajra (pearl millet), ragi (Eleucine), and minor millets as "nutri-cereals" and allocated Rs 300 crore in the 2011-12 Union Budget for their popularization.

In its draft National Food Security Bill, the National Advisory Council (NAC), headed by Shrimati Sonia Gandhi, has included millets among the staple grains that should be made available to food-insecure families in both rural and urban India at highly subsidized rates through the public distribution system. If Parliament approves and implements this bill, there will be revived interest in the cultivation and consumption of these nutrition-rich and climate-resilient crops. Agrobiodiversity hot spots can then become "happy spots" and will witness the dawn of an era of biohappiness, where rural and tribal families can convert bioresources into jobs and income on an environmentally sustainable and socially equitable basis.

Another significant recent development is the initiation of a project on "Alleviating Poverty and Malnutrition in Agrobiodiversity Hotspots" with financial support from the Canadian International Food Security Research Fund (CIFSRF). The project is administered by the Canadian International Development Agency (CIDA) and the International Development

Research Center of Canada (IDRC) and involves partnerships with the MSSRF; the University of Alberta, Canada; Bioversity International; the World Agroforestry Center (ICRAF); and the World Food Program (WFP). This 5-year project (2011–16) will help to revitalize the in situ on-farm conservation traditions of tribal and rural families in the Kolli Hills area of Tamil Nadu, the Wayanad district of Kerala, and the Koraput district of Orissa. The MSSRF has been working with them for over 15 years. The contributions of the tribal families of Koraput have been recognized through the Equator Initiative Award at the 2002 UN Conference on Sustainable Development held at Johannesburg and the 2011 Genome Savior Award by the Plant Variety Protection and Farmers' Rights Authority of the Government of India. Thus, two decades of research and education conducted by the MSSRF in the area of orphan crops have led to important research investment and public policy initiatives at the national and international levels. The expansion of the food basket by increasing the number of crops that go into the daily diet will also stabilize food security systems.

Through the CIFSRF, the IDRC also supports another project for strengthening rural food security through the production, processing, and value-addition of nutritious millets. This project is being implemented in collaboration with McGill University, Canada, and the University of Agricultural Sciences, Dharwad. In addition, the MSSRF coordinates the project activities assigned to the Himalayan Environmental Studies and Conservation Organization (HESCO), Dehradun. This project capitalizes on the progress previously made by the MSSRF in these crops with support received from the International Fund for Agricultural Development and Biodiversity International.

Price volatility and hunger: Operation 2015

Nearly 70% of the income of the poor is spent in buying food. Therefore, high prices are responsible for reducing food intake, thus leading to the persistence of hunger. Figure 1 depicts the extent of price volatility in recent years for rice, wheat, maize, and oil (petroleum products).

Figure 1
World Commodity Prices, Jan 2000 - Jun 2011

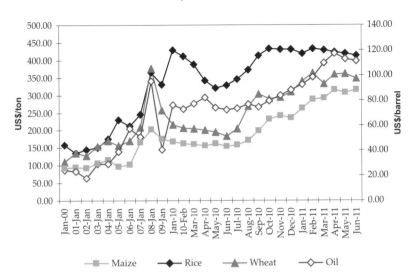

Source: FAO and US Energy Information Administration
(data updated as of 06/29/2011)

The agriculture ministers of the G-20 nations who met in Paris on June 22–23, 2011, have emphasized that "small scale agricultural producers represent the majority of the food insecure in developing countries. Increasing their production and income would directly improve access to food among the most vulnerable and improve supply for local and domestic markets." In addition, the ministers decided to establish an Agricultural Market Information System, initially in wheat, rice, maize, and soybeans, to improve the agricultural market outlook and forecasts at the national and global levels.

The MSSRF's work in this area has three major dimensions. The first is the development of village-level food security systems on the basis of community gene, seed, grain, and water banks that will help to store and distribute local nutritious grains like millets and pulses. The second encompasses the training of a cadre of "Community Hunger Fighters" well-versed in the science and art of overcoming both chronic and hidden hunger. The third dimension of the MSSRF's work in the management of price volatility is a dynamic and location-specific market information system through Gyan Chaupals or Village Knowledge Centers. Many such centers, now operating for over 15 years, provide timely information on the monsoon and the market. The behavior of the monsoon and the market determines farmers' well-being. Therefore, the Gyan Chaupals operated by local women and men give priority to empowering farm women and men with timely information on weather and market behavior. In addition, they provide information on food quality and safety, as well as on the entitlements of farm households to various government schemes.

The tribal areas where the MSSRF is working in Tamil Nadu, Kerala, and Odisha, as well as the Vidharba region of Maharashtra, have yet to achieve the progress necessary for the reduction of hunger and poverty to reach the 2015 target set by the first UN Millennium Development Goals. Therefore, the MSSRF, in association with other partners, has launched a program titled "Operation 2015" to help these areas achieve the UNMDG 1 by 2015. The program consists of the following features:

- Adoption of a lifecycle approach in nutrition support programs
- Promoting a "deliver as one" method with reference to nutrition, clean drinking water, sanitation, environmental hygiene, and primary health care
- Concurrent attention to small farm productivity improvement and producer-oriented marketing
- Encouraging a food-cum-fortification approach (particularly, fortification of salt with iron and iodine) to counteract chronic calorie deprivation and micronutrient deficiencies
- Establishing a cadre (at least one woman and one man in every village) trained as Climate Risk Managers and Community Hunger Fighters.

Thus, the MSSRF hopes that the challenge of price volatility can be fought at the local community level as well as at national and global levels.

Seawater farming

From 1990 onward, the MSSRF has been working on integrated coastal zone management, with concurrent attention to the seaward and landward sides of the shoreline, to strengthen both the ecological security of coastal areas and the livelihood security of coastal communities. Therefore, it developed a Coastal Systems Research (CSR) methodology. Research activities have included the conservation and restoration of mangrove wetlands, development of a Participatory Mangrove Forest Management System, generation of awareness of the importance of mangrove and non-mangrove bioshields in reducing the strength of coastal storms and tsunamis, and the breeding of salinity-tolerant rice, pulses, and other crops important to coastal agriculture by transferring genes for salinity tolerance from mangrove species through marker-assisted selection of recombinant DNA technology. Eighteen years of sustained research in this field has led to international patents for the novel genetic combinations produced by MSSRF scientists for tolerance to abiotic stresses like salinity and drought. These include

- US patent for the dehydrin gene from avicennia marina, responsible for making plants salt tolerant (Dr. Ajay Parida, Dr. Preeti Mehta, and Dr. Gayatri Venkataraman);
- US patent for the glutathione S-transferase gene from prosopis juliflora, making plants drought tolerant (Dr. Ajay Parida and Dr. Suja George)

Three more patents—for the phytosulfokine-α precursor sequence from avicienna marina creating stress tolerance, the antiporter gene from porteresia coarctata creating stress tolerance, and the superoxidase dismutase gene for creating abiotic stress tolerance in plants—have been filed and are going through the approval process.

Marker-assisted breeding has resulted in developing location-specific transgenic lines in popular indica varieties (IR64, IR20, Ponni, and ADT 43) with 99.5% purity and enhanced salinity tolerance of 400 mM of NaCl.

The MSSRF's work led to the rehabilitation and replanting of 2400 ha of mangroves in Tamil Nadu, Andhra Pradesh, and Odisha. The 2011 Coastal Regulation Zone Notification (January 6, 2011) by the Government of India derives its scientific basis from the MSSRF's research during the past 20 years and from two reports submitted by committees chaired by me.

On the basis of projects proposed by the MSSRF, India's Ministry of Environment and Forests (MoEF) and Department of Science and Technology (DST) have sanctioned funds for effective use of sea water to not only raise bioshields but also initiate sea water farming projects involving integrated agroforestry and mariculture techniques. The MoEF support comes through the Society of Integrated Coastal Management (SICOM). Seawater constitutes nearly 97% of global water resources, and Mahatma Gandhi rightly noted that it is a very important social resource. In 1930, Gandhiji's salt march supported manufacturing salt in the Dandi beach region in violation of the existing government regulations. In the same year, C Rajagopalachari and Sardar Vedaratnam Pillai organized a salt satyagraha at Vedaranyam in Tamil Nadu. The MSSRF organized a workshop at Vedaranyam on December 26, 2010, to highlight the need for undertaking conversion of sea water into fresh water through halophytes possessing food and other economic value. The DST included the sea water farming project under its Winning, Augmentation, and Renovation (WAR) for Water mission. Steps have been initiated for establishing a genetic garden of halophytes in Vedaranyam, both to conserve the genetic resources of halophytes and spread economically attractive and environmentally sustainable sea water farming methods. With a potential rise in sea level, halophytes will become crops of the future in coastal areas.

Preserving agricultural and biodiversity heritage sites

During 2010-11, two important MSSRF initiatives achieved wider impact. First, the Tamil Nadu government established genetic heritage gardens on the basis of the description of eco-systems in the classical Sangam literature. These were set up at

Kurinji (hill)–Yercaud, Salem District;
Mullai (forest)–Sirumalai, Dindigul District;
Marudham (wetland)–Maruthanallur,
    Kumbakonam, Thanjavur District;
Neithal (coastal area)–Thirukadaiyur,
    Nagapattinam District; and
Palai (arid land)–Achadipirambu, Ramanathapuram District.

In such genetic heritage gardens, the flora and fauna characteristic of each ecosystem will be preserved to spread understanding of the value of such ecosystems. The garden in the Taramani campus of the MSSRF also contains a replica of these five ecosystems as described 2000 years ago.

The other important initiative relates to obtaining recognition for two Globally Important Agricultural Heritage Sites (GIAHS) under the FAO's GIAHS program. The project proposal seeking recognition for the Koraput rice genetic heritage site in Odisha has been prepared and forwarded to the FAO. Here, tribal families have conserved a veritable mine of valuable genes in rice for hundreds of years. Recognition under the FAO's GIAHS program will confer prestige upon those conserving vanishing varieties and dying wisdom.

Another globally important agricultural heritage site is the Kuttanad area of Kerala where, for over a century, farmers have been farming below sea level. This system, developed by farm families through practical experience, involves rice cultivation during the monsoon season and fish during the non-rainy season. Unlike in the Netherlands, the Kuttanad farmers erect only low-cost temporary dykes. The GIAHS designation for the below sea-level farming system developed by the Kuttanad farm families will provide recognition to the pioneers of this technology and refine it further. This refinement will prove particularly useful in the event of a rise in sea level resulting from global warming, which seems very likely. Establishing a Regional Training Center for Below Sea-Level Farming is proposed in Kuttanad for the benefit of countries in this region—the Maldives, Sri Lanka, Bangladesh, and Thailand—that may have to undertake farming below sea level during this century.

Land and water care: Role of the Global Soil Partnership

Since 2000, the MSSRF, with financial support from the Tata Trusts and in association with the Punjab Agricultural University, Ludhiana, and the Jawaharlal Nehru Krishi Vishwavidyalaya, Jabalpur, has been conducting detailed studies on rainwater harvesting and efficient use and watershed development and management. This project's current emphasis is on maximizing employment and income-generation opportunities for the watershed community through both on-farm and non-farm enterprises. Therefore, the program is known as "Bio-industrial Watershed" development. It promotes small-scale, market-linked, microcredit supported enterprises. Land-use decisions are also water-use decisions, and therefore, an integrated approach to land and water care is necessary to achieve an evergreen revolution leading to enhancement in perpetual productivity without associated ecological harm. Because land is a shrinking resource for agriculture, and because there is a growing tendency to "grab" prime farmland for non-farm purposes such as real estate and biofuel production, I proposed, in my capacity as Chairman of the FAO's High Level External Committee (HLEC) on the UN Millennium Development Goals, the establishment of the Global Soil Partnership (GSP) for Food Security and Climate Change Adaptation and Mitigation in October 2009. Both HLEC and the Director General of the

FAO have accepted this suggestion. The MoEF has invited the MSSRF to assist in developing strategies for sustainable food and nutrition security within the framework of a green economy. Obviously, a National Soil and Water Care program involving all stakeholders, particularly farmers' associations, must be an integral component of India's Rio +20 program.

Human resource development

The MSSRF's institution-building philosophy has always been to concentrate on brains and not bricks. The sustained growth of the MSSRF's Gyan Chaupal movement is a good example of the value of this approach. It is equally important that initiatives such as Village Knowledge Centers are based on the principle of dynamic and location-specific information delivered in the local languages, based on a demand-driven approach. Local communities should also have a sense of ownership, as otherwise it will not be sustainable. The Jamsetji Tata National Virtual Academy, which currently has nearly 1500 rural women and men as Fellows and 35 foreign Fellows, has become a valuable institutional device to build the self-esteem and capability of rural women and men belonging to socially and economically underprivileged families. In a recent review of the project, the reviewers concluded that the Academy has helped to convert ordinary people into extraordinary individuals.

Research strategies for social impact

It will be clear from the foregoing that the bottom line of the programs undertaken by the MSSRF during the last twenty years has been the well-being of rural and tribal families in an environmentally and socially sustainable manner. Unless we place faces before figures in our programs dealing with human beings, we will not know whether the steps we have taken are really beneficial to those for whose welfare they are intended. The greatest emphasis has to be placed on anticipatory research for meeting the challenges of climate change and participatory research with rural and tribal families to ensure economic, environmental, and social sustainability.

Food security in an era of climate change

On the basis of a proposal I had made three years ago, the FAO launched a Global Soil Partnership for Food Security and Climate Change Adaptation and Mitigation at a multi-stakeholder conference held in Rome from September 7–9, 2011. Despite all the advances made in capture and culture fisheries, nearly 90% of human food requirements will have to come from the soil. Land is becoming a diminishing resource for agriculture, despite the growing understanding that the future of food security will depend upon the sustainable management of land resources and the conservation of prime farm land for agriculture. The National Commission on Farmers emphasized in its report submitted in 2006 the urgent need for replacing the 1894 Land Acquisition Law with a 21st century legislation that safeguards the interests of farmers and farming. Shri Jairam Ramesh is to be complimented for introducing in Parliament a National Land Acquisition and Rehabilitation and Resettlement Bill focused on not only acquisition but also rehabilitation and resettlement of the affected families.

A High Level Panel of Experts (HLPE) set up under my chairmanship in 2010 by the UN Committee on Food Security (CFS) has recently submitted to the CFS a Report on Land Tenure and International Investments in Agriculture, which analyzes the potential impact of land acquisitions, particularly in Africa, on food security. It has been estimated that about 50–80 million hectares of farm land in developing countries has recently been the subject of negotiations by international investors; two-thirds of these farmlands in Sub-Saharan Africa are widely recognized as hotspots for endemic hunger. We found little evidence that such large-scale land acquisitions have helped to provide food and jobs to the local population. More than three-quarters of the land deals have yet to demonstrate improvements in agricultural output. The HLPE identified several steps that governments should take toward more effective and equitable land tenure systems, starting with creating more transparent systems for registering, tracking, and protecting

196

land rights, particularly those of women, tribal families, and other vulnerable groups who depend on common property resources for the security of their livelihoods. The satellite and aerial imagery used in biophysical surveys are blind to the rights and institutions that govern how land is actually used. According to the World Bank, the "land rush" is not likely to slow in the future. As a result, the landless labor population will grow, leading to greater social unrest in the rural areas of developing countries.

The loss of land for food security must be measured not only in quantitative terms but also as regards land use. According to the US Department of Agriculture, in 2011, American farmers for the first time harvested more maize for ethanol production than for food or feed. In Europe, about 50% of the rapeseed crop is likely to be used for biofuel production. The plant–animal–man food chain (particularly, beef and poultry products) will need several times more land to produce a calorie of meat compared to a calorie of cereal or vegetable.

The sudden escalation in rice and wheat prices observed in 2008 resulted largely from a steep increase in the price of fossil fuels that drove up input costs. The growing diversion of farm land for fuel production in industrialized countries; increasing consumption of meat by affluent sections of society; and loss of farm land for other uses such as roads, houses, and industries will probably cause acute food scarcity, severe price volatility, and high food inflation by the end of this decade. Several experts have noted that "the Arab Spring" had its genesis in high food inflation. That is my reason for stressing that the future belongs to nations with grains, not guns.

On the basis of widespread consultations, the FAO has recently prepared "Voluntary Guidelines on the Responsible Governance of Tenure of Land, Fisheries, and Forests in the Context of National Food Security." These voluntary guidelines will be considered at the next meeting of the CFS scheduled to be held in October 2011. Elements in these guidelines merit consideration by the Parliamentarian committee, which will explore the provisions of our National Land Acquisition

Bill. For example, one provision states, "Subject to their national law and legislations and in accordance with national context, states should expropriate only where rights to land (including associated buildings and other structures), fisheries, or forests are required for a public purpose. In no way should expropriation or forced eviction be made for private purposes." The Voluntary Guidelines also recommend that "states should ensure that women and girls have equal tenure rights and access to land, fisheries, and forests, independent of their civil or marital status." Business models should involve steps that generate employment opportunities and strengthen the livelihood security of the poor. "Food security first" should be the motto of our Land Acquisition Bill. Large-scale investment for biofuels is a risk and must be avoided, unless there are situations, as for example in Brazil, where such investments provide a win–win situation for both food and energy security. Land tenure is key to protecting land rights. Central and state governments should have accessible systems for registering, tracking, and protecting land rights, including customary rights and common property resources.

In 1981, FAO member states adopted a World Soil Charter, containing a set of principles for the optimum use of the world's land resources and improvement of their productivity and conservation for future generations. The World Soil Charter called for a commitment by governments and land users to manage the land for long-term advantage rather than short-term expediency.

International interest in the conservation and management of soil resources for food security and climate change adaptation and mitigation has grown in recent years because of increasing diversion of farmland for non-farm uses. In May 2011, a Global Soil Forum was formed at a conference held at the Institute for Advanced Sustainability Studies in Potsdam, Germany, for enhancing investment in soil resources assessment and management. The Global Soil Forum, with financial support from Germany and several other donors, will help to identify key technological options to enhance and sustain soil-based ecosystem services to safeguard long-term food security. To emphasize the need to conserve soil biodiversity, the European Union has prepared a comprehensive European Soil Biodiversity Atlas.

Over 15 years ago, the Global Water Partnership (GWP) was formed to stimulate attention and action at the national, regional, and global levels in the area of sustainable water security. The GWP was conferred the status of an international organization by the government of Sweden in 2002. India is also a partner in GWP activities. Land use decisions constitute water use decisions, and therefore, the formation of GSP to work closely with the GWP is a timely initiative. In particular, the GSP will address urgent problems such as soil degradation, conservation of soil biodiversity, gender and social equity, climate change, and soil health management for an evergreen revolution in agriculture. The GSP will provide a multi-disciplinary and multi-institutional platform for mobilizing the power of partnership in managing threats to food security arising from climate change and "land rush."

Soil anemia breeds human anemia. Deficiency of micronutrients in the soil results in micronutrient malnutrition in children, women, and men because the crops grown in such soils tend to be deficient in the nutrients needed to relieve hidden hunger. With the addition of the GSP to the already existing GWP and with the likely adoption of the Voluntary Guidelines on the Responsible Governance of Tenure of Land and Other Natural Resources, we have global instruments for assisting nations to safeguard and strengthen the ecological foundations of sustainable agriculture and overcoming endemic, hidden, and transient hunger. What is needed is the conversion of global instruments and guidelines into socially sustainable and equitable national regulations as recommended in the HLPE report on Land Tenure. The National Land Acquisition and Rehabilitation and Resettlement Bill, currently under Parliament's consideration, has a much wider significance than just preventing land grab. The critical role soil plays in food security and climate change adaptation and mitigation must be widely understood.

Along with oceans, soils offer opportunities for storing carbon. For example, it is estimated that global net primary productivity (NPP) may be about 120 Gt/c/year. Most of it is returned to the atmosphere through plant and soil respiration. If 10% of NPP can be retained in the terrestrial biosphere such as wetlands and mangrove ecosystems, 12 Gt/c/year can become a part of a terrestrial carbon bank. Increasing the soil carbon pool by 1 t/c/ha/year in the root zone can increase food production by 30–50 million tons. Thus, soil carbon banks represent a win-win situation for both food security and climate change mitigation.

Managing our soil and water resources in a sustainable and equitable manner needs a new political vision, which can be expressed through the proposed Land Acquisition Bill. The year 2012 marks the 20th anniversary of the Rio Earth Summit and the 40th anniversary of the Stockholm Conference on the Human Environment. Thus, it is an appropriate occasion to launch a Soil and Water Security Movement through education, social mobilization through Gram Sabhas, and legislation such as the Land Acquisition Bill.

Mahatma Gandhi's articulation of the role of food in a human being's life in his 1946 speech at Naokhali, now in Bangladesh, is the most powerful expression of the importance of making access to food a basic human right. Gandhiji also wanted the pathway to ending hunger to be an opportunity for everyone to earn their daily bread because the process of ending hunger should not erode human dignity. Unfortunately, this message was forgotten after the country became independent in 1947, and government departments began referring to those receiving some form of social support as "beneficiaries." The designation "beneficiary" is also applied to the women and men who toil for eight hours in sun and rain under the MGNREGA. Sixty-five years after Gandhiji's Naokhali speech, we find that India houses the world's largest number of under- and malnourished children, women, and men. There are more people going to bed partially hungry now than the entire population of India in 1947.

Recent articles by P. Sainath in The Hindu (September 26 and 27, 2011) vividly depict the extent of deprivation and destitution prevalent in rural India. Rural deprivation and agrarian distress cause the growth of urban slums and suffering. The recent submission of the Union Planning Commission to the Supreme Court on the amount needed per day per person in urban and rural India to meet his/her needs in the areas of nutrition, education, and health care (i.e., Rs. 35 per person per day in urban India and Rs. 26 in rural India) has shown how disconnected this important organization has become from the real life of the poor. This context holds at least a ray of hope in the draft National Food Security Bill of 2011 accessible on the website of the Ministry of Consumer Affairs, Food, and Public Distribution, now under the charge of the humanist, Prof. K. V. Thomas. This draft will ultimately go through a Select Committee of Parliament, and I hope that the final version designed to make access to food a legal right, rather than a mere token of political patronage, will help to erase India's current image as the land of the malnourished. The stated aim of the draft bill is "to provide for food and nutritional security, in the human life cycle approach, by ensuring access to an adequate quantity of quality food at affordable prices, for people to live a life with dignity." To achieve this goal, we must ensure that every child, woman, and man has physical, economic, and social (in terms of gender) access to a balanced diet (i.e., the necessary calories and protein), micronutrients (iron, iodine, zinc, Vitamin A, Vitamin B_{12}, etc.), and clean drinking water, as well as sanitation and primary health care.

A life-cycle approach to food security implies attention to human nutritional needs from conception to cremation. The most vulnerable but most neglected segment is the first 1000 days of a child's life, covering the period from conception through the child's first two years of life. During this period, tremendous brain development occurs. Obviously, during this period the child can be reached only through the mother. Therefore, the life-cycle approach to food security starts with pregnant women. The high incidence of children with low birth weight (i.e., less than 2.5 kg at birth) results from maternal and fetal undernutrition. Such children suffer from several disabilities in later life, including impaired cognitive ability. Denying a child even at birth an opportunity for the full expression of its innate genetic potential for physical and mental development is the cruelest form of inequity. The Integrated Child Development Service (ICDS) must be redesigned and implemented in two time frames (0–2 and 3–6 years).

From the perspective of legal rights, the draft bill addresses only the issue of economic access to food. The other two components of food security—availability of food, which is a function of production, and absorption of food in the body, which is a function of clean drinking water—sanitation, and primary health care cannot easily be made into legal entitlements. To make food for all a legal right, we must adopt a universal Public Distribution System (PDS) with common but differentiated entitlements regarding the cost and quantity of food grains. The draft bill adopts the nomenclature suggested by the NAC and divides the population into priority, that is, those who need adequate social support, and general, that is, those who can afford to pay a higher price for food grains. The initial prices proposed are Rs. 3, 2, and 1 per kg for rice, wheat, and millet, respectively, for the priority group, and 50% of the minimum support price (MSP) for the general group. In a universal PDS system, both self-selection and well-defined exclusion criteria operated by elected local bodies will help to eliminate those who are not in need of social support for their daily bread. In fact, it is the general group that should be financially supporting the provision of highly subsidized food to the economically and socially underprivileged sections of our society. For the well-to-do, the aim of the universal PDS should be to ensure physical access to food.

The widening of the food basket by including a wide range of nutri-cereals (normally called "coarse cereals") along with wheat and rice is a very important feature of the Food Security Bill. Nutri-cereals such as *bajra, ragi, jowar,* and *maize* constitute "health foods," and their inclusion in the PDS, along with wheat and rice, will stimulate increased production by farmers. Nutri-cereals are usually cultivated in rainfed areas, and they are more climate-resilient. Therefore, in an era of climate change, they will play an increasingly important role in human nutrition security. During 2010-11, our farm women and men produced 86 million tons of wheat, 95 million tons of rice, and 42 million tons of nutri-cereals (coarse cereals). The production of nutri-cereals, grown in dry farming areas, will increase if procurement and consumption rise. Thus, adding these grains will help to concurrently strengthen food grain availability and nutrition security.

The bill's other components, which do not involve legal commitments, refer to agricultural production, procurement, and safe storage of grains, clean drinking water, and sanitation. The temptation to provide cash instead of grains to the Priority Group should be avoided. The government can print currency notes; however, only farmers, who constitute nearly two-thirds of our population, can produce grains. Giving cash will reduce interest in procurement and safe storage, which in turn will affect production. The "Crop Holiday" declared by farmers in the East Godavari District of Andhra Pradesh is a wake-up call. A committee set up by the Andhra Pradesh government and chaired by Dr. Mohan Kanda has found that the following factors partially formed the basis of the decision of a large number of farm families to not grow rice this *Kharif* season. First, the MSP presently offered does not cover the cost of production; the MSP fixed by the government of India was Rs. 1080 per quintal for common varieties, whereas the cost of production was Rs. 1270 per quintal. Second, procurement is sluggish because it is largely performed by the rice mills. Third, late release of canal water, credit and other essential input unavailability, and delayed crop insurance dues settlement also affect the morale and interest of farm families. Thus, farmers are facing serious economic, ecological, and farm management difficulties. The government should seriously consider adopting as a general policy the formula suggested by the National Commission on Farmers (NCF) that MSP should be C2 plus 50% (i.e., total cost of production plus 50%).

Finally, the bill provides for establishing Food Security Commissions at the state and central levels. The two essential ingredients for successful implementation of the legal right to food are political will and farmers' skill. Therefore, it will be appropriate if the state-level Food Security Commissions are chaired by farmers with an outstanding record of successful farming. They will then help to ensure adequate food supply to feed the PDS. At the national level, the following composition proposed by the NCF in their final report submitted in October 2006 would help to ensure adequate political will and oversight. The NCF's suggestion was to set up a National Food Security and Sovereignty Board at the central level, chaired by the Prime Minister. The other members could be the concerned central government ministers, political party leaders in Parliament, several chief ministers of surplus and deficit states, and several leading farmers and experts. Unless we develop and introduce methods of ensuring effective political and farmers' participation in successfully implementing the Food Security Bill, we will be unable to overcome the problems currently faced by the PDS in certain places, arising from corruption in the distribution of entitlements.

The 2011 National Food Security Bill provides the last chance for mounting a frontal attack on poverty-induced hunger and for achieving Mahatma Gandhi's desire that the God of Bread be present in every home and hut in our country. Gandhi's message for achieving a green economy with inclusive growth is the following:

"Unsustainable lifestyles and unacceptable poverty should become problems of the past, to achieve harmony with nature and with each other."

This is the pathway to achieve the goal of the Blue Planet Prize: to keep our planet ever blue.

References

1. Swaminathan, M.S. 1990. Agriculture and food systems in Proceedings of the Second World Climate Conference, Geneva, World Meteorological Organisation.
2. National Commission on Farmers 2006. Fifth and Final Report, Vol I. Ministry of Agriculture. Government of India. New Delhi. www. kisanayog.gov.in.
3. Swaminathan, M.S. 2010. *From Green to Evergreen Revolution, Indian Agriculture: Performance and Challenges*. New Delhi, Academic Foundation. 410 pp.
4. Swaminathan, M.S. 2010. *Science and Sustainable Food Security: Selected Papers of M S Swaminathan*, IISc Press Bangalore and World Scientific Publishing Company Singapore. 420 pp.
5. Swaminathan, M.S. 2011. *Towards an Era of Biohappiness: Biodiversity and food, Health and Livelihood Security*. World Scientific, Chennai. 170 pp.
6. MSSRF Annual Report.

Agriculture and Food Security

Robert Watson

There is no doubt that the Earth's environment is changing on all scales, from local to global, resulting largely from human activities. The climate is warming at a rate faster than at any time during the last 10,000 years, biodiversity is being lost at an unprecedented rate, fisheries are in decline in most of the world's oceans, and soils and water are degrading in many parts of the world. Much of this environmental degradation is because of the unsustainable production and use of energy, water, food, and other biological resources. However, in turn, environmental degradation is undermining poverty alleviation; livelihoods of the poor; human health; and food, water, and human security.

Understanding the interconnections among these environmental and developmental issues is essential for developing and implementing informed, cost-effective, and socially acceptable policies, practices, and technologies on the local, regional, and global scales. Because these environmental and development issues are closely interlinked, we must ensure that policies and technologies addressing one issue do not affect other aspects of the environment and human well-being negatively. Cost-effective and equitable approaches to address these issues exist or can be developed but will require political will and moral leadership.

The major indirect drivers of change are primarily demographic, economic, sociopolitical, technological, and cultural. These drivers are clearly changing: the world's population and the global economy are growing, the world is becoming more interdependent, and there are major changes in information technology and biotechnology. Increases in population and wealth will create increasing demands for food, water, energy, and other biological resources.

Total food production has nearly trebled since 1960, per capita production has increased by 30%, and food prices and the percentage of undernourished people have fallen. However, the benefits have been uneven, and more than one billion people still go to bed hungry each night. Furthermore, intensive and extensive food production has caused environmental degradation.

The major challenges facing agriculture and food security, as identified by the UK Go-Science Foresight report, *The Future of Food and Farming*, include (i) balancing future demand and supply sustainably, (ii) addressing the threat of future volatility in the food system, (iii) ending hunger, (iv) meeting the challenges of a low emissions world, and (v) maintaining biodiversity and ecosystem services while feeding the world.

It is clear that to achieve food security for all in an environmentally sustainable manner will require a radical redesign of the global food system. Business-as-usual will not work, and inaction or no change is not an option. Furthermore, leaders must recognize that policies and decisions outside the food system are equally critical, such as a climate change policy.

A key issue is price volatility. Food prices have exhibited significant volatility during the last several years, with prices for some commodities doubling for periods of time. There are various reasons for these increases that are unlikely to disappear in the coming decades, possibly including (i) poor harvests because of variable weather that might be related to human-induced climate change, (ii) low food stocks, (iii) increased biofuel use, (iv) increased demand in rapidly growing economies, (v) high energy prices, increasing costs of mechanization and fertilizers, (vi) speculation on the commodity markets during periods of low stocks, and (vii) export bans by large exporting countries to protect domestic supplies.

Agriculture affects the environment; for example, tillage and irrigation methods can lead to salinization and erosion of soils; fertilizers, rice production, and livestock contribute to greenhouse gas emissions; and extensification into grasslands and forests leads to loss of biodiversity at the genetic, species, and landscape levels. One of the key challenges facing the world is to increase agricultural productivity while reducing its environmental footprint through sustainable intensification. As noted earlier, environmental degradation in turn reduces agricultural productivity.

The demand for food is likely to double in the next 25–50 years, primarily in developing countries. Furthermore, the type and nutritional quality of food demanded will change, such as an increased demand for meat. We need sustained growth in the agricultural sector to feed the world, enhance rural livelihoods, and stimulate economic growth. Yet, these new demands are arising at a time when, in addition to the aforementioned challenges, the world will have less labor as a result of disease and rural–urban migration, less water because of competition from other sectors, distorted trade policies resulting from OECD subsidies, land policy conflicts, loss of genetic, species, and ecosystem biodiversity, increasing levels of air and water pollution, and human-induced climate change.

We can feed the world today with affordable food while providing a viable income for the farmer; however, business-as-usual will not work. We can address most of today's hunger problems with the appropriate use of current technologies, particularly appropriate agro-ecological practices (e.g., no/ low till, integrated pest management, and integrated natural resource management); however, these must be coupled with decreased post-harvest losses.

Emerging issues such as climate change and new plant and animal pests may increase our future need for higher productivity and require advanced biotechnologies, including genetic modification, to address future food demands. However, leaders must fully understand the risks and benefits of these technologies on a case-by-case basis. The public and private sectors should increase their investments in research and development, extension services, and weather and market information.

Farmers must be central to all initiatives taken; local and traditional knowledge must be integrated with agricultural knowledge, science, and technology developed by universities and government laboratories. Innovation that involves all relevant stakeholders along the complete food chain is essential. Therefore, we must recognize the critical role of women and empower them through education, property rights, and financial access.

In addition, we must employ global-scale policy reforms, including eliminating both OECD production subsidies and tariff escalation on processed products, and recognizing the special needs of the least developed countries through non-reciprocal market access. Governments should pay farmers to maintain and enhance ecosystem services similar to the agri-environment schemes of the EU Common Agricultural Policy.

Current and Projected State of the Global and Regional Environment
Implications for Environmental, Economic, and Social Sustainability

Robert Watson

Most countries are attempting to achieve environmentally and socially sustainable economic growth, coupled with food, water, energy, and human security at a time of enormous global changes, including environmental degradation on the local, regional, and global scales. Key issues include climate change, loss of biodiversity and ecosystem services (provisioning, regulating, cultural, and supporting), local and regional air pollution, and land and water degradation.

There is no doubt that the Earth's environment is changing on all scales, from local to global, resulting in large measure from human activities. The stratospheric ozone layer has been depleted, the climate is warming at a rate faster than at any time during the last 10,000 years, biodiversity is being lost at an unprecedented rate, fisheries are in decline in most of the world's oceans, air pollution is an increasing problem in and around many of the major cities in the world, large numbers of people live in water-stressed or water-scarce areas, and large areas of land are being degraded. Much of this environmental degradation is because of the unsustainable production and use of energy, water, food, and other biological resources, and is already undermining efforts to alleviate poverty and stimulate sustainable development, and worse, the future projected changes in the environment are likely to have even more severe consequences.

Understanding the interconnections among these environmental issues is essential for developing and implementing
informed, cost-effective, and socially acceptable policies, practices, and technologies on the local, regional, and global scales.
Because environmental issues are closely interlinked, we must
ensure that policies and technologies addressing one environmental issue do not affect other aspects of the environment or
human well-being negatively; for example, we must identify
climate change response measures that are beneficial and do
not adversely affect biodiversity. Cost-effective and equitable
approaches to address these issues exist or can be developed;
however, they will require political will and moral leadership.
While the substantial measures needed to prevent environmental degradation from undermining growth and poverty
alleviation are not yet established, a combination of technological and behavioral changes, coupled with pricing and effective
policies (including regulatory policies), are needed to address
these global challenges at all spatial scales and across all sectors.

The major indirect drivers of change are primarily demographic, economic, socio-political, technological, cultural,
and religious. These drivers are clearly changing: the world's
population and the global economy are growing, the world is
becoming more interdependent, and major changes are occurring in information technology and biotechnology. The world's
population is likely to increase from about 7 billion people today to 9–10 billion people by 2050. This increase in population will be accompanied by an increase in GDP globally of a
factor of 3–4, with developing countries increasingly driving
global economic growth. By 2030, at least half of the purchasing power of the global economy will stem from developing
countries. Broad-based growth in developing countries sustained over the next 25 years could significantly reduce global
poverty. At the same time, we must recognize that the benefits
from growth and globalization could be undermined by failure to properly manage global environmental issues, particularly mitigating and adapting to climate change and reducing

212

the loss of biodiversity and degradation of ecosystem services.

Climate change

There is no doubt that the composition of the atmosphere and the Earth's climate have changed since the industrial revolution, predominantly resulting from human activities, and it is inevitable that these changes will continue regionally and globally. The atmospheric concentration of carbon dioxide has increased by over 30% since the pre-industrial era, primarily from the combustion of fossil fuels and deforestation. Global mean surface temperatures have already increased by about 0.85°C; an additional 0.5–1.0°C is inevitable because of past emissions; and they are projected to increase by an additional 1.2–6.4°C between 2000 and 2100, with land areas warming more than oceans and high latitudes warming more than the tropics. Precipitation is more difficult to predict, but is likely to increase at high latitudes and in the tropics and decrease significantly in the sub-tropics, with an increase in heavy precipitation events and a decrease in light precipitation events, leading to more floods and droughts.

Changes in temperature and precipitation are causing, and will continue to cause, other environmental changes, including rising sea levels; retreating mountain glaciers; melting of the Greenland ice cap; shrinking Arctic Sea ice, particularly in summer; increasing frequency of extreme weather events such as heat waves, floods, and droughts; and intensification of cyclonic events such as hurricanes in the Atlantic.

The Earth's climate, which is projected to change at a faster rate than it did during the last century, is projected to adversely affect freshwater, food and fiber, natural ecosystems, coastal systems and low-lying areas, and human health and social systems. The impacts of climate change will probably be extensive, primarily negative, and cut across many sectors. Temperature increases, which will increase the thermal growing season at temperate latitudes, including in the United States and Europe, will probably cause increased agricultural productivity for temperature changes below 2–3°C, but decrease it with larger changes. However, agricultural productivity is likely to be negatively affected by almost any changes in climate throughout the tropics and subtropics, areas with high levels of hunger and malnutrition. Water quality and availability in many arid- and semi-arid regions is likely to decrease, whereas the risk of floods and droughts in many regions of the world will increase. Vector- and water-borne diseases, heat stress mortality and extreme weather-event deaths, and threats to nutrition in developing countries are likely to increase. Millions of people could be trapped in areas of abject poverty or displaced by sea-level rise and flooding. These climate change impacts will most likely adversely affect populations in developing countries. Climate change, coupled with other stresses, can lead to local and regional conflict and migration, depending on the social, economic, and political circumstances.

The goal, agreed upon at the 2009 ministerial session of the UNFCCC in Copenhagen and endorsed in Cancun and Durban, to limit global temperature changes to 2°C above preindustrial levels is appropriate to avoid the most severe consequences of human-induced climate change; however, it must be recognized as a stretch target and, unless political will changes drastically in the near future, it will not be met. Therefore, we should be prepared to adapt to global temperature changes of 4–5°C. In addition, we must recognize that we cannot address mitigation and adaptation separately.

Mitigating climate change will require getting the price right; evolution of low-carbon technologies (production and use of energy); and behavior change by individuals, communities, and private and public sectors (see paper by Goldemberg and Lovins). In addition to transitioning to a low-carbon energy system, it is critical to reduce emissions from forests by reducing forest degradation and deforestation, sequestering carbon through reforestation, afforestation, and agroforestry, and from agricultural systems through conservation tillage, reducing emissions from the use of fertilizers, and from livestock and rice production.

In addition, to mitigating the emissions of greenhouse gases, we must adapt to climate change. However, mitigation is essential because there are physical, technological, behavioral, and financial limits to the amount of adaptation that we can achieve: there are physical limits to adaptation on small, low-lying islands, technological limits to flood defenses, behavioral limits to where people live and why, and financial limits for adaptation activities. The more we mitigate, the less we will have to adapt. Nevertheless, we know that adaptation is essential and must be mainstreamed, particularly into sectoral and national economic planning in developing countries because of their heightened vulnerability to climate change impacts.

Loss of biodiversity and degradation of ecosystem services

Throughout the world, biodiversity is being lost at the genetic, species, and landscape levels, and ecosystems and their services are being degraded because of conversion of natural habitats, over-exploitation, pollution, introduction of exotic species, and climate change, which in many instances cause tremendous harm to both people and the environment. In particular, the emphasis on provisioning services to meet the increased need for food (crops and livestock) and, to a lesser extent, fiber, water, and energy for an increasing population has resulted in a decline in biodiversity and degradation of many ecosystems. The Millennium Ecosystem Assessment reported that 15 of the 24 services evaluated were in decline, four were improving worldwide, and five were improving in some regions of the world but declining in others. The UK National Ecosystem Assessment reported that 30–35% of the ecosystem services evaluated were in decline, 20% were improving, and 45–50% were relatively stable. Although climate change has not been a major cause of biodiversity loss over the last 100 years, it is likely to be a major threat in all biomes during the next 100 years. Climate change is likely to exacerbate biodiversity loss and adversely affect most ecological systems, particularly coral reefs and mountainous and polar ecosystems, potentially resulting in significant adverse changes in ecosystem goods and services. A recent assessment estimated that every 1°C increase in global mean surface temperature up to 5°C would eventually result in a 10% loss of species.

Biodiversity is central to human well-being, providing a variety of ecosystem services on which humankind relies, including provisioning (e.g., food, freshwater, wood and fiber, and fuel), regulating (e.g., of climate, flood, and diseases), culture (e.g., esthetic, spiritual, educational, and recreational), and supporting (e.g., nutrient cycling, soil formation, and primary production). These ecosystem services, which contribute to human well-being, including our security, health, social relations, and freedom of choice and action, are declining.

The benefits that we derive from the natural world and its constituent ecosystems are critically important to human well-being and economic prosperity, but are consistently undervalued in economic analysis and decision making. Human well-being and a future thriving and sustainable green economy crucially require effective conservation and sustainable use of ecosystems. Failure to include the valuation of non-market values in decision making produces less efficient resource allocation; however, a major challenge is to develop systems to appropriate the values of non-market ecosystem services for land managers.

Therefore, addressing the issue of biodiversity and ecosystem services requires changing the economic background of decision making. Leaders must (i) ensure that the value of all ecosystem services, not only those bought and sold in the market, are taken into account when making decisions; (ii) remove subsidies to agriculture, fisheries, and energy that harm people and the environment; (iii) introduce payments to landowners in return for managing their lands in ways that protect ecosystem services, such as water quality and carbon storage, that are of value to society; and (iv) establish market mechanisms to reduce nutrient releases and carbon emissions in the most cost-effective manner.

Furthermore, leaders must improve policy, planning, and management by integrating decision making between different departments and sectors and international institutions to ensure that policies focus on the protection and sustainable use of ecosystems. This approach will require (i) empowering marginalized groups to influence decisions affecting ecosystem services and recognizing in law the local communities' ownership of natural resources; (ii) restoring degraded ecosystems and establishing additional protected areas, particularly in marine systems, and providing greater financial and management support to those that already exist; and (iii) using all relevant forms of knowledge and information about ecosystems in decision making, including the knowledge of local and indigenous groups.

In addition, success will require influencing individual and community behavior. Thus, leaders must provide broad access to information about ecosystems and decisions affecting their services, provide public education on why and how to reduce consumption of threatened ecosystem services, and establish reliable certification systems to give people the choice to buy clearly labeled sustainably harvested products. We must also develop and use environment-friendly technologies, thus requiring investments in agricultural science and technology for the purpose of increasing food production with minimal harmful trade-offs.

Innovation and Grassroots Action

Bunker Roy

**"The Earth has enough for every man's need
but not for one man's greed." - Gandhi**

At the outset, it must be said that since Rio 1992, community-based groups in the poorer, most inaccessible rural areas around the world have demonstrated the power of grassroots action to change policy at regional and national levels. In consultation with communities, innovative methods and approaches have been implemented and indeed been scaled up to cover thousands of communities living on less than $1/day.

Unfortunately, though, they have not been collectively visible enough to catch the attention of the policymakers and power brokers who formulate crucial and serious global policies without engaging with them at the cutting-edge levels.

Fully acknowledging the tremendous contribution of such grassroots action and showing them the respect and recognition they deserve, we must now urgently bring them into mainstream thinking and convey the belief all is not lost, and that the planet can still be saved, thus exposing the doom and gloom skeptics.

New ideas have been implemented as a result of collective grassroots actions that have lessons we can learn from only if we have the humility and ability to listen. Broadly speaking, several of the lessons learned can be summarized as follows:

1. There is no urban solution to a fundamentally rural poverty problem. The simple solutions by which the rural poor have tackled the issues of climate change already

exist; however, we have yet to implement a mechanism to learn from them. There are best practices with the potential to scale up that must be highlighted.

2. The answer to addressing the critical issues of poverty and climate change is NOT technical but social. The problems of corruption, funds wastage, poor technological choices, and lack of transparency or accountability are social problems for which innovative solutions are emerging from the grassroots. For instance, the idea and practice of public hearings and social audits came from people who were fed up with government inaction in India. The processes have now been institutionalized and benefit nearly 600,000 villages in India.

3. Grassroots groups have found the value and relevance of a south–south partnership that uses and applies traditional knowledge, village skills, and practical wisdom between communities and across continents, producing low-cost community-based solutions that have had a tremendous impact on improving the quality of life. Migration from rural to urban areas has decreased. Dependency on urban and technology skills has decreased.

4. The empowerment of women is the ultimate sustainable rural solution. By improving their capacity and competence to provide basic services in the rural areas (for instance, training them to be solar engineers), they could become the new role models that the world seeks.

5. The long term answer is NOT a centralized system but a demystified and decentralized system, where the management, control, and ownership of technology lies in the hands of the communities themselves and is not dependent on formally qualified professionals from outside the villages.

6. Listen and learn how poor communities around the world see the problems of energy, water, food, and livelihoods as interdependent and integrated as part of a living ecosystem and not separately.

Without using the written or spoken word and through sign language alone, 604 illiterate rural grandmothers aged 35–50 have been trained as solar engineers and in six months have solar electrified over 45,000 houses, reaching more than 1,083 villages in 63 countries across the world at a total cost of $5 million—the cost of 2 Millennium Villages in Africa.

If a grandmother is selected from any part of the developing world, India's government pays the airfare and six months' training costs in India. The funds for the hardware have been provided by the GEF Small Grants Program, UNWOMEN, UNESCO, the Skoll Foundation, and individual philanthropists.

The traditional practice of collecting rainwater for drinking and irrigation needs to be revived. It has been used, tested, and proved over hundreds of years. However, ever since formally qualified engineers arrived on the scene, this practice has been devalued, and the technological solution of exploiting (and thus, abusing) groundwater through powerful, polluting drilling rigs for installing deep-well pumps has seriously depleted groundwater. Thousands of open wells for irrigation and hand pumps for drinking water have gone dry.

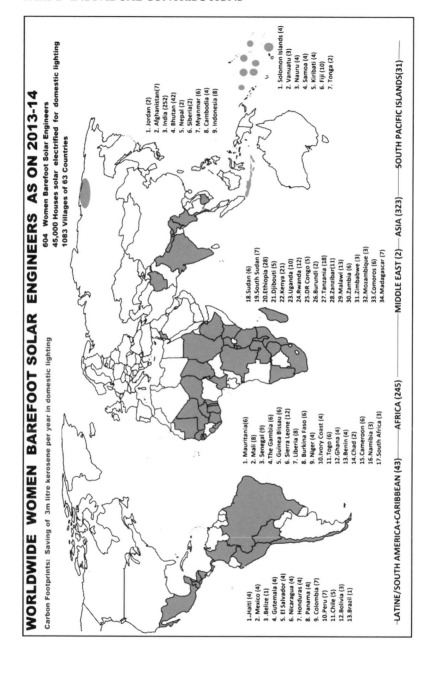

WORLDWIDE WOMEN BAREFOOT SOLAR ENGINEERS AS ON 2013-14

Carbon Footprints: Saving of 3m litre kerosene per year in domestic lighting

604 Women Barefoot Solar Engineers
45,000 Houses solar electrified for domestic lighting
1083 Villages of 63 Countries

ASIA (323)
1. Jordan (2)
2. Afghanistan(7)
3. India (252)
4. Bhutan (42)
5. Nepal (2)
6. Siberia(2)
7. Myanmar (6)
8. Cambodia (4)
9. Indonesia (8)

SOUTH PACIFIC ISLANDS(31)
1. Solomon Islands (4)
2. Vanuatu (3)
3. Nauru (4)
4. Samoa (4)
5. Kiribati (4)
6. Fiji (10)
7. Tonga (2)

AFRICA (245)
1. Mauritania(6)
2. Mali (8)
3. Senegal (9)
4. The Gambia (6)
5. Guinea Bissau (6)
6. Sierra Leone (12)
7. Liberia (8)
8. Burkina Faso (6)
9. Niger (4)
10. Ivory Coast (4)
11. Togo (6)
12. Ghana (4)
13. Benin (4)
14. Chad (2)
15. Cameroon (6)
16. Namibia (3)
17. South Africa (3)
18. Sudan (6)
19. South Sudan (7)
20. Ethiopia (28)
21. Djibouti (5)
22. Kenya (21)
23. Uganda (10)
24. Rwanda (12)
25. DR Congo (5)
26. Burundi (2)
27. Tanzania (18)
28. Zanzibari(11)
29. Malawi (13)
30. Zambia (6)
31. Zimbabwe (3)
32. Mozambique (3)
33. Comoros (6)
34. Madagascar (7)

MIDDLE EAST (2)

LATINE/SOUTH AMERICA+CARIBBEAN (43)
1. Haiti (4)
2. Mexico (4)
3. Belize (1)
4. Gutemala (4)
5. El Salvador (4)
6. Nicaragua (4)
7. Honduras (4)
8. Panama (4)
9. Colombia (7)
10. Peru (7)
11. Chile (5)
12. Bolivia (3)
13. Brazil (1)

222

To combat this problem, water must be collected from the roofs of public buildings (schools, dispensaries, etc.) into underground tanks for drinking and sanitation purposes.

Small dams must be constructed to support ground water recharge, thus revitalizing the dry open wells and hand pumps, reclaiming collective assets worth millions of dollars.

In over 1,500 rural primary schools nearly 500,000 children are benefiting from the rain water collected covering 40 districts in 17 States of India. Nearly 10 billion litres of rain water have been collected in small dams and the roofs of schools.

We need simple practical solutions multiplied over a large scale around the world, costing little money but having tremendous long-term impact.

Adapting to Climate Change

Saleemul Huq

Climate change impacts have begun, and further impacts are inevitable. While some of the impacts in certain parts of the world may have short-term benefits, most of the impacts, particularly in poorer countries in Asia, Africa, and Latin America, will damage poor countries and communities.

All countries, both developed and developing, must adapt to the impacts of climate change over the next few decades. However, there are limits to how effectively they can adapt. Adaptation becomes more difficult if temperatures rise more than 2°C, which is of significant concern because the world is on a pathway to becoming 3–5°C warmer than its pre-industrial temperature.

The good news is that many countries, starting with the least developed, have already begun taking steps to plan climate change adaptation and attempt to mainstream these steps into development planning, such as Bangladesh, which has developed and begun implementing a long-term Climate Change Strategy and Action Plan.

All countries, both rich and poor, must develop their own national adaptation plans. Although many adaptation actions will be country- and location-specific, opportunities exist for learning lessons across countries, south–south and south–north.

The most effective adaptation strategy is mitigation to limit the magnitude of climate change, particularly given the significant physical, financial, technological, and behavioral limits to adaptation.

Adaptation is essential

For the next two, or even three, decades, the amount of warming of nearly 1°C attributable to human-induced climate change is now inevitable because of past greenhouse gas emissions and the time lags in the atmospheric system. This warming is now unavoidable, and no amount of greenhouse gas mitigation will prevent it. Therefore, the world can expect certain climate change impacts, and all countries must deal with them. Although certain parts of the world may experience some beneficial impacts, most of them will be adverse and will fall disproportionately on poorer countries and communities.

Therefore, climate change adaptation must be a part of all national development plans of both developing and developed countries, as well as at the global level. As the poorer countries already have difficulty coping with the current climate impacts, they will need financial and technical assistance to adapt to the additional burden of climate change impacts.

While most of the adaptation actions will be at the local and national levels, there are few that transcend national boundaries and require global solutions. These include transboundary water systems that may dry up and transboundary population migration beyond their national borders because of environmental degradation in their current locations.

Limits to adaptation

While adaptation to climate change is now unavoidable, its attainable results are limited. Unlike mitigation, which avoids climate change (a ton of greenhouse gas not emitted means zero impact), adaptation does not entirely eliminate them, although it can reduce the amount of impact. Mere adaptation always leaves residual impacts.

Furthermore, as the temperature rises more than 2°C, by 3–4°C, the residual impacts will increase. Thus, adaptation at higher temperatures has only limited effectiveness. Therefore, mitigation remains the best form of adaptation and must remain the first strategy for tackling climate change.

226

This approach is significant as the current emission trajectory will lead to a 3.5–4°C increase in global temperatures.

Least developed countries taking the lead

The good news is that many countries have already taken significant steps to start planning and implementing climate change adaptation. The first countries to have implemented a National Adaptation Program of Action (NAPA) have been the 48 least developed countries (LDCs). These exercises identified the vulnerable sectors and communities and prioritized urgent and immediate adaptation actions. Many LDCs have implemented many of the adaptation actions.

Several LDCs have gone beyond the NAPAs and developed longer-term strategic climate change plans. One such country is Bangladesh, which was one of the first LDCs to develop such plans that its government is now implementing with a Climate Change Trust Fund of US$300 million of its own money.

Another example is Nepal, which was one of the last LDCs to finish its NAPA, benefitting from other LDCs' experiences, and which developed an adaptation plan that allocated 80% of all climate change resources to the most vulnerable communities for independent use through the development of Local Adaptation Plans of Action (LAPAs).

International cooperation on adaptation

Although most of the adaptation plans and actions will remain location- and country-specific, many lessons can be shared across countries. One of the first lessons about adaptation planning resulting from nearly 50 LDCs' NAPAs is that adaptation is less about technical interventions and much more about societal and institutional capacities to deal with a changing environment. These institutional issues are similar in all countries, regardless of level of development; therefore, even rich countries can apply the lessons learned from the poorest countries.

Thus, when it comes to climate change adaptation, international cooperation and lesson sharing across countries will probably be south–south and south–north.

227

Focus on the most vulnerable countries and communities

While the impacts of climate change will affect all countries eventually, those affected first are the poorest countries and communities. Therefore, financial and technical assistance from the global level must focus on assisting the efforts of the poorest countries and communities.

This initiative requires working with those communities and enhancing their adaptive capacities, as well as empowering them to adapt independently. This approach means supporting the growing numbers of communities around the world who are already practicing community-based adaptation to climate change.

Conclusion

In the end, the most effective adaptation strategy is mitigation to limit the magnitude of climate change, particularly given adaptation's significant physical, financial, technological, and behavioral limits.

The Importance of Good Governance

Camilla Toulmin

There are serious shortcomings in the decision-making systems on which we rely in government, business, and society overall. Building more effective governance and institutions is central to achieving more sustainable patterns of development—globally, nationally, and locally. Yet, the central importance of governance issues is often neglected, partly because of the differing definitions of "governance" and the intangibility of these norms and structures. An analysis of governance needs to ask, "How, where, and by whom are decisions made?"; "Who gets to write the rules by which decisions are made?"; "What gets decided, and who gains what?"; and "How can people monitor the decision-making process?" Governance is more than just a question of institutional architecture and how elements relate to each other. Each of these elements presents issues of credibility and legitimacy concerning the processes by which rules are made and remade, interpreted and reinterpreted.

The rules and institutions for decision making are influenced by vested interests, each with very different levels of influence on the process. For example, lobbyists spend a large amount of time and money trying to influence the way elected representatives vote in many legislatures. We must also see governance as a dynamic phenomenon, an ongoing process of negotiation between interests, played out in a series of arenas and institutions, nationally and globally. The legitimacy of technical evidence marshaled within such negotiations is critical and often contested, as has been evident from the climate change talks.

Governance involves much more than the ensemble of

government frameworks and includes multiple and overlapping governance systems, with the private sector, civil society, sub-national, and local levels engaged in making decisions in relation to their interests. A widespread assumption exists that governments are the central actors in governance; however, a deeper investigation reveals that government is often an instrument of its own and others' interests, rather than playing the role of an objective arbiter. The existence of plural and overlapping systems of governance can lead to competition between rival structures and institutional "shopping."

Transformation of governance systems must accommodate a far broader range of interests (poor and rich, young and old, future and present) and ensure access to information regarding the likely impacts of different tactics. Subsidiarity, control at the lowest possible level, should be a central principle for sustainable development governance to assure that decisions about resource allocation and use are made at the appropriate level by the appropriate authority for the resource in question. Shifting power to lower levels is vital to bring in local knowledge, increase accessibility to decision making, and ensure a broader range of voices in the debate. Innovations must ensure that the marginalized have a voice that counts through, for example, coalition building, organization, and mobilization for those voices' more effective influence. Public hearings, social audits, and participatory budgeting can bring the voices of marginalized groups to the fore.

At the national level, effective changes in governance require a transparent means for people to hold those in power to account. Parliamentary and press oversight are key alongside freedom of information; however, in many countries, these mechanisms remain weak. The accountability challenge is compounded by alliances cemented between government officials and powerful individuals and corporations. The international nature of much of the corporate sector involved in natural resource use means that even the governments of the countries in which they are headquartered have limited influence on their actions and decisions.

Globally, we urgently need better means to agree upon and implement measures to achieve our collective goals. Given the large numbers of states and their separate jurisdictions, we need more effective and far-reaching international institutions and rules; yet, nation-states are unwilling to submit to collective agreements that constrain their freedom of maneuver. Equally, greater control over international financial and corporate actors is needed to reduce their ability to escape fiscal and other responsibilities through freedom of movement between jurisdictions. Global efforts to address climate change have resulted in a complex international governance architecture, which has largely replicated geopolitical and global economic power relations among nations. These evolving governance arrangements allow little room for the priorities of weaker countries and marginalized people to be heard and addressed. Growing reliance on the G20 as a forum for sorting out global problems risks disempowering the large number of smaller, less economically prominent nations.

Development policymakers and practitioners are increasingly turning to markets as a tool for addressing sustainability and alleviating poverty. Yet, market governance also presents major challenges. Markets and business have the potential to generate new and decent jobs and use natural assets more sustainably. However, market signals and incentives must be established in ways that mobilize businesses and others to support sustainable growth, create the "missing markets" for environmental goods and services, and ensure more equitable participation. In addition, they need government to ensure the institutional and regulatory infrastructure that allows markets to operate effectively, such as support of property rights. A second worry concerns the lack of accountability of market chains and transnational operations that can evade national laws and regulatory frameworks. A third relates to finding the incentives for environmentally sustainable practices that pertain to the mainstream, as opposed to 'niche' sustainable businesses.

Governance failures also occur because decisions are being made in sectoral compartments, with environmental, social, and economic dimensions being addressed by separate competing structures. At government level, this means moving sustainable development concerns from beyond the environment ministries to focus on finance, planning, health, and education ministries as entry points. Cross-ministerial buy-in demands that sustainability be led by the head of government, and that environmental and social valuations are brought into decision making. In business, environment and social issues must move from CSR departments into core business operations, with companies required to report in terms of the triple bottom line. In society, more generally, groups such as NGOs must work together to bridge divides and recognize not only common interests but also trade-offs between different objectives.

Biodiversity
Conserving the Foundation of Sustainable Development

Will R. Turner,[1]* Russell A. Mittermeier,[1]
Julia Marton-Lefèvre,[2] Simon N. Stuart,[2]
Jane Smart,[2] Josephine M. Langley,[2]
Frank W. Larsen,[1] and Elizabeth R. Selig[1]

Biodiversity – the variety of species, genes, ecosystems, and ecological processes that make up life on Earth – is integral to the fabric of all the world's cultures. Biodiversity underpins ecosystem services, sustains humanity, and is foundational to the resilience of life on Earth. In addition, it is the source of benefits, often immeasurable, that sustain human lives, livelihoods, communities, and economies. The economic value of biodiversity is enormous. Yet, we are at risk of losing much of biodiversity and the benefits it provides humanity. As humankind's footprint has swelled, unsustainable use of land, ocean, and freshwater resources has produced extraordinary global changes, from habitat loss and invasive species to anthropogenic climate change. Threats to terrestrial and aquatic biodiversity are diverse, persistent, and in some cases, increasing. Action is critical; without it, current high rates of species loss are projected to continue what is becoming the sixth mass extinction event in Earth's history, while current losses in two-thirds of ecosystem services will soon amount to an estimated $500 billion annually in lost benefits. Fortunately, however, action is also possible: biodiversity losses can be stopped and

[1] Conservation International, 500 Crystal Drive Ste 500, Arlington, VA 22202, USA
[2] International Union for Conservation of Nature (IUCN), 28 rue Mauverney, CH-1196 Gland, Switzerland
* Address correspondence to w.turner@conservation.org.

reversed by concerted planning on the basis of adequate data, a well-managed protected areas network, and transformational shifts in the public and private sectors that value the role of natural capital in economic development.

Introduction. *Biodiversity, the variability among living organisms and ecosystems, is foundational to the resilience of life on Earth.*

Biodiversity, or biological diversity, is defined by the Convention on Biological Diversity (CBD) as "the variability among living organisms," including "diversity within species, between species and of ecosystems."[3] Biodiversity often serves as a measure of the health of biological systems. Ecosystems are distinguished from each other by the composition and interactions of species within and between these systems. A healthy population of organisms, community of species, or ecosystems can recover from disturbance and threat, if provided with sufficient opportunity for feeding, growth, and reproduction. Loss of species, declining populations or size of organisms, and changing dynamics between species can represent the system's reduced health. Within species, genetic diversity influences the ability to respond to threats, adapt to a changing environment, and evolve in the face of long-term changes.

Benefits of biodiversity. *Biodiversity underpins ecosystem services and sustains humanity; its economic value is enormous; biodiversity is the most fundamental element of green economic development.*

Biodiversity is the source of the benefits, or ecosystem services that humans receive from nature. Thus, it is a fundamental component of natural capital that, along with produced and human capital, underpins human communities and economies. For example, fish are among the most important food sources (FAO Fisheries and Aquaculture Department 2010), and the fishing industry contributes US $225–240 billion/year

---

[3] http://www.cbd.int/doc/legal/cbd-en.pdf

234

to the global economy (Dyck & Sumaila 2010). Plant pollination by insect, bird, and other animal pollinators is essential for about one in three food crops worldwide (Daily & Ellison 2002). Species are a storehouse of genetic material that has provided more than half of all commercial medicines – even more in developing nations (Chivian & Bernstein 2008) – and may harbor undiscovered cures for cancer, malaria, or the next emerging infectious disease. Natural patterns and processes inspire a vast array of novel materials, energy sources, technological devices, and other innovations (Benyus 2009). Biodiversity loss has been compared to burning down all the world's libraries without knowing the content of 90% of the books. As species vanish, so do the sources of our crops and the genes we use to improve agricultural resilience, the inspiration for products, and the structure and function of the ecosystems that support human communities and all life on Earth (McNeely et al. 2009). Beyond material goods and livelihoods, biodiversity contributes to security, resilience, and freedom of choices and actions (Millennium Ecosystem Assessment 2005). Species extinctions inflict cultural, spiritual, and moral costs – perhaps less tangible, but no less important than direct economic costs. All societies value plants and animals for their own sake, and wild species are integral to the fabric of all of the world's cultures (Wilson 1984).

Threats. *Biodiversity is being lost at alarming rates; threats to terrestrial and aquatic biodiversity are diverse, persistent, and, in some cases, increasing.*

Earth's species and the benefits they provide humanity are in trouble. As human populations have increased from a few hundred million 1000 years ago to seven billion in 2011, unsustainable consumption in developed nations and dire poverty in developing countries are together destroying the natural world. Agricultural expansion, urbanization, and industrial development have spread significantly through wild lands; overexploitation threatens the viability of populations; invasive species degrade and alter the structure of ecosystems; chemical pollution impairs biochemical processes in the soil, air, and water; and rapidly spreading diseases put entire branches of the tree of life at risk (Millennium Ecosystem Assessment 2005; Vitousek et al. 1997; Wake & Vredenburg 2008). The higher density of people in some areas puts particular strain on ecosystems to provide food and fuel, and to clean the water, break down the waste, and control the spread of disease.

Extinction, irreversible, may be the gravest consequence of the biodiversity crisis. Human activities have elevated the rate of species extinction to a thousand or more times the background rate (Pimm et al. 1995). Habitat destruction, which even in an era of climate change may remain the dominant threat to biodiversity (Sala et al. 2000), is driving extinctions around the world (Brooks et al. 2002). Growing impacts of climate change will be felt worldwide as modified precipitation and temperature, rising oceans, and climate-driven habitat loss threaten a substantial fraction of species with extinction (Thomas et al. 2004) and drive desperate human populations to additional environmental degradation (Turner et al. 2010). Other threats, even if less widespread, are felt severely in particular regions. Introduced predators have devastated island biodiversity, where species evolved in the absence of domestic cats, rats, and other invasive predators (Steadman 1995). Introduced plants are having massive impacts on hydrology and biodiversity in many ecosystems, particularly those with Mediterranean vegetation (Groves & di Castri 1991). Exploitation for macro- and micronutrients (e.g., bush meat) for medicine and pet trade threatens species in several regions, particularly Sub-Saharan Africa and Southeast Asia (van Dijk et al. 2000). Chitridiomycosis, a fungal disease, is recognized as a dominant driver of amphibian decline and extinction worldwide (Stuart et al. 2004; Wake & Vredenburg 2008).

Multiple indications of continuing decline in biodiversity exist in all three of its components—ecosystems, species, and genes. The Millennium Ecosystem Assessment (2005) concluded that 60% of ecosystem services worldwide have become

236

degraded in the past 50 years, primarily from unsustainable use of land, freshwater, and ocean resources. Most major habitats have declined in this period, and at the species level, the IUCN Red List of Threatened Species (IUCN 2008) states that 22% of the world's mammals are threatened and at risk of extinction worldwide, as well as nearly one-third of amphibians, one in eight birds, and 28% of conifers.

Marine ecosystems and species have experienced substantial declines in the last several decades as well (Butchart et al. 2010), with populations of exploited marine species declining an average 84% in abundance (Lotze & Worm 2009). Globally, 35% of mangrove area (Valiela et al. 2001) and 15% of seagrass area have been lost (Waycott et al. 2009), and an estimated 32% of coral species are threatened (Carpenter et al. 2008). The loss of foundation species or top-level predators can cause shifts from highly productive ecosystems to less complex ones with reduced ecosystem services (Estes et al. 2011; Springer et al. 2003). Human activities now threaten every part of the oceans, with 41% of the ocean strongly affected by multiple human activities (Halpern et al. 2008). Currently, climate-related threats have the highest cumulative impact on marine ecosystems (Halpern et al. 2008), with increased ocean temperatures, ocean acidification, sea-level rise, increased ultraviolet radiation, and increased storm frequency and intensity (Harley et al. 2006; IPCC 2007) producing shifts in species' ranges, ocean productivity, species composition, and population dynamics (Hoegh-Guldberg & Bruno 2010). Open ocean and coastal regions are also highly affected by fishing as vast new areas of the ocean have been opened to commercial fishing (Swartz et al. 2010), and technology has facilitated an unprecedented level of exploitation, leading to collapse of several major fisheries (Myers & Worm 2003). Land-based activities can cause direct habitat destruction and result in run-off of sediments and nutrients in sensitive coastal habitats (Mcculloch et al. 2003). Population density and growth are very high in coastal regions around the world, with roughly half of all humans living within 200 km of the coast, with the result that the most highly affected marine regions in the world are in coastal areas because they experience the full set of coastal and open ocean threats (Halpern et al. 2008). Although some large areas of the ocean remain comparatively unaffected, particularly near the poles, even these areas will probably be at risk in the future if climate change continues at current rates, and illegal, unregulated, and unreported fishing in these areas remains relatively uncontrolled.

Responses. *Stopping biodiversity loss depends critically on sufficient data, effective planning, a well-managed protected areas network, and transformational shifts in the public and private sectors to green economic development. The CBD is our international umbrella for biodiversity, and its 2020 Aichi targets—particularly targets 11 and 12—are critical.*

To end global biodiversity loss, we must channel limited available resources to conservation and green economic development in those regions that need it most. Biodiversity is not evenly distributed on our planet. It is heavily concentrated in certain areas with exceptionally high concentrations of endemic species found nowhere else, and many (but not all) of these areas are those at the greatest risk of disappearing because of heavy human impact. For example, the biodiversity hotspots are a set of 35 regions of high endemism that collectively has lost more than 85% of its original habitat size (Mittermeier et al. 2011; Myers 1988; Myers et al. 2000). Although their combined remnant natural vegetation comprises a scant 2.3% of the world's land area (3.4 million km^2), these regions harbor more than 50% of all plant species and 43% of all terrestrial vertebrates as endemics. Considering threatened species only— those assessed as critically endangered, endangered, or vulnerable on the IUCN Red List of Threatened Species (IUCN 2008)—60% of threatened mammals, 63% of threatened birds, and 79% of threatened amphibians are found exclusively within the hotspots. These regions harbor an irreplaceable concentration of biodiversity in a very small and highly threatened portion of our planet. While conservation in these areas is more difficult because of ongoing threats, scarce information, and limited local financial capacity, action in these places is required. Indeed, failure in the hotspots will translate to loss of nearly half of all terrestrial species even if we are successful everywhere else, not to mention an almost unthinkably large contribution to greenhouse gas emissions and extensive human suffering resulting from the loss of ecosystem services upon which the human populations of the hotspots ultimately depend. A few highly diverse regions remain largely intact, including the high-biodiversity wilderness areas of Amazonia, Congo, and the island New Guinea (Mittermeier et al. 2003). Furthermore, some 18 "megadiversity" countries (Mittermeier et al. 1997) account for more than two-thirds of all biodiversity–terrestrial, freshwater, and marine–a concept that led to the creation of the Like-Minded Group of Megadiverse Countries in the CBD.

Understanding the natural and human dimensions of biodiversity conservation requires good data. The Global Mammal Assessment (Schipper et al. 2008) and related efforts provide updated data on the status and distribution of species, while population, poverty, and other data sets provide important socioeconomic context. Successful conservation requires accurate, timely data on biodiversity, threats, and benefits to humanity at finer scales. Data on marine regions remains sparse compared to information on terrestrial systems (Sala & Knowlton 2006), and our lack of knowledge about freshwater systems is even more pronounced. However, research is making substantial strides on knowledge of aquatic biodiversity through, for example, efforts such as the Global Freshwater Biodiversity Assessment (Darwall et al. 2005) and the Global Marine Species Assessment, which includes comprehensive status assessments conducted for reef-forming corals (Carpenter et al. 2008), and similar work underway for thousands of other species.

The establishment and effective management of a comprehensive set of protected areas (Bruner et al. 2001) must continue to be the cornerstone of efforts to halt the loss of biodiversity. These areas may be in the form of national parks or strict biological reserves, or may come in a variety of other forms, depending on local context, including indigenous reserves, private protected areas, and community conservation agreements. Efforts must focus on ensuring long-term persistence and equitable management of the areas already protected and strategically add new protected areas in the highest priority intact, unprotected habitats as indicated by systematic efforts to identify gaps in protected areas networks (e.g., Rodrigues et al. 2004).

Maintaining the resilience of biodiversity in the face of climate change is another major challenge for planning and policy. Changing precipitation and temperature have begun forcing species to follow their preferred environmental conditions; yet, these movements will often be both difficult for species to make and complex for researchers to predict (Loarie et al. 2009; Tewksbury et al. 2008), and further climate change will likely produce a complex mosaic of climates shifted in space, climates that disappear, and entirely novel climates (Williams et al. 2007). Thus, to be successful, conservation planning must begin to systematically plan actions in both space and time. Protecting the sites where species currently exist is essential, particularly sites where species are at greatest current risk, including key biodiversity areas (Eken et al. 2004) and Alliance for Zero Extinction sites–locations harboring the sole remaining populations of the most threatened species (Ricketts et al. 2005). If we lose these sites now, we will not have another chance to save the species they contain. However, this is only the beginning. We must also protect habitats where species will exist in the future and "stepping stones" to facilitate movement to these new ranges. Biologists are increasing their ability to anticipate and plan for these needs (Hannah et al. 2007). To be successful, conservation in a changing climate will require a very strong focus on ending further habitat destruction as quickly as possible.

In 2002, world leaders committed through the CBD "to achieve by 2010 a significant reduction of the current rate of biodiversity loss..." (Balmford & Bond 2005). Results fell short of this target; most indicators of the state of biodiversity (e.g., population trends and extinction risk) declined, with no significant recent reductions in rate, whereas indicators of pressures on biodiversity (e.g., resource consumption, invasive alien species, and climate change impacts) increased (Butchart et al. 2010; CBD 2010b). In October 2010, world leaders met in Nagoya, Japan at the CBD Conference of the Parties (COP10) and adopted a strategic plan for biodiversity and 20 biodiversity targets – the so-called Aichi Biodiversity Targets – for 2011–2020. The Aichi targets (CBD 2010a) now articulate much of the action required to secure the planet's life-support systems. In the Aichi targets, countries settled on a target for the global coverage of protected areas, comprising 17% of land and 10% of oceans by 2020. Currently, the global network of protected areas (PAs) covers 12.9% of Earth's land surface (IUCN & UNEP-WCMC 2010) and only about 1.17% of the total ocean area (CBD 2010b). Thus, fulfillment of this global land target would expand the global coverage of PAs by about 4% by 2020, and the agreed target represents more than a tenfold increase over the currently protected ocean area. CBD parties, and indeed the world, together must maintain the sense of urgency and level of ambition toward achieving the targets to ensure the necessary change in our investment and action.

Nevertheless, the agreement on the CBD policy target of global coverage of 17% of land as PAs by 2020 is based on perceptions of political feasibility rather than science-based understanding of PA needs to sustain planetary health. The question of how much nature needs to be protected to prevent biodiversity loss and ensure important ecosystem services is critical and presents many challenges. First, little is known about Earth's biodiversity: only 2.5% of known species have been assessed for their conservation status (Stuart et al. 2010), and only a small fraction of the estimated total number of species have been described by science. Second, the understanding of ecosystem services remains poor for a range of important issues such as the ecological underpinnings of ecosystem services (Kremen & Ostfeld 2005). Finally, we face limited understanding of tipping

241

points in ecological systems and cannot yet predict the potential threshold effects of climate change and other anthropogenic pressures on biodiversity and ecosystem services.

The Intergovernmental Science-Policy Platform on Biodiversity and Ecosystem Services (IPBES, www.ipbes.net), modeled after the influential IPCC for climate change, is in the process of being established. IPBES will provide an interface between the scientific community and policymakers and will conduct regular and timely assessments of knowledge on biodiversity and ecosystem services and their interconnections (Perrings et al. 2011). IPBES must catalyze the effort to set science-driven targets for protecting biodiversity and ecosystem services and create the necessary understanding of societal dependence on natural ecosystems among decision makers.

The Millennium Development Goals (MDGs) constitute a set of goals and targets for 2015, designed to inspire efforts to improve people's lives, that is, halving extreme poverty.[4] The people for whom the benefits from protecting biodiversity matter most are the world's poor, who depend disproportionately on nature for critical services such as clean water, livelihoods, and insurance against hard times, making biodiversity conservation and development two intertwined challenges (Sachs et al. 2009; TEEB 2009; Turner et al. 2012). Therefore, leaders must integrate the development and environmental sustainability agenda to address these two linked issues in a meaningful manner. The upcoming UN Conference on Sustainable Development in 2012 (Rio+20) will provide an opportunity for the international community to address this challenge.

References

1. Balmford, A., and W. Bond. 2005. Trends in the state of nature and their implications for human well-being. *Ecology Letters* 8:1218–1234.
2. Benyus, J. 2009. Borrowing nature's blueprints: Biomimicry in J. A. McNeely, R. A. Mittermeier, T. M. Brooks, F. Boltz, and N. Ash, editors.

[4] www.un.org/millenniumgoa

The Wealth of Nature: Ecosystem Services, Biodiversity, and Human Well-Being. CEMEX, Mexico City.

3. Brooks, T. M., R. A. Mittermeier, C. G. Mittermeier, G. A. B. da Fonseca, A. B. Rylands, W. R. Konstant, P. Flick, J. D. Pilgrim, S. Oldfield, G. Magin, and C. Hilton-Taylor. 2002. Habitat loss and extinction in the hotspots of biodiversity. *Conservation Biology* 16:909–923.

4. Bruner, A. G., R. E. Gullison, R. E. Rice, and G. A. B. da Fonseca. 2001. Effectiveness of parks in protecting biological diversity. *Science* 291:125–128.

5. Butchart, S. H. M., M. Walpole, B. Collen, et al. 2010. Global biodiversity: Indicators of recent declines. *Science* 328:1164–1168.

6. Carpenter, K. E., M. Abrar, G. Aeby, et al. 2008. One-third of reef-building corals face elevated extinction risk from climate change and local impacts. *Science* 321:560–563.

7. CBD 2010a. Decision X/2. The Strategic Plan for Biodiversity 2011-2020 and the Aichi Biodiversity Targets. Convention on Biological Diversity, Montreal.

8. CBD 2010b. Global Biodiversity Outlook 3. Convention on Biological Diversity, Montreal.

9. Chivian, E., and A. Bernstein, editors. 2008. *Sustaining Life: How Human Health Depends on Biodiversity*. Oxford University Press, New York.

10. Daily, G. C., and K. Ellison 2002. *The New Economy of Nature: The Quest to Make Conservation Profitable*. Island Press, Washington, DC.

11. Darwall, W., K. Smith, T. Lowe, and J.-C. Vié 2005. *The Status and Distribution of Freshwater Biodiversity in Eastern Africa*. IUCN, Gland, Switzerland.

12. Dyck, A. J., and U. R. Sumaila. 2010. Economic impact of ocean fish populations in the global fishery. *J. Bioeconomics* 12:227–243.

13. Eken, G., L. Bennun, T. M. Brooks, et al. 2004. Key biodiversity areas as site conservation targets. *BioScience* 54:1110–1118.

14. Estes, J. A., J. Terborgh, J. S. Brashares, et al. 2011. Trophic downgrading of planet Earth. *Science* 333:301–306.

15. FAO Fisheries and Aquaculture Department 2010. The State of World Fisheries and Aquaculture. Food and Agriculture Organization, Rome.

16. Groves, R. H., and F. di Castri 1991. *Biogeography of Mediterranean Invasions*. Cambridge University Press, Cambridge.

17. Halpern, B. S., S. Walbridge, K. A. Selkoe, et al. 2008. A global map of human impact on marine ecosystems. *Science* 319:948–952.

18. Hannah, L., G. Midgley, S. Andelman, M. Araújo, G. Hughes, E. Martinez-Meyer, R. Pearson, and P. Williams. 2007. Protected area needs in a changing climate. *Front. Ecol. Environ.* 5:131–138.

19. Harley, C. D. G., A. R. Hughes, K. M. Hultgren, B. G. Miner, C. J. B. Sorte, C. S. Thornber, L. F. Rodriguez, L. Tomanek, and S. L. Williams. 2006. The impacts of climate change in coastal marine ecosystems. *Ecology Letters* 9:228–241.

20. Hoegh-Guldberg, O., and J. F. Bruno. 2010. The impact of climate

change on the world's marine ecosystems. *Science* 328:1523–1528.

21. IPCC 2007. *Climate Change 2007: The Fourth Assessment Report of the Intergovernmental Panel on Climate Change*. IPCC, Geneva, Switzerland.

22. IUCN 2008. 2008 IUCN Red List of Threatened Species. <www.iucnredlist.org>. Downloaded on 10 Sep 2009.

23. IUCN and UNEP-WCMC 2010. The World Database on Protected Areas (WDPA). UNEP-WCMC, Cambridge, UK.

24. Kremen, C., and R. S. Ostfeld. 2005. A call to ecologists: measuring, analyzing, and managing ecosystem services. *Frontiers in Ecology and the Environment* 3:540–548.

25. Loarie, S. R., P. B. Duffy, H. Hamilton, G. P. Asner, C. B. Field, and D. D. Ackerly. 2009. The velocity of climate change. *Nature* 462:1052–1055.

26. Lotze, H. K., and B. Worm. 2009. Historical baselines for large marine animals. *Trends in Ecology & Evolution* 24:254–262.

27. Mcculloch, M., S. Fallon, T. Wyndham, E. Hendy, J. Lough, and D. Barnes. 2003. Coral record of increased sediment flux to the intter Great Barrier Reef since European settlement. *Nature* 421:727–730.

28. McNeely, J. A., R. A. Mittermeier, T. M. Brooks, F. Boltz, and N. Ash 2009. *The Wealth of Nature: Ecosystem Services, Biodiversity, and Human Well-Being*. CEMEX, Mexico City.

29. Millennium Ecosystem Assessment 2005. *Ecosystems and Human Well-being: Synthesis*. Island Press, Washington, DC.

30. Mittermeier, R. A., C. G. Mittermeier, T. M. Brooks, J. D. Pilgrim, W. R. Konstant, G. A. B. da Fonseca, and C. Kormos. 2003. Wilderness and biodiversity conservation. *Proc. Natl. Acad. Sci. U.S.A.* 100:10309–10313.

31. Mittermeier, R. A., P. Robles Gil, and C. G. Mittermeier 1997. *Megadiversity*. CEMEX, Mexico.

32. Mittermeier, R. A., W. R. Turner, F. W. Larsen, T. M. Brooks, and C. Gascon. 2011. Global biodiversity conservation: The critical role of hotspots. Pages 3–22 in F. E. Zachos, and J. C. Habel, editors. *Biodiversity Hotspots*. Springer, Berlin Heidelberg.

33. Myers, N. 1988. Threatened biotas: 'Hotspots' in tropical forests. *Environmentalist* 1988:187–208.

34. Myers, N., R. A. Mittermeier, C. G. Mittermeier, G. A. B. da Fonseca, and J. Kent. 2000. Biodiversity hotspots for conservation priorities. *Nature* 403:853–858.

35. Myers, R. A., and B. Worm. 2003. Rapid worldwide depletion of predatory fish communities. *Nature* 423:280–283.

36. Perrings, C., A. K. Duraiappah, A. Larigauderie, and H. Mooney. 2011. The Biodiversity and Ecosystem Services Science-Policy Interface. *Science* 331:1139–1140.

37. Pimm, S. L., G. J. Russell, J. L. Gittleman, and T. M. Brooks. 1995. The future of biodiversity. *Science* 269:347.

38. Ricketts, T. H., E. Dinerstein, T. Boucher, et al. 2005. Pinpointing

and preventing imminent extinctions. *Proc. Natl. Acad. Sci. U.S.A.* 102:18497–18501.

39. Rodrigues, A. S. L., H. R. Akcakaya, S. J. Andelman, et al. 2004. Global Gap Analysis: Priority Regions for Expanding the Global Protected-Area Network. *BioScience* 54:1092–1100.

40. Sachs, J. D., J. E. M. Baillie, W. J. Sutherland, et al. 2009. Biodiversity conservation and the Millennium Development Goals. *Science* 325:1502–1503.

41. Sala, E., and N. Knowlton. 2006. Global Marine Biodiversity Trends. *Annual Review of Environment and Resources* 31:93–122.

42. Sala, O. E., F. S. Chapin, III, J. J. Armesto, et al. 2000. Global biodiversity scenarios for the year 2100. *Science* 287:1770–1774.

43. Schipper, J., J. S. Chanson, F. Chiozza, et al. 2008. The status of the world's land and marine mammals: Diversity, threat, and knowledge. *Science* 322:225–230.

44. Springer, A. M., J. A. Estes, G. B. v. Vliet, T. M. Williams, D. F. Doak, E. M. Danner, K. A. Forney, and B. Pfister. 2003. Sequential megafaunal collapse in the North Pacific Ocean: An ongoing legacy of industrial whaling? *Proceedings of the National Academy of Sciences of the United States of America* 100:12223–12228.

45. Steadman, D. W. 1995. Prehistoric extinctions of Pacific island birds: Biodiversity meets zooarchaeology. *Science* 267:1123–1131.

46. Stuart, S. N., J. S. Chanson, N. A. Cox, B. E. Young, A. S. L. Rodrigues, D. L. Fischman, and R. W. Waller. 2004. Status and trends of amphibian declines and extinctions worldwide. *Science* 306:1783–1786.

47. Stuart, S. N., E. O. Wilson, J. A. McNeely, R. A. Mittermeier, and J. P. Rodriguez. 2010. The barometer of life. *Science* 9:177.

48. Swartz, W., E. Sala, S. Tracey, R. Watson, and D. Pauly. 2010. The spatial expansion and ecological footprint of fisheries (1950 to present). *PLoS One* 5:e15143.

49. TEEB 2009. The Economics of Ecosystems and Biodiversity for National and International Policy Makers. UNEP, Bonn.

50. Tewksbury, J. J., R. B. Huey, and C. A. Deutsch. 2008. Putting the heat on tropical animals. *Science* 320:1296–1297.

51. Thomas, C. D., A. Cameron, R. E. Green, et al. 2004. Extinction risk from climate change. *Nature* 427:145–148.

52. Turner, W. R., B. A. Bradley, L. D. Estes, D. G. Hole, M. Oppenheimer, and D. S. Wilcove. 2010. Climate change: Helping Nature survive the human response. *Conservation Letters* 3:304–312.

53. Turner, W. R., K. Brandon, T. M. Brooks, C. Gascon, H. K. Gibbs, K. Lawrence, R. A. Mittermeier, and E. R. Selig. 2012. Global biodiversity conservation and the alleviation of poverty. *BioScience* 62:85–92.

54. Valiela, I., J. L. Bowen, and J. K. York. 2001. Mangrove forests: One of the world's threatened major tropical environments. *BioScience* 51:807–815.

55. van Dijk, P. P., B. L. Stuart, and A. G. J. Rhodin. 2000. Asian turtle trade. *Chelonian Research Monographs* 2:1–164.

56. Vitousek, P. M., H. A. Mooney, J. Lubchenco, and J. M. Melillo. 1997. Human domination of earth's ecosystems. *Science* 277:494–499.

57. Wake, D. B., and V. T. Vredenburg. 2008. Are we in the midst of the sixth mass extinction? A view from the world of amphibians. *Proc. Natl. Acad. Sci. U.S.A.* 105:11466–11473.

58. Waycott, M., C. M. Duarte, J. B. Carruthers, et al. 2009. Accelerating loss of seagrasses across the globe threatens coastal ecosystems. *Proc. Natl. Acad. Sci. U.S.A.* 106:12377–12381.

59. Williams, J. W., S. T. Jackson, and J. E. Kutzbach. 2007. Projected distributions of novel and disappearing climates by 2100 AD. *Proc. Natl. Acad. Sci. U.S.A.* 104:5738–5742.

60. Wilson, E. O. 1984. *Biophilia*. Harvard University Press, Boston.

Climate Change
Protecting Biodiversity and
Harnessing Nature's Climate Solutions

Will R. Turner,[1]* Russell A. Mittermeier,[1]
Julia Marton-Lefèvre,[2] Simon N. Stuart,[2] Jane Smart,[2]
David G. Hole,[1] Elizabeth R. Selig[1]

Earth's climate continues to change at unprecedented rates, with dramatic global, regional, and local changes that will, with increasing severity, undermine food security and freshwater security, particularly in the developing world, and produce severe changes in the ecosystems that support all life. The loss of biodiversity and natural ecosystems from dangerous levels of climate change portend a serious threat to human communities via the loss of ecosystem services. Ecosystems are critical for mitigating climate change. Tropical forests, coastal marine ecosystems, and others play large roles in global biochemical cycles, are widely available, and can be deployed immediately to reduce atmospheric greenhouse gas concentrations without waiting for new technology. An effective mechanism for Reducing Emissions from Deforestation and Forest Degradation (REDD) must be implemented and financed, and must recognize the role of traditionally high-forest, low-deforestation countries. Natural ecosystems will save lives and sustain livelihoods in myriad ways as Earth's climate changes, and the services provided by healthy, diverse ecosystems will become ever more crucial in the face of climate change. Yet, the

[1] Conservation International, 500 Crystal Drive Ste 500, Arlington, VA 22202, USA
[2] International Union for Conservation of Nature (IUCN), 28 rue Mauverney,
  CH-1196 Gland, Switzerland
* Address correspondence to w.turner@conservation.org.

global community's attempts to address climate change have been inadequate. The costs of climate change, already projected at 5% or more of global GDP, could one day exceed global economic output if leaders do not take action. We have the ability to reduce or avoid many of these impacts. Biodiversity, in particular, is foundational to solving the climate crisis because conservation can decelerate climate change while increasing the adaptive capacity of people and ecosystems alike. The opportunities to harness nature's climate change solutions are essential, immediate, and fleeting. We must act now.

Introduction

Earth's climate continues to change at an unprecedented rate (Kiehl 2011). Emissions from fossil fuels have accelerated over the past decade (Raupach et al. 2007), with the fleeting reduction during the financial crisis of 2008-2009 being followed by further rapid growth (Peters et al. 2012), and our planet is steadily heading toward a concentration of greenhouse gases in the atmosphere that is unprecedented during the past 20 million years (Beerling & Royer 2011). The implications of this trend for dramatic global, regional, and local changes in, among others, temperature, precipitation patterns, sea-level rise, ice-sheet and glacier loss, and the frequency of extreme climatic events, are underscored by a review of research covering the period since the IPCC's 2007 assessment report (Good et al. 2010). Indeed, analyses suggest that currently, there is little or no chance of maintaining the global mean surface temperature at or below 2°C (Anderson & Bows 2011). The impacts of a 2°C rise on human societies and the natural world that supports them is likely to be severe and pervasive (Solomon et al. 2007), and the consequences of exceeding this value are dire (New et al. 2011). Among the greatest risks, even at increases in global mean temperature well below 4°C, is the potential for exceeding one or more tipping points in the Earth's system–from irreversible melt of the Greenland ice sheet to dieback of the Amazon rainforest (Lenton 2011). Meanwhile, slower-onset, chronic changes will have equally profound impacts, with reductions in food

248

security (Lobell et al. 2008) and freshwater security (McDonald et al. 2011), particularly in the developing world, amplified by equally severe changes in the natural world–from likely significant numbers of species doomed to extinction (Thomas et al. 2004) to many of the world's coral reefs in terminal decline (Veron et al. 2009). The magnitude and severity of such impacts underscore the urgent need for rapid and substantive progress to mitigate climate change and help the world adapt to its impacts.

Climate change impacts on biodiversity and ecosystem services. *The loss of biodiversity and natural ecosystems from dangerous levels of climate change portend a serious threat to human communities via the loss of ecosystem services.*

Anthropogenic climate change has the potential to dramatically disrupt biodiversity at all levels of organization–from individuals to populations to entire ecosystems. Organisms are already displaying a range of responses to contemporary climate change, including changes in phenology (Parmesan 2006), abundance (Moritz et al. 2008), and evolutionary processes (Karell et al. 2011). These changes are paralleled by shifts in species' ranges as they attempt to track shifting climatic niches. Indeed, evidence from the paleoecological record of past climate change (Graham & Grimm 1990) together with recent documented changes in species' distributions (Chen et al. 2011) and modeled simulations of future range shifts (Hole et al. 2009) indicate that species' responses to projected climate change over the coming decades could substantially alter present-day patterns of biodiversity. In addition, species responses are highly individualistic, depending on factors such as individual dispersal capability and the responses of interacting species such as competitors, predators, or prey (Traill et al. 2010). Furthermore, projected rates of climate change in both terrestrial (Loarie et al. 2009) and marine (Burrows et al. 2011) environments are likely to be of such magnitude that many species will be unable to keep pace with their shifting envelope–an outcome that is already becoming apparent (Devictor et al. 2008). As a result, changes in community composition and structure and the emergence of novel species' assemblages will probably characterize the future as they did the past (Williams & Jackson 2007). This disassembly and reassembly of ecosystems together with inevitable extinctions will affect ecosystem function and resulting service provision (Traill et al. 2010). This era of uncertainty and rapid change will pose unprecedented challenges to our ability to achieve global goals for sustaining biodiversity and the communities that depend upon it.

Climate change impacts on ecosystem services are still relatively poorly characterized, largely because of our lack of understanding of the complex web of interacting species that comprise any ecosystem, each of which will respond to climate change in its own individual manner. Yet, accumulating evidence suggests that the implications of climate change for the provision of ecosystem services are profound (Millennium Ecosystem Assessment 2005; Schroter et al. 2005; Traill et al. 2010). Ecosystems that are most susceptible to climate change impacts will be those whose sustained provision of services is probably most at risk. For example, montane cloud forests are highly susceptible to a climate change-driven lifting of the cloud base (Still et al. 1999), with consequent ramifications for future downstream provision of freshwater services (Bruijnzeel 2004). The nature and magnitude of changes in service provision will potentially be the greatest, but also most uncertain, in ecosystems whose biota disassemble and reassemble as a result of climate change to such a degree that no-analog communities form (Harborne & Mumby 2011; Hoegh-Guldberg & Bruno 2010). The impacts of such changes in ecosystem structure and function will have significant consequences for attained service provision to human communities across spatial scales (Millennium Ecosystem Assessment 2005). For example, at local scales, shifts in pollinator abundance and distribution will affect pollination services (Traill et al. 2010). Indeed, we can expect a wide range of negative impacts across the panoply of provisioning, regulating, cultural, and supporting services as climate change reshuffles the web of life.

Climate change effects on the ocean will be diverse and profound. Rising ocean temperatures have led to widespread die-offs on coral reefs from bleaching events (Veron et al. 2009) and slowed coral growth because of ocean acidification (Lesser & Farrell 2004). Ocean acidification – a decrease in ocean pH – can have similarly devastating consequences for other ecosystems and species. Many species need particular levels of chemicals in the ocean to build their shells; as these levels change, populations must shift their energy and resources from reproduction to simply maintaining their individual growth rates, which can lead to considerable declines in the number of individuals in a population. Over the next few decades, ocean acidification is predicted to affect corals and many shell-builders of commercial importance, including crabs, lobsters, mussels, and clams. Furthermore, rising sea levels threaten several coastal ecosystems such as mangroves and seagrass beds, particularly where development inhibits their ability to migrate inland with rising seas. Meanwhile, at regional to global scales, significant changes in the potential of global fisheries catches – both positive and negative – are projected under climate change (Cheung et al. 2010). In combination, these climate change impacts are both severe and global in reach, and can affect every marine ecosystem in the world, including relatively pristine areas of the ocean.

Nature is essential for mitigating climate change. *Ecosystems are critical for mitigating climate change. Tropical forests, coastal marine ecosystems, and others strongly affect global biochemical cycles, are widely available, and can be deployed immediately to reduce atmospheric greenhouse gas concentrations without waiting for new technology. An effective mechanism for REDD must be implemented and financed, and must recognize the role of traditionally high-forest, low-deforestation countries.*

Natural ecosystems are a major force in mitigating global warming. First, forests, peatlands, oceans, and other ecosystems strongly affect carbon and other global biogeochemical cycles. The oceans sequester about two gigatons of carbon a year, while reducing deforestation and forest degradation rates by half would cut global emissions by about a gigaton of carbon a year – substantially more than the emissions of all passenger cars combined. Restoring marginal and degraded lands to natural habitats could sequester an additional 0.65 gigatons annually (McKinsey & Company 2009). Second, the maintenance and restoration of natural habitats are among the most cost-effective, widely accessible solutions available in the effort to reduce greenhouse gas concentrations. Ecosystem restoration (e.g., replanting a forest on previously degraded land) may remain for several decades the only realistic large-scale mechanism for removing the CO_2 already in the atmosphere (Hansen et al. 2008).

Ecosystem-based adaptation. *Natural ecosystems will save lives and sustain livelihoods in myriad ways as Earth's climate changes. The services provided by healthy, diverse ecosystems will become ever more crucial in the face of climate change because they can help us deal with impacts such as changing hydrology, rising sea levels, and changes in the range of disease-carrying organisms and other pests.*

Although it is critical that the world mitigates aggressively to "avoid the unmanageable," we must equally crucially address the impacts already with us and those to which we are committed to "manage the unavoidable." Adaptation to climate change comprises a wide range of approaches in response to experienced or expected climate change exposures. It is becoming clear that the maintenance and restoration of natural ecosystems are among the cheapest, safest, and most readily implemented solutions at our disposal to lessen the impacts of climate change on people (Turner et al. 2009). Ecosystem-based approaches to adaptation (EbA) harness nature's capacity to buffer human communities against the adverse impacts of climate change through the sustainable delivery of ecosystem services. They are generally deployed in the form of targeted management, conservation, and restoration activities and are often focused on specific ecosystem services with the potential to reduce climate change exposures. For example, mangrove forests and coastal marshes can help dissipate the energy of storm surges along exposed coastlines (Costanza et al. 2008; Das & Vincent 2009; Shepard et al. 2011). Therefore, restoring or conserving mangrove ecosystems can help protect coastal communities from the projected rise in the number of powerful tropical storms under climate change (Emanuel 2005). EbA presents a potentially broad scope of options for reducing vulnerability to diverse climate change impacts. Ecosystems deliver services that can help meet adaptation needs across multiple human development sectors (Andrade et al. 2010; World Bank 2009), including disaster risk reduction (through flood regulation and storm surge protection), food security (from fisheries to agroforestry), sustainable water management (via water purification and flow regulation), and livelihoods diversification (through increasing resource-use options or tourism). Although people have used the natural environment to cope with climatic variability for millennia, the potential for natural infrastructure to provide adaptation services is gaining increasing attention at all levels because of the urgent need to find tractable, flexible, cost-effective adaptation interventions that reduce vulnerability under rapid anthropogenic climate change.

A great advantage of ecosystems as a climate solution is that they play multiple roles simultaneously. Beyond mitigation, the climate adaptation services provided by healthy, diverse ecosystems will become increasingly important in the face of climate change because they can help us deal with impacts such as changing freshwater flows, rising sea levels, and shifts in disease-carrying organisms and other pests. For example, mangroves store carbon, support fisheries, harbor diverse species, and can reduce storm impacts. In addition, ecosystems support livelihoods by providing income and food alternatives that will be important where climate change disrupts current sources. Such diversification is helpful for all, particularly for the most vulnerable communities and countries with the least capacity to cope with climate change.

Although the known value of nature in reducing climate change and its impacts is high, there may be more value in what remains to be discovered. Several decades ago, few imagined that the carbon stored in natural ecosystems would become critical for combating climate change. What breadth of untapped innovation for addressing climate change – the "option value" of biodiversity – might lie in the diverse wildlands of the world? Agriculture is one area in which this untapped innovation could prove particularly valuable. When changes in patterns of precipitation and temperature begin testing the physiological limits of current crops, farmers may benefit greatly from wild relatives and novel cultivars better suited to the new conditions (Sheehy et al. 2005).

Harnessing nature to fight climate change impacts, and the costs of inaction. *The global community's attempts to address climate change have been inadequate. The costs of climate change, already estimated at 5% or more of global GDP, could one day exceed global economic output if leaders do not take action. Biodiversity is foundational to solving the climate crisis because conservation can decelerate climate change while increasing the adaptive capacity of people and ecosystems alike. The opportunities to harness nature's climate change solutions are essential, immediate, and fleeting. We must act now.*

The global community's attempts to address climate change thus far have been entirely inadequate. Currently, there is little chance of avoiding global mean temperature increases of 2°C or more (Anderson & Bows 2011), the so-called "guard-rail" recognized by the Copenhagen Accord in 2009 as the limit necessary to avoid "dangerous" climate change, despite the growing view that this limit might itself be too high (New et al. 2009). It is true that individual ecosystems and regions are likely to exhibit high variability in their responses to continued climatic change depending on their degree of exposure to climatic perturbations and specific tolerances of their component species. For example, under the combined pressures of increasing ocean temperatures, ocean acidification, and other environmental impacts, coral reefs could face rapid and terminal decline worldwide by mid-the 21st century if CO_2 levels exceed 450 ppm (Veron et al. 2009). Other ecosystems, such as the humid tropical forests of South and insular Asia, could be relatively unaffected (Zelazowski et al. 2011), although evidence suggests that tropical biodiversity may experience greater impact from climate change than previously thought (Tewksbury et al. 2008). Overall, the direct impacts of climate change on people and ecosystems will probably be substantial and primarily negative, particularly in the developing world, where exposure to climatic changes are likely to be highest and the potential to adapt lowest (Parry et al. 2007). For example, food security will probably be reduced in many regions of the developing world as the yields of many agricultural staples fall (Lobell et al. 2008; Thornton et al. 2011) and fisheries productivity declines (Cheung et al. 2010) while exposure to climatic extremes (e.g., droughts, floods, and storms) increases.

Without concerted action, the costs of climate change will exceed 5%, or perhaps 20%, of global GDP (Stern 2007). The consequences of continued inaction are ominous. The risk of breaching one or more tipping points in the Earth's system—including shifts in the West African monsoon, West Antarctic ice-sheet collapse, Amazon forest dieback, and shutdown of the Atlantic thermohaline circulation—increases with increasing climatic change, with estimates of threshold levels for tipping points at global mean temperature change from 0.5–6°C of warming (Lenton et al. 2008). In such circumstances, total costs may approach and exceed global GDP. Continued failure to implement substantive mitigation actions will also result in significant adaptation costs. Current estimates of global adaptation need range from $49–171 billion per year, although these are recognized as gross underestimates (Parry et al. 2009). Similarly, reactive conservation actions will cost substantially more than proactive ones (Hannah et al. 2007). Even if we take strong mitigation measures now, along with the actions required to adapt to the climatic changes already locked into the system, we must ensure that we minimize the unintended, harmful consequences of inadequately planned or inappropriate responses to climate change for biodiversity and people (Turner et al. 2010).

Our responses to climate change must harness nature as a solution if we are to avoid further compromising the integrity of the planet upon which we depend. We cannot restrict our actions to engineered fixes, such as constructing sea walls to protect against sea-level rise or desalination facilities to address water scarcity. Because human responses will be diverse, addressing the threats of climate change will require coordination across various sectors, including conservation and development. By focusing on ecosystems and their benefits to people, we can improve resilience and ensure that we and other species will survive for generations to come. We must proactively identify and secure key intact ecosystems and the climate services they provide, restore lost or degraded ones, and limit future losses, all in partnership with the communities who need those services most.

Climate mitigation and adaptation, for both nature and people, can no longer be thought of as separate problems, for they will not be solved in isolation. If human adaptation to climate change compromises forests or other ecosystems, this loss will speed climate change. Likewise, adaptation actions can also reduce biodiversity—for example, reforestation using sigle-species stands. It is important that ensembles of native species be used for reforestation activities. These losses will increase the need for adaptation even as our capacity to accommodate it diminishes. An integrated approach makes this cycle virtuous: by conserving biodiversity, we decelerate climate change while increasing the adaptive capacity of people and ecosystems alike. Achieving such an integrated approach will pose challenges: the broad interest of humanity is up against powerful short-term political and economic interests. Yet, these are challenges we must conquer. The opportunities to harness nature's climate change solutions are essential, immediate, and fleeting. We must act now.

References

1. Anderson, K., and A. Bows. 2011. Beyond 'dangerous' climate change: Emission scenarios for a new world. *Philosophical Transactions of the Royal Society a-Mathematical Physical and Engineering Sciences* 369:20–44.

2. Andrade, A. P., B. F. Herrera, and R. G. Cazzolla, editors. 2010. *Building Resilience to Climate Change: Ecosystem-based adaptation and lessons from the field.* IUCN, Gland, Switzerland.

3. Beerling, D. J., and D. L. Royer. 2011. Convergent Cenozoic CO(2) history. *Nature Geoscience* 4:418–420.

4. Bruijnzeel, L. A. 2004. Hydrological function of tropical forests: not seeing the soil for the trees? *Agriculture, Ecosystems and Environment* 104:185–228.

5. Burrows, M. T., D. S. Schoeman, L. B. Buckley, et al. 2011. The Pace of Shifting Climate in Marine and Terrestrial Ecosystems. *Science* 334:652–655.

6. Chen, I. C., J. K. Hill, R. Ohlemueller, D. B. Roy, and C. D. Thomas. 2011. Rapid Range Shifts of Species Associated with High Levels of Climate Warming. *Science* 333:1024–1026.

7. Cheung, W. W. L., V. W. Y. Lam, J. L. Sarmiento, K. Kearney, R. Watson, D. Zeller, and D. Pauly. 2010. Large-scale redistribution of maximum fisheries catch potential in the global ocean under climate change. *Global Change Biology* 16:24–35.

8. Costanza, R., O. Pérez-Maqueo, M. L. Martinez, P. Sutton, S. J. Anderson, and K. Mulder. 2008. The value of coastal wetlands for hurricane protection. *Ambio* 37:241–248.

9. Das, S., and J. R. Vincent. 2009. Mangroves protected villages and reduced death toll during Indian super cyclone. *Proc. Natl. Acad. Sci. U.S.A.* 106:7357–7360.

11. Devictor, V., R. Julliard, D. Couvet, and F. Jiguet. 2008. Birds are tracking climate warming, but not fast enough. *Proceedings of the Royal Society B-Biological Sciences* 275:2743–2748.

12. Emanuel, K. 2005. Increasing destructiveness of tropical cyclones over the past 30 years. *Nature* 436:686–688.

13. Good, P., S. N. Gosling, D. Bernie, J. Caesar, R. Warren, N. W. Arnell, and J. A. Lowe. 2010. *An updated review of developments in climate science research since the IPCC Fourth Assessment Report.* Page 177. Met Office Hadley Center, Exeter, UK, Walker Institute, University of Reading, UK, Tyndall Center, University of East Anglia, Norwich, UK.

14. Graham, R. W., and E. C. Grimm. 1990. Effects of global climate change

on the patterns of terrestrial biological communities. *Trends in Ecology & Evolution* 5:289–292.

15. Hannah, L., G. Midgley, S. Andelman, M. Araújo, G. Hughes, E. Martinez-Meyer, R. Pearson, and P. Williams. 2007. Protected area needs in a changing climate. *Front. Ecol. Environ.* 5:131–138.

16. Hansen, J., M. Sato, P. Kharecha, et al. 2008. Target atmospheric CO_2: Where should humanity aim? *The Open Atmospheric Science Journal* 2:217–231.

17. Harborne, A. R., and P. J. Mumby. 2011. Novel Ecosystems: Altering Fish Assemblages in Warming Waters. *Current Biology* 21:R822–R824.

18. Hoegh-Guldberg, O., and J. F. Bruno. 2010. The impact of climate change on the world's marine ecosystems. *Science* 328:1523–1528.

19. Hole, D. G., S. G. Willis, D. J. Pain, L. D. Fishpool, S. H. M. Butchart, Y. C. Collingham, C. Rahbek, and B. Huntley. 2009. Projected impacts of climate change on a continent-wide protected area network. *Ecology Letters* 12:420–431.

20. Karell, P., K. Ahola, T. Karstinen, J. Valkama, and J. E. Brommer. 2011. Climate change drives microevolution in a wild bird. *Nature Communications* 2:1–7.

21. Kiehl, J. 2011. Lessons from Earth's Past. *Science* 331:158–159.

22. Lenton, T. M. 2011. Early warning of climate tipping points. *Nature Climate Change* 1:201–209.

23. Lenton, T. M., H. Held, E. Kriegler, J. W. Hall, W. Lucht, S. Rahmstorf, and H. J. Schellnhuber. 2008. Tipping elements in the Earth's climate system. *Proceedings of the National Academy of Sciences of the United States of America* 105:1786–1793.

24. Lesser, M. P., and J. H. Farrell. 2004. Exposure to solar radiation increases damage to both host tissues and algal symbionts of corals during thermal stress. *Coral Reefs* 23:367–377.

25. Loarie, S. R., P. B. Duffy, H. Hamilton, G. P. Asner, C. B. Field, and D. D. Ackerly. 2009. The velocity of climate change. *Nature* 462:1052–1055.

26. Lobell, D. B., M. B. Burke, C. Tebaldi, M. D. Mastrandrea, W. P. Falcon, and R. L. Naylor. 2008. Prioritizing climate change adaptation needs for food security in 2030. *Science* 319:607–610.

27. McDonald, R. I., P. Green, D. Balk, B. M. Fekete, C. Revenga, M. Todd, and M. Montgomery. 2011. Urban growth, climate change, and freshwater availability. *Proceedings of the National Academy of Sciences of the United States of America* 108:6312–6317.

28. McKinsey & Company 2009. Pathways to a Low-Carbon Economy: Version 2 of the Global Greenhouse Gas Abatement Cost Curve.

29. Millennium Ecosystem Assessment 2005. *Ecosystems and Human Wellbeing: Synthesis*. Island Press, Washington, D.C..

30. Moritz, C., J. L. Patton, C. J. Conroy, J. L. Parra, G. C. White, and S. R. Beissinger. 2008. Impact of a century of climate change on small-mammal communities in Yosemite National Park, USA. *Science* 322:261–264.

31. New, M., D. Liverman, and K. Anderson. 2009. Mind the gap. *Nature Reports Clim. Change* 3:143–144.
32. New, M., D. Liverman, H. Schroder, and K. Anderson. 2011. Four degrees and beyond: The potential for a global temperature increase of four degrees and its implications. *Phil. Trans. R. Soc. A* 369:6–10.
33. Parmesan, C. 2006. Ecological and evolutionary responses to recent climate change. Pages 637–669. Annual Review of Ecology Evolution and Systematics.
34. Parry, M., N. Arnell, P. Berry, et al. 2009. Assessing the Costs of Adaptation to Climate Change: A Review of the UNFCCC and Other Recent Estimates, London, UK.
35. Parry, M., O. Canziani, J. Palutikof, P. van der Linden, and C. Hanson. 2007. Climate Change 2007: Impacts, Adaptation and Vulnerability. Contribution of Working Group II to the Fourth Assessment Report of the Intergovernmental Panel on Climate Change, Cambridge, UK.
36. Peters, G. P., G. Marland, C. Le Quere et al., T. Boden, J. G. Canadell, and M. R. Raupach. 2012. Rapid growth in CO_2 emissions after the 2008-2009 global financial crisis. *Nature Climate Change* 2:2–4.
37. Raupach, M. R., G. Marland, P. Ciais, C. Le Quere, J. G. Canadell, G. Klepper, and C. B. Field. 2007. Global and regional drivers of accelerating CO_2 emissions. *Proceedings of the National Academy of Sciences of the United States of America* 104:10288–10293.
38. Schroter, D., W. Cramer, R. Leemans, et al. 2005. Ecosystem service supply and vulnerability to global change in Europe. *Science* 310:1333–1337.
39. Sheehy, J., A. Elmido, C. Centeno, and P. Pablico. 2005. Searching for new plants for climate change. *J. Agric. Meteorol.* 60:463–468.
40. Shepard, C. C., C. M. Crain, and M. W. Beck. 2011. The Protective Role of Coastal Marshes: A Systematic Review and Meta-analysis. *PloS one* 6:e27374.
41. Solomon, S., D. Qin, M. Manning, M. Marquis, K. Averyt, M. M. B. Tignor, H. L. Miller, and C. Z. 2007. Climate Change 2007: The Physical Science Basis. Contribution of Working Group I to the Fourth Assessment Report of the Intergovernmental Panel on Climate Change.
42. Stern, N. 2007. *The Economics of Climate Change: The Stern Review.* Cambridge University Press, Cambridge.
43. Still, C. J., P. N. Foster, and S. H. Schneider. 1999. Simulating the effects of climate change on tropical montane cloud forests. *Nature* 398:608–610.
44. Tewksbury, J. J., R. B. Huey, and C. A. Deutsch. 2008. Putting the heat on tropical animals. *Science* 320:1296–1297.
45. Thomas, C. D., A. Cameron, R. E. Green, et al. 2004. Extinction risk from climate change. *Nature* 427:145–148.
46. Thornton, P. K., P. G. Jones, P. J. Ericksen, and A. J. Challinor. 2011. Agriculture and food systems in sub-Saharan Africa in a 4 degrees C+ world. *Philosophical Transactions of the Royal Society a-Mathematical*

Physical and Engineering Sciences 369:117–136.

47. Traill, L. W., M. L. M. Lim, N. S. Sodhi, and C. J. A. Bradshaw. 2010. Mechanisms driving change: Altered species interactions and eco-system function through global warming. *Journal of Animal Ecology* 79:937–947.

48. Turner, W. R., B. A. Bradley, L. D. Estes, D. G. Hole, M. Oppenheimer, and D. S. Wilcove. 2010. Climate change: Helping Nature survive the human response. *Conservation Letters* 3:304–312.

49. Turner, W. R., M. Oppenheimer, and D. S. Wilcove. 2009. A force to fight global warming. *Nature* 462:278–279.

50. Veron, J. E. N., O. Hoegh-Guldberg, T. M. Lenton, et al. 2009. The coral reef crisis: The critical importance of < 350 ppm CO_2. *Marine Pollution Bulletin* 58:1428–1436.

51. Williams, J. W., and S. T. Jackson. 2007. Novel climates, no-analog communities, and ecological surprises. *Frontiers in Ecology and the Environment* 5:475–482.

52. World Bank 2009. Convenient Solutions to an Inconvenient Truth: Ecosystem-based Approaches to Climate Change. World Bank, Washington, D.C..

53. Zelazowski, P., Y. Malhi, C. Huntingford, S. Sitch, and J. B. Fisher. 2011. Changes in the potential distribution of humid tropical forests on a warmer planet. *Philosophical Transactions of the Royal Society a-Mathematical Physical and Engineering Sciences* 369:137–160.

Ecosystem Services
Accounting for the Benefits that Nature Provides to Humanity

Will R. Turner,[1]* Russell A. Mittermeier,[1]
Rachel Neugarten,[1] Julia Marton-Lefèvre,[2]
Simon N. Stuart,[2] Jane Smart[2]

Human well-being has historically enjoyed ecosystem bene-fits free of charge and exerts an increasing demand for them. Species from all branches of the tree of life and a variety of hab-itats around the globe provide ecosystem services both directly and indirectly, with biodiversity as their foundation. Ecosystem services are pervasive, benefiting people in diverse socioeco-nomic conditions, across virtually every economic sector and over a range of spatial scales, now and in the future. Although the global economic value of ecosystem services may be im-possible to measure, it almost certainly rivals or exceeds aggre-gate global GDP, and ecosystem benefits frequently outweigh costs of their conservation. Yet, leaders seldom consider envi-ronmental benefits in conventional economic decision-making, and costs and benefits often do not accrue to the same commu-nity or at the same time or place. Thus, a range of ecosystem services are vanishing rapidly, with enormous consequences for current and future human well-being. To stop biodiversity loss and maintain the services humanity depends on, leaders must incorporate the value of ecosystem services and natural capital into national accounting and decision-making processes

[1] Conservation International, 500 Crystal Drive Ste 500, Arlington, VA 22202, USA
[2] International Union for Conservation of Nature (IUCN), 28 rue Mauverney,
  CH-1196 Gland, Switzerland
* Address correspondence to w.turner@conservation.org.

across all sectors of society, access to ecosystem benefits and costs of ecosystem conservation must be shared equitably, and biodiversity and ecosystem services must be seen as the most fundamental components of green economic development.

Introduction. *Ecosystem services are the benefits that ecosystems contribute to human well-being.*

Ecosystem services are "the benefits people obtain from ecosystems" (Millennium Ecosystem Assessment 2005) or "the direct and indirect contributions of ecosystems to human well-being" (TEEB 2009). Humans are fundamentally dependent on the flow of ecosystem services for food provision, water purification, waste and nutrient cycling, climate stabilization, recreational and spiritual fulfillment, and other needs. In economic terms, ecosystems should be considered capital assets worthy of careful valuation and investment because they sustain both lives and livelihoods (Turner & Daily 2007). This "natural capital," along with human and produced capital, is one of the cornerstones of societies and economies. Natural capital plays a large role in supporting human communities and a disproportionate role in supporting the rural poor.

Between 1960 and 2000, the demand for ecosystem services grew significantly because world population doubled to six billion, and the global economy increased more than sixfold. To meet this demand, food production increased roughly two-and-a-half times, water use doubled, wood harvests for pulp and paper production tripled, installed hydropower capacity doubled, and timber production increased by more than half (Millennium Ecosystem Assessment 2005).

Biodiversity and ecosystem services. *Biodiversity is the foundation of the ecosystem services that humanity depends on; all branches of the tree of life and a variety of habitats around the globe provide these services both directly and indirectly.*

Ecosystem services are produced by all branches of the tree of life–the many species of plants, insects, microbes, and mammals that populate the planet. For example, fish are among the most important sources of food for much of the world's population. The fishing industry contributes between US$225–240 billion per year to the global economy (Dyck & Sumaila 2010). In coastal and island communities, reef-based resources are the primary source of income and food for 30 million people (TEEB 2010).

Many other species provide valuable services to humanity. Birds act as pollinators, scavengers, seed dispersers, seed predators, and ecosystem engineers (Whelan et al. 2008) and provide an important global food source and significant recreational and economic values in the form of nature-based tourism.

Mammals, both wild and domesticated, also provide a significant source of food to the global population, as along with significant recreational values in the form of hunting, wildlife tourism, and the pet trade. Bats and many other mammals provide services such as seed dispersal, pollination, pest control, and fertilization (Kunz et al. 2011). Collectively, insects, birds, and bats reduce agricultural crop losses caused by pests as well as costs of pesticide use, services estimated to range between $54 billion and $1 trillion globally (Kunz et al. 2011). In addition, migratory mammals, birds, and fish transport energy and nutrients between ecosystems (de Groot et al. 2002).

Amphibians also help cycle nutrients (VanCompernolle et al. 2005) and, like many mammal, birds, and fish species, can serve as cultural symbols. For example, the Wet'suwet'en people in British Columbia are organized into frog, beaver, wolf, and fireweed clans.

Invertebrates such as insects, prawns, and crabs play an important role in nutrient cycling, breaking down waste, and making it available directly as food or as nutrients in soil. In addition, they pollinate crops, control pests, and provide food for fish and wildlife. Pollinators are necessary for producing about one in three of the world's food crops (Daily & Ellison 2002). Wild insects provide services estimated to be worth at least US$57 billion per year in the United States alone (Losey & Vaughan 2006). Commercial beekeeping generates US$213 million per year in Switzerland (TEEB 2010). Furthermore, invertebrates provide raw ingredients for many medicines. For example, chemicals derived from mollusks such as cone snails have been turned into powerful painkillers (Becker & Terlau 2008).

Many species of trees are used for timber and fuel wood. Forests also provide protection from floods and landslides, erosion control, climate stabilization, food crops, and habitat for wildlife. Worldwide, forests are estimated to provide US$4.7 trillion in total ecosystem services (Costanza et al. 1997). The value of living trees has been recognized in some cities. For example, 400,000 trees were planted in Canberra, Australia, to improve urban air quality, reduce energy costs for air conditioning, sequester and store carbon, and regulate microclimate. In total, these services are estimated at US$20m–67m in value provided or savings to the city for the period 2008–2012 (TEEB 2010). Trees also provide significant esthetic, recreational, and cultural values. Hospital patients that looked out on a modest stand of trees fared much better than those that had a view of a building wall (Daily & Ellison 2002). Other flowering and non-flowering plants make up a significant portion of the world's food crops, help clean water, cycle nutrients, prevent soil erosion, and absorb heat-trapping atmospheric gases and other pollutants. Like animals, plants can also be the source of life-saving medicines. For example, substances extracted from the Madagascar periwinkle, an endangered flowering plant, are used to treat leukemia. Microorganisms, the most abundant life form by far, provide countless services: they purify groundwater, detoxify and decompose wastes, regulate climate, and improve soil fertility (Lavelle et al. 2006).

The ocean provides a range of important ecosystem services including food provision, recreational and tourism opportunities, coastal protection, climate regulation, and a source of livelihoods. Marine ecosystems provide the majority of all ecosystem service value (Costanza et al. 1997). More than 1.5 billion people rely on the oceans for 20% of their animal protein (FAO Fisheries and Aquaculture Department 2010). Beyond fishing, the world's oceans also play a critical role in regulating global climate change (Levitus et al. 2005; Turner et al. 2009). Although the ocean's vegetated habitats (mangroves, seagrasses, and salt marshes) have only 0.05% of the total biomass of terrestrial plants, they store a disproportionate amount of carbon globally per year, and therefore are among the most efficient carbon sinks on the planet (Laffoley & Grimsditch 2009).

Variation itself–within or among species–often underpins ecosystem services. Agricultural crops with higher genetic diversity can better adapt to changing environmental conditions, and therefore are more likely to survive pest or pathogen outbreaks or climate fluctuations. The diversity of animals that eat fruit and disperse seeds influences the functioning of forest ecosystems; thus, their ability to sequester and store carbon (Brodie & Gibbs 2009; Howe & Smallwood 1982; Kone et al. 2008). Plant species richness also influences nutrient cycling, carbon sequestration, and other services (Maestre et al. 2012).

The breadth of services. *Ecosystem services benefit people in a variety of socioeconomic conditions, across virtually every economic sector and over a range of spatial scales, now and in the future.*

The Millennium Ecosystem Assessment (2005) grouped ecosystem services into four categories: provisioning services that produce food, water, timber, and fiber; regulating services that mitigate climate and flooding, purify water, and process wastes; supporting services that underpin photosynthesis, nutrient cycling, and soil formation; and cultural services such as spiritual, esthetic, and recreational benefits.

Primary production, the process by which organisms such as plants, algae, or bacteria transform energy and carbon dioxide into biomass, is considered the most fundamental supporting service (McNeely et al. 2009). Nutrient cycling of carbon, nitrogen, phosphorus, and sulfur is also a critical supporting service as it maintains ecosystem productivity and reduces the dangerous accumulation of nutrients that can threaten ecological and human health.

Important regulating services provided by ecosystems include the sequestration and cycling of greenhouse gases such as carbon dioxide and methane and other pollutants such as sulfur dioxide that cause climate change and affect air quality. These pollutants are released by human activities including burning fossil fuels, growing crops and livestock, and clearing forests and have negative impacts on ecosystem and human health. Furthermore, ecosystems help process wastes, protecting soil and water quality. Intact and functioning ecosystems can also reduce the frequency, intensity, and damage resulting from natural disasters such as floods, tropical storms, and landslides. Natural habitats provide refuges for people and animals fleeing natural and man-made disasters and can provide emergency supplies of food, water, shelter, and fuel. Many species provide regulating services in the form of pollination and the control of insects and other pests, which directly affect food production and the spread of disease.

Provisioning services are the most direct form of benefits from nature. They include the direct harvest of food from fishing, hunting, and gathering as well as the harvest of timber, fuel, and fiber. In addition, they support the grazing of livestock and crop cultivation and production of fuel and energy from firewood and charcoal, biomass fuel, grain ethanol, or animal dung. Natural products are also used in medicine, biomimicry, and genetic resources. Nature provides a "library" of genetic material with values for medical, industrial, and agricultural products (Daily & Ellison 2002). At least half of the medicines in use have natural components (Chivian & Bernstein 2008). Genetic resources that offer or inspire important drugs arise from taxa as disparate as reptiles, flowering plants, and microbes. For example, a drug derived from Gila monster saliva is used to treat diabetes (Triplitt & Chiquette 2006), and a chemical from the Madagascar periwinkle is used to fight cancer (Gentry 1993).

Biodiversity also provides many non-material benefits to

humanity, including recreation, tourism, esthetic and spiritual values, cultural identity, and opportunities for education and scientific research. It is difficult to quantify these values; however, in many cases, the value of cultural services may outweigh the market value of converting or exploiting ecosystems, providing one of the strongest arguments for conserving biodiversity to sustain human well-being.

All the ecosystem services described above are supported, directly or indirectly, by the diversity of life on Earth—its genes, species, populations, and ecosystems. Diverse life forms provide the basic materials for the production of food and medicine, biological control of pests and pathogens, genetic material for crops and cures, and experiences that heal the body and soothe the soul. As valuable as the known benefits of biodiversity may be, there may be even greater value in what we have yet to discover. Indeed, humanity remains every bit as dependent on nature in solving 21st century problems such as climate change (Turner et al. 2009) and multiple-drug-resistant pathogens (e.g., vancomycin, a powerful antibiotic, originating in bacteria from interior Borneo; Moellering 2006) as it has always been for more basic services such as food and water provision. As these and many other examples demonstrate (McNeely et al. 2009) time and again, biodiversity offers solutions to challenges we could not have anticipated. If we succeed in protecting only the biodiversity on which we can put a price in today's markets, we will fail. Our failure will not be measured by merely the intrinsic value of nature and our ethical responsibilities to it or the "existence" value of nature—its value to the identities of local communities and people around the globe who benefit from nature's existence, whether experienced directly or from afar. If we fail to protect biodiversity beyond what can be immediately priced, we will also fail in retaining the benefits of nature for human well-being in the long term. Thus, any discussion of "tradeoffs" between biodiversity and human well-being presents a false choice; the real tradeoff is between short-term benefits to a limited set of people and the long-term well-being of humanity.

The value of nature.   *The global economic value of ecosystem services may be impossible to measure, but almost certainly rivals or exceeds aggregate global GDP; these benefits of ecosystems frequently outweigh costs of their conservation.*

By 1997, the total economic value of ecosystem services globally was estimated at US\$33 trillion per year (Costanza et al. 1997), nearly twice the global aggregate GDP.

The global protected area network is a critical core of our efforts to preserve our collective natural capital. For example, nearly a third (33 out of 105) of the world's largest cities obtains a substantial portion of their drinking water directly from PAs (Dudley & Stolton 2003). The value of maintaining natural ecosystems and their wide range of services frequently far outweighs the value of converting them to supply a limited range of provisioning services, with global estimates of benefits relative to costs ranging from 3:1 (Turner et al. 2012) to 100:1 (Balmford et al. 2002).

The broken economic compass and the cost of inaction. *Leaders seldom consider environmental benefits in conventional economic decision-making, and costs and benefits often do not accrue to the same community or the same time or place. Thus, a range of ecosystem services are vanishing rapidly, with enormous consequences for current and future human well-being.*

Although the benefits of ecosystems are substantial, the value of ecosystem services and natural capital are seldom considered in economic decision-making, with the result that the actions of our governments, banks, corporations, and other institutions are guided by what economist Pavan Sukhdev calls a "broken economic compass" (Sukhdev 2011). The value of ecosystem services and the costs of losing them are treated as mere externalities in conventional decision-making.

The result of this disconnect is the continued rapid loss of ecosystems and their services. More than half of the services studied during the Millennium Ecosystem Assessment (2005), including freshwater, fisheries, pest control, air and water purification, climate regulation, and natural hazard regulation were either degraded or being used at unsustainable levels. Water from over-pumped aquifers is used to produce much of the world's grain (Brown 2001). Globally, deforestation claims over nine million hectares of land every year. Nearly a fifth of the planet's coral reefs have been lost, and another fifth have been degraded in the past few decades. Two-thirds of oceanic fisheries are being fished at or beyond their sustainable yield (Millennium Ecosystem Assessment 2005). The loss of marine biodiversity affects the ocean's ability to provide food and maintain water quality (Worm et al. 2006). Lower marine diversity was also associated with decreased stability, increasing rates of resource collapse, and decreased recovery potential. Between 10–30% of the world's mammals, birds, and amphibians are at risk of extinction (Millennium Ecosystem Assessment 2005). The burning of fossil fuels, deforestation, and other changes in land use have increased the amount of carbon in the atmosphere by about a third (from 280 to 376 ppm in 2003).

Changes in ecosystem extent, function, or species abundances can have major impacts on the delivery of critical services. Population growth is expected to slow and level off mid-century; nonetheless, global GDP is predicted to multiply three- to sixfold, driving ever higher the levels of demand for ecosystem services (Millennium Ecosystem Assessment 2005).

It is challenging to quantify the costs of lost or degraded ecosystem services; however, the evidence suggests that such costs are substantial and growing. The single greatest cost might be that of lost future opportunities. Fewer than 10%, or perhaps even 1%, of the Earth's species have been described, much less studied (Novotny et al. 2002). The opportunity to learn from, enjoy, or discover new sources of food and medicine dwindles with every species that disappears. Because of the complexity of interactions between many species, a single extinction can cause cascading effects on other species that are important to humans and the functioning of ecosystems that provide many other services.

Exploitation of species or destruction of ecosystems can have severe consequences for human well-being. The destruction of coastal wetlands and mangrove forests results in increased human mortality and economic damage from tropical cyclones (Costanza et al. 2008; Das & Vincent 2009). Trade in wildlife for human consumption contributes to the spread of diseases, such as the 2003 outbreak of Severe Acute Respiratory Syndrome (SARS) in East Asia (Guan et al. 2003). In Africa, the degradation of rangeland has caused a decrease in livestock production with an estimated cost of US$7 billion per year, nearly the GDP of Ethiopia (Brown 2001). Declining soil fertility and erosion has resulted in the abandonment of nearly half of Kazakhstan's cropland during 1980–2000, resulting in declining wheat harvests and an annual economic loss of US$900 million.

In the early 1990s, the Newfoundland cod fishery collapsed because of overfishing, resulting in the loss of tens of thousands of jobs and at least US$2 billion in income support and retraining (Millennium Ecosystem Assessment 2005). Globally, fisheries are estimated to underperform by US$50 billion annually (TEEB 2010). Terrestrial biodiversity losses over the last decade are estimated to have cost the global economy US$500 billion per year (TEEB 2009). Economic losses from natural catastrophes (fires, floods, storms, droughts, and earthquakes) totaled approximately US$70 billion in 2003–a tenfold increase since the 1950s (Millennium Ecosystem Assessment 2005). In coming decades, the effects of a changing climate, including increased frequency and intensity of natural disasters, will increase the importance of and demand for the services provided by species and ecosystems (Turner et al. 2009).

The costs of losing ecosystems are borne disproportionately by the poor, who are more directly dependent on nature for the provision of food, water, shelter, energy, and livelihoods. Thus, the destruction of ecosystems exacerbates existing inequality, resulting in increased poverty and conflict (Millennium

Ecosystem Assessment 2005). This situation complicates efforts to improve human well-being, such as global efforts to achieve the Millennium Development Goals agreed upon by the UN General Assembly in 2000.

Fixing the broken economic compass. *Leaders must incorporate the value of ecosystem services and natural capital into national accounting and decision-making processes across all sectors of society; biodiversity and ecosystem services must be seen as the most fundamental components of green economic development; and access to ecosystem benefits and costs of ecosystem conservation must be shared equitably.*

Incorporating the value of nature in decision-making is complicated by a series of disconnects between those who receive the benefits of ecosystems and those who incur the costs of their conservation. Although the costs of conserving ecosystems are most often incurred by those nearby, many benefits can accrue over large distances, for example, in water provision, climate regulation, and recreation. A temporal disconnect also exists: though costs are often felt immediately and acutely, benefits are often not obtained until the future. Furthermore, different services are of greater or lesser importance to different people, communities, and institutions (Kremen et al. 2000).

These disconnects will not resolve themselves; however, understanding them can point the way to solutions. Among these are "Payment for Ecosystem Services," which are financial transfers from service beneficiaries to would-be resource stewards or those whose behavior must change to secure ecosystems (Wunder et al. 2008).

Mechanisms such as payments for ecosystem services can create incentives for conserving or enhancing services. In some cases, the conservation of certain services (such as carbon sequestration) results in synergistic production of other services (such as freshwater and other biodiversity benefits; Larsen et al. 2011). Such mechanisms can also alleviate poverty and promote sustainable development if they are carefully designed and implemented (Turner et al. 2012). Understanding synergies and tradeoffs between services requires knowing the value and location of services. Efforts to map the costs and benefits of ecosystem services are beginning at scales ranging from global (TEEB 2010), national (Moilanen et al. 2011, the World Bank's Wealth Accounting and Valuation of Ecosystem Services initiative, and others), to local (Beier et al. 2008; O'Farrell et al. 2010). Mechanisms such as payments for ecosystem services and Reducing Emissions from Deforestation and Forest Degradation are just beginning to reconcile the disconnects between the costs and benefits of services, develop markets and institutions for previously unvalued services, and share benefits equitably. Nonetheless, leaders must make sweeping changes in policies, institutions, and practices to fix the broken compass and reverse the degradation of ecosystems while meeting increasing demands for services in coming decades.

References

1. Balmford, A., A. Bruner, P. Cooper, et al. 2002. Economic reasons for conserving wild nature. *Science* 297:950–953.
2. Becker, S., and H. Terlau. 2008. Toxins from cone snails: Properties, applications and biotechnological production. *Applied Microbiology and Biotechnology* 79:1–9.
3. Beier, C. M., T. M. Patterson, and F. S. Chapin. 2008. Ecosystem services and emergent vulnerability in managed ecosystems: A geospatial decision-support tool. *Ecosystems* 11:923–938.
4. Brodie, J. F., and H. K. Gibbs. 2009. Bushmeat hunting as climate threat. *Science* 326:364–365.
5. Brown, L. R. 2001. *Eco-economy: Building an Economy for the Earth*. W. W. Norton & Co., New York.
6. Chivian, E., and A. Bernstein, editors. 2008. *Sustaining Life: How Human Health Depends on Biodiversity*. Oxford University Press, New York.
7. Costanza, R., R. dArge, R. deGroot, et al. 1997. The value of the world's ecosystem services and natural capital. *Nature* 387:253–260.
8. Costanza, R., O. Pérez-Maqueo, M. L. Martinez, P. Sutton, S. J. Anderson, and K. Mulder. 2008. The value of coastal wetlands for hurricane protection. *Ambio* 37:241–248.
9. Daily, G. C., and K. Ellison 2002. *The New Economy of Nature: The Quest to Make Conservation Profitable*. Island Press, Washington, D.C..

10. Das, S., and J. R. Vincent. 2009. Mangroves protected villages and reduced death toll during Indian super cyclone. *Proc. Natl. Acad. Sci. U.S.A.* 106:7357–7360.
11. de Groot, R. S., M. A. Wilson, and R. M. J. Boumans. 2002. A typology for the classification, description, and valuation of ecosystem functions, goods and services. *Ecological Economics* 41:393–408.
12. Dudley, N., and S. Stolton 2003. *Running pure: The importance of forest protected areas to drinking water*. World Bank and WWF, Washington, D.C..
13. Dyck, A. J., and U. R. Sumaila. 2010. Economic impact of ocean fish populations in the global fishery. *J. Bioeconomics* 12:227–243.
14. FAO Fisheries and Aquaculture Department 2010. *The State of World Fisheries and Aquaculture*. Food and Agriculture Organization, Rome.
15. Gentry, A. 1993. Tropical forest biodiversity and the potential for new medicinal plants in A. D. Kinghorn, and M. F. Balandrin, editors. *Human Medicinal Agents from Plants*. American Chemical Society, Washington, D.C..
16. Guan, Y., B. J. Zheng, Y. Q. He, et al. 2003. Isolation and characterization of viruses related to the SARS coronavirus from animals in Southern China. *Science* 302:276–278.
17. Howe, H. F., and J. Smallwood. 1982. Ecology of seed dispersal. *Ann Rev. Ecol. Syst.* 13:201–228.
18. Kone, I., J. E. Lambert, J. Refisch, and A. Bakayoko. 2008. Primate seed dispersal and its potential role in maintaining useful tree species in the Taï region, Côte-d'Ivoire: Implications for the conservation of forest fragments. *Tropical Conservation Science* 1:293–306.
19. Kremen, C., J. O. Niles, M. G. Dalton, G. C. Daily, P. R. Ehrlich, J. P. Fay, D. Grewal, and R. P. Guillery. 2000. Economic incentives for rain forest conservation across scales. *Science* 288:1828–1832.
20. Kunz, T. H., E. B. de Torrez, D. Bauer, T. Lobova, and T. H. Fleming. 2011. Ecosystem services provided by bats. *Annals of the New York Academy of Sciences* 1223:1–38.
21. Laffoley, D., and G. Grimsditch 2009. The Management of Natural Coastal Carbon Sinks. International Union for Conservation of Nature, Gland, Switzerland.
22. Larsen, F. W., M. C. Londoño-Murcia, and W. R. Turner. 2011. Global priorities for threatened species, carbon storage, and freshwater services: Scope for synergy? *Conservation Letters* 4:355–363.
23. Lavelle, P., T. Decaëns, M. Aubert, S. Barot, M. Blouin, F. Bureau, P. Margerie, P. Mora, and J.-P. Rossi. 2006. Soil invertebrates and ecosystem services. *European Journal of Soil Biology* 42:S3–S15.
24. Levitus, S., J. Antonov, and T. Boyer. 2005. Warming of the world ocean, 1955–2003. *Geophys. Res. Lett.* 32:L02604.
25. Losey, J. E., and M. Vaughan. 2006. The economic value of ecological services provided by insects. *BioScience* 56:311–323.
26. Maestre, F. T., J. L. Quero, N. J. Gotelli, et al. 2012. Plant species richness and ecosystem multifunctionality in global drylands. *Science*

335:6065.

27. McNeely, J. A., R. A. Mittermeier, T. M. Brooks, F. Boltz, and N. Ash 2009. *The Wealth of Nature: Ecosystem Services, Biodiversity, and Human Well-Being*. CEMEX, Mexico City.

28. Millennium Ecosystem Assessment 2005. *Ecosystems and Human Well-being: Synthesis*. Island Press, Washington, D.C..

29. Moellering, R. C. 2006. Vancomycin: A 50-year reassessment. Clinical Infectious Diseases 42 (Supplement 1):S3–S4.

30. Moilanen, A., B. J. Anderson, F. Eigenbrod, A. Heinemeyer, D. B. Roy, S. Gillings, P. R. Armsworth, K. J. Gaston, and C. D. Thomas. 2011. Balancing alternative land uses in conservation prioritization. *Ecological Applications* 21:1419–1426.

31. Novotny, V., Y. Bassett, S. E. Miller, G. D. GWeiblen, B. Bremer, L. Cizek, and P. Drozd. 2002. Low host specificity of herbivorous insects in a tropical forest. *Nature* 416:841–844.

32. O'Farrell, P. J., B. Reyers, D. C. Maitre, et al. 2010. Multi-functional landscapes in semi arid environments: Implications for biodiversity and ecosystem services. *Landscape Ecology* 1231–1246.

33. Sukhdev, P. 2011. Focusing on GDP growth fails to account for the value of nature, July 2011 blog post. *The Guardian*, London.

34. TEEB 2009. The Economics of Ecosystems and Biodiversity for National and International Policy Makers. UNEP, Bonn.

35. TEEB 2010. The Economics of Ecosystems and Biodiversity: Mainstreaming the Economics of Nature: A Synthesis of the Approach, Conclusions and Recommendations of TEEB. UNEP, Bonn.

36. Triplitt, C., and E. Chiquette. 2006. Exenatide: From the Gila monster to the pharmacy. *Journal of the American Pharmacists Association* 46:44–52.

37. Turner, R. K., and G. C. Daily. 2007. The ecosystem services framework and natural capital conservation. *Environmental and Resource Economics* 39:25–35.

38. Turner, W. R., K. Brandon, T. M. Brooks, C. Gascon, H. K. Gibbs, K. Lawrence, R. A. Mittermeier, and E. R. Selig. 2012. Global biodiversity conservation and the alleviation of poverty. *BioScience* 62:85–92.

39. Turner, W. R., M. Oppenheimer, and D. S. Wilcove. 2009. A force to fight global warming. *Nature* 462:278–279.

40. VanCompernolle, S. E., R. J. Taylor, K. Oswald-Richter, J. Jiang, B. E. Youree, J. H. Bowie, M. J. Tyler, and e. al. 2005. Antimicrobial peptides from amphibian skin potently inhibit human immunodeficiency virus infection and transfer of virus from dendritic cells to T cells. *J. Virology* 79:11598–11606.

41. Whelan, C. J., D. G. Wenny, and R. J. Marquis. 2008. Ecosystem services provided by birds. *Annals of the New York Academy of Sciences* 1134:25–60.

42. Worm, B., E. Barbier, N. Beaumont, et al. 2006. Impacts of biodiversity loss on ocean ecosystem services. *Science* 314:787–790.

43. Wunder, S., S. Engel, and S. Pagiola. 2008. Taking stock: A comparative

analysis of payments for environmental services programs in developed and developing countries. *Ecological Economics* 65:834–852.

Annex I

The Blue Planet Prize Laureates who contributed to the paper (in no special order)

- PROF. SIR BOB WATSON, Chief Scientific Adviser of the UK Department for Environment, Food and Rural Affairs
- LORD (ROBERT) MAY OF OXFORD, former Chief Scientific Adviser to the UK Government and President of Royal Society of London
- PROF. PAUL EHRLICH, Stanford University
- PROF. HAROLD MOONEY, Stanford University
- DR. GORDON HISASHI SATO, President, Manzanar Project Corporation
- PROF. JOSÉ GOLDEMBERG, Secretary for the environment of the State of São Paulo, Brazil and Brazil's interim Secretary of Environment during the Rio Earth Summit in 1992
- DR. EMIL SALIM, former Environment Minister of the Republic of Indonesia
- DR. CAMILLA TOULMIN, Director of the International Institute for Environment and Development
- DR. SALEEMUL HUQ, Senior Fellow, Climate Change Group, International Institute for Environment and Development
- MR. BUNKER ROY, Founder of Barefoot College
- DR. SYUKURO MANABE, Senior Scientist, Princeton University
- DR. JULIA MARTON-LEFÈVRE, Director-General of the International Union for the Conservation of Nature
- DR. SIMON STUART, Chair of the Species Survival Commission of the International Union for the Conservation of Nature
- DR. RUSSELL MITTERMEIER, President of Conservation International
- DR. WILL TURNER, Vice President of Conservation Priorities and Outreach, Conservation International

- PROF. KARL-HENRIK ROBÈRT, Blekinge Institute of Technology, Founder of the Natural Step
- DR. JAMES HANSEN, NASA Goddard Institute for Space Studies
- LORD (NICHOLAS) STERN OF BRENTFORD, Professor, the London School of Economics
- DR. AMORY LOVINS, Chair and Chief Scientist, Rocky Mountain Institute
- DR. GENE LIKENS, Director of the Carey Institute of Ecosystem Studies
- DR. GRO HARLEM BRUNDTLAND, former Prime Minister of Norway and Director-General of the World Health Organization, now Special Envoy on Climate Change for UN Secretary General Ban Ki-moon
- DR. SUSAN SOLOMON, Senior Scientist, Aeronomy Laboratory, National Oceanic and Atmospheric Administration
- PROF. M. S. SWAMINATHAN, Founder Chairman, M. S. Swaminathan Research Foundation

The above titles are as of February 2012.

Laureates' profiles when they were awarded The Blue Planet Prize

1992 (1st)

Dr. Syukuro Manabe (USA)

Member of the Senior Executive Service of the Geophysical Fluid Dynamics Laboratory at the National Oceanic and Atmospheric Administration

For pioneering research, predicting climate change by numerical models and quantifying the effects of greenhouse gases

1992 (1st)

International Institute for Environment and Development

(Founded in UK)

For pioneering scientific research and implementation activities for the realization of sustainable development in a wide range of fields, including agriculture, energy, and urban planning

1993 (2nd)

IUCN-The World Conservation Union

(Headquartered in Switzerland)

For outstanding research and the application of scientific strategies to the conservation of natural resources and the promotion of biological diversity on an international scale

1996 (5th)

M. S. Swaminathan Research Foundation (Founded in India)

For leading the way toward the realization of sustainable agriculture and rural development through research into soil improvement and genetic engineering of plant species and the application of these findings

279

1997 (6th)

Conservation International

(Headquartered in Washington, D.C., USA)

For protecting the earth's biological diversity through research into ways to conserve ecosystems while improving the lives of local people

1999 (8th)

Dr. Paul R. Ehrlich (USA)

Director of the Center of Conservation Biology, Stanford University

For co-funding the new science of conservation biology, co-authoring the theory of co-evolution and for promoting environmental conservation by warning of a population explosion

2000 (9th)

Dr. Karl-Henrik Robèrt (Sweden)

Chairman of the Natural Step (NGO)

For scientifically formulating the principles and theoretical framework required to establish a sustainable society and for enhancing the environmental awareness of businesses, municipalities and others

2001 (10th)

Lord (Robert) May of Oxford (Australia)

President of Royal Society of London

For developing mathematical ecology, the means to predict changes in animal populations that serves as a fundamental tool for ecological conservation planning

2002 (11th)

Prof. Harold A. Mooney (USA)

Professor, Department of Biological Sciences, Stanford University

For pioneering work in the field of plant physiological ecology, for providing objective measures of how plant ecologies are influenced by their environments, and for his conservation efforts

2003 (12th)

Dr. Gene E. Likens (USA)

President and Director, Institute of Ecosystem Studies

Dr. F. Herbert Bormann (USA)

(right)

Oastler Professor of Ecosystem Ecology, Emeritus, Yale University

For pioneering an approach that has become a model for the scientific world, and for the comprehensive understanding of ecosystems through long-term measurement of the flows of water and chemical substances in watersheds

2004 (13th)

Dr. Susan Solomon (USA)

Senior Scientist, Aeronomy Laboratory, National Oceanic and Atmospheric Administration

For pioneering work in identifying the mechanism that produces the Antarctic ozone hole and momentous contributions towards the protection of the ozone layer

2004 (13th)

Dr. Gro Harlem Brundtland (Norway)

Chairman, World Commission of Environment and Development
Former Prime Minister of Norway
Director-General Emeritus, WHO

For putting forward globally the innovative concept of sustainable development, an idea that aims to balance environmental conservation with economic growth

2005 (14th)

Dr. Gordon Hisashi Sato (USA)

Director Emeritus, W. Alton Jones Cell Science Center. Inc.
Chairman of the Board, A&G Pharmaceutical, Inc.
President, Manzanar Project Corporation

For developing a new mangrove planting technology in Eritrea and through its utilization thus showing the possibility of building a sustainable local community in the poorest area of the world

2006 (15th)

Dr. Emil Salim (Indonesia)

Professor, Faculty of Economics and Post Graduate Course, University of Indonesia
Former Minister of Population and Environment, Republic of Indonesia

For contributing in establishing the concept of sustainable development and furthering global environmental policies through various United Nation's committees especially as the chairman of the Preparatory Committee for the World Summit on Sustainable Development

2007 (16th)

Dr. Amory B. Lovins (USA)

Chairman and Chief Scientist, Rocky Mountain Institute

For his contributions to leading global energy strategy for protection of the global environment by efficient utilization of energy through his advocacy of the concept of the "soft energy path" and invention of the Hypercar

2008 (17th)

Prof. José Goldemberg (Brazil)

Professor, Institute of Electrotechnics and Energy, University of São Paulo
Former Rector, University of São Paulo

For making major contributions in formulating and implementing many policies associated with improvements on energy use and conservation, in devising a pioneering concept of "technological leapfrogging" for the developing countries for their sustainable development and in exhibiting strong leadership in preparation for the 1992 Rio Earth Summit

2009 (18th)

Lord (Nicholas) Stern of Brentford (UK)
Professor, the London School of Economics

Having reported the economic and social impact of and actions against climate change in The Economics of Climate Change with the approach of using cutting edge natural sciences and economics, he provided a clear cut policy regarding the global warming, which has had a major impact on the world

2010 (19th)

Dr. James Hansen (USA)
Director at Goddard Institute for Space Studies (NASA)
Adjunct professor in the Department of Earth and Environmental Sciences at Columbia University

For having predicted global warming in the early stage and warned that it would very probably cause destructive results for life on Earth, he called on the governments and the public to take immediate action to reduce and mitigate the impact of climate change

2010 (19th)

Dr. Robert Watson (UK)
Chief Scientific Adviser of the UK Department for Environment, Food and Rural Affairs
Chair of Environmental Science and Science Director at Tyndall Centre for Climate Change Research, the University of East Anglia

For having organized the famous scientific project to derive scientific evidence of the depletion of the Ozone Layer, he eventually endorsed the Montreal Protocol. Later as Chair of IPCC, he played a significant role in coordinating and bridging science and policy for protecting the world environment

2011 (20th)

Barefoot College (Founded in India)

Having supported rural villagers in underdeveloped nations and created a model for autonomous regional social development through unique educational programs that emphasize traditional ideas and self-respect

Information on Blue Planet Prize laureates corresponds to their titles and positions at the time Prize was awarded.

Annex II

About the Blue Planet Prize

In 1992, the year of the Rio Earth Summit, the Asahi Glass Foundation established the Blue Planet Prize, an award presented to individuals or organizations worldwide in recognition of outstanding achievements in research and their application that have helped provide solutions to global environmental problems.

The Prize is offered in hopes of encouraging efforts to bring about the healing of the Earth's fragile environment.

The award's name was inspired by the remark "the Earth was blue," uttered by the first human in space, Russian cosmonaut Yuri Gagarin, upon viewing our planet from space. The Blue Planet Prize was so named in hopes that our blue planet will be a shared asset capable of sustaining human life far into the future.

About the Asahi Glass Foundation

The Asahi Glass Foundation was established in 1933 as the Asahi Foundation for Chemical Industry Promotion, to commemorate the twenty-fifth anniversary (1932) of the founding of Asahi Glass Co., Ltd. Over most of its first half century, the Foundation focused primarily on fostering research in the field of applied chemistry.

In 1990, the Foundation undertook an overall redesign of its programs, expanding the scope of its activities and establishing its commendation program. At the same time it was renamed as the Asahi Glass Foundation. Since then, the activities of the Foundation have focused on its grant and commendation programs.